AFRICAN ETHNOGRAPHIC STUDIES OF THE 20TH CENTURY

Volume 61

SOCIAL CHANGE IN MODERN AFRICA

SOCIAL CHANGE IN MODERN AFRICA

Studies Presented and Discussed at the First
International African Seminar,
Makerere College, Kampala, January 1959

Edited by
AIDAN SOUTHALL

LONDON AND NEW YORK

First published in 1961 by Oxford University Press for the International African Institute.

This edition first published in 2018
by Routledge
2 Park Square, Milton Park, Abingdon, Oxon OX14 4RN

and by Routledge
711 Third Avenue, New York, NY 10017

Routledge is an imprint of the Taylor & Francis Group, an informa business

© 1961 International African Institute

All rights reserved. No part of this book may be reprinted or reproduced or utilised in any form or by any electronic, mechanical, or other means, now known or hereafter invented, including photocopying and recording, or in any information storage or retrieval system, without permission in writing from the publishers.

Trademark notice: Product or corporate names may be trademarks or registered trademarks, and are used only for identification and explanation without intent to infringe.

British Library Cataloguing in Publication Data
A catalogue record for this book is available from the British Library

ISBN: 978-0-8153-8713-8 (Set)
ISBN: 978-0-429-48813-9 (Set) (ebk)
ISBN: 978-1-138-59824-9 (Volume 61) (hbk)
ISBN: 978-0-429-48644-9 (Volume 61) (ebk)

Publisher's Note
The publisher has gone to great lengths to ensure the quality of this reprint but points out that some imperfections in the original copies may be apparent.

Disclaimer
The publisher has made every effort to trace copyright holders and would welcome correspondence from those they have been unable to trace.

SOCIAL CHANGE IN MODERN AFRICA

Studies presented and discussed at the First
International African Seminar, Makerere College,
Kampala, January 1959

EDITED BY
AIDAN SOUTHALL

Foreword by
DARYLL FORDE

Published for the
INTERNATIONAL AFRICAN INSTITUTE
by the
OXFORD UNIVERSITY PRESS
LONDON   NEW YORK   TORONTO
1961

Oxford University Press, Amen House, London E.C.4

GLASGOW NEW YORK TORONTO MELBOURNE WELLINGTON
BOMBAY CALCUTTA MADRAS KARACHI KUALA LUMPUR
CAPE TOWN IBADAN NAIROBI ACCRA

© International African Institute 1961

Printed in Great Britain by
Butler & Tanner Ltd., Frome and London

FOREWORD

Over recent years the amount and scope of research on the contemporary social and cultural life of African peoples have greatly increased. Various African and metropolitan governments have set up advisory bodies and provided funds for such studies, and a number of research centres, some of them associated with universities and colleges, have been established in Africa itself.

These researches often require a prolonged analysis of the data obtained in the field, and the fact that they are not infrequently undertaken as short-term engagements after which the investigators are drawn into other duties commonly imposes a considerable delay before results are available for publication. Informal discussion and exchange of information and ideas among those concerned with particular problems goes forward in the meantime; but this tends to be artificially separated into a number of distinct channels, according to the facilities provided within particular territories or by the academic institutions of the different countries to which research workers are attached and to which they return. Thus, early and effective personal contacts and discussions between scholars of different nationalities, who may be concurrently engaged in different parts of Africa on researches on similar studies, do not naturally follow. Indeed, such contacts and discussions are often least available to the younger research workers while they are actually working on their field data.

The need for greater inter-territorial exchange within Africa itself has not been ignored. For West Africa a biennial inter-territorial conference of field sciences (Conférence Internationale des Africanistes de l'Ouest), in which social scientists participate, was established soon after the war. In East Africa informal Anglo-Belgian social studies conferences have been organized jointly by the East African Institute of Social Research and the Institut pour la Recherche Scientifique en Afrique Centrale. More comprehensively, the Commission for Technical Co-operation in Africa

South of the Sahara, with the co-operation of the Belgian authorities, held a conference at Bukavu in 1955 to make a general review of the opportunities and needs for social science research in Africa, which gave an opportunity to those responsible for its organization and development to acquaint themselves with current work and plans in all territories.

The International African Institute which, from its inception more than thirty years ago, has sought to promote international co-operation in African cultural and social studies through its field research fellowships, its publications, its information service, and the annual meeting of its Council, obtained the support of UNESCO some years ago for the organization in Africa of a small international conference of specialists on one of the most complex and challenging fields of study: the social implications of industrialization and urbanization. The success of this conference which met at Abidjan in the Ivory Coast in 1954, in presenting and analysing comparable data from a wide range of territories and in defining the scope of problems and methods of research, can be judged from the extensive use that has been made of the volume in which the papers prepared for it and the reports of its findings were published.[1] But it was also remarkable for the fact that so many of its participants, actively engaged in research in different parts of Africa, were meeting one another for the first time, and had hitherto had little or no knowledge of each other's work, theoretical approach, or further plans. The contacts established at that conference led to a number of subsequent exchanges of information and discussions of problems on methods of research and the interpretation of field material. The Council of the International African Institute accordingly approved a project to further such international interchanges in the field of African studies by organizing a series of small seminars to be held in Africa. Each was to be devoted to a different topic, and the fifteen to twenty participants were to be selected from among those actively engaged in relevant field researches in different territories. The Ford Foundation generously responded to an approach for

---

[1] Forde, D. (ed.), *The Social Implications of Industrialization and Urbanization in Africa South of the Sahara.* UNESCO, 1956.

assistance for this project by making a grant to the Institute to enable it to organize four such seminars.

This volume presents some of the findings of the first Seminar which met for ten days at Makerere College, Kampala, in January 1959. Its subject, 'Kinship, Status and Neighbourhood under Modern Economic Conditions in Tropical Africa', was selected to focus attention on small-scale, inter-personal relations. It considered, with reference to data already available in this field, the relevance of different conceptional approaches and methods of systematic analysis, and also appraised on this basis the character of the significant patterns and underlying factors in these relations, where paid employment and money incomes had come to predominate in the economic life of the community.

The participants in the Seminar prepared for circulation in advance of its meetings short studies of relevant material from their own investigations and a number of themes were selected for detailed discussion. The substantive results are presented in this volume.

A detailed record of the Seminar meetings was taken, but it was neither intended nor was it feasible to attempt during that short period to systematize the outcome of the discussions in a series of definitive statements. On some questions the work was exploratory in character. There were also among the participants differences of interest and emphasis concerning the selection and definition of problems and the methods of analysis. These find expression in the revised and shortened versions of their papers. Indeed, one of the main objects was to secure an exchange of views with reference to a common topic among field workers, who had approached it in different ways and in diverse contexts. On the basis of the discussions at the Seminar, including the comparative reviews of particular topics and problems which it took up, Professor Southall has provided in an Introductory Survey a general review of the aspects discussed, illustrating these from the material in the studies presented and also by reference to some other published sources. While thus providing a background to the series of more specialized papers presented in this volume, he has also taken the opportunity to make his own appraisal of some of the main factors involved and the recurrent processes at work in the field of changing social relationships in urban Africa.

It is hoped that the publication of these studies will not only stimulate further discussion among social scientists, administrators, and others, who are concerned with particular inquiries and programmes, but will also be of use to all those who are more generally interested in contemporary developments in tropical Africa.

I should like on behalf of the Institute to take this opportunity of thanking all the participants for their co-operation in the preparation of the Seminar as well as for their long hours of work during its meetings. Our thanks are especially due to Professor Southall for his skill and patience as Chairman and local organizer. We are also grateful to the Principal of Makerere College and the Warden of its Mary Stuart Hall for accommodating the Seminar, and to the secretarial staff of the East African Institute of Social Research for the very considerable additional work that they undertook in connexion with it. The assistance of the Ford Foundation is greatly appreciated, not only because it has made possible the holding of this and subsequent seminars but also for its recognition of the Institute's endeavours to further international co-operation in African studies.

DARYLL FORDE

CONTENTS

Foreword by Professor Daryll Forde   v
Director, International African Institute

PART ONE. INTRODUCTORY SUMMARY
By Professor A. W. Southall
Director, East African Institute of Social Research

I	Social Change, Demography, and Extrinsic Factors	1
II	Norms and Status Symbols	14
III	Small Groups and Social Networks	25
IV	Kinship, Tribalism, and Family Authority	31
V	The Position of Women and the Stability of Marriage	46

PART TWO. SPECIAL STUDIES

I   PROFESSOR M. GLUCKMAN. *University of Manchester*
Anthropological Problems arising from the African Industrial Revolution   67

II   Mr. E. W. ARDENER. *Nigerian Institute for Social and Economic Research*
Social and Demographic Problems of the Southern Cameroons Plantation Area   83

III   Dr. GORDON WILSON. *Ministry of African Affairs, Nairobi*
Mombasa—A Modern Colonial Municipality   98

IV   DR. M. BANTON. *Social Science Research Centre, University of Edinburgh*
The Restructuring of Social Relationships   113

V   Dr. W. B. SCHWAB. *Temple University, Philadelphia*
Social Stratification in Gwelo   126

VI   MR. J. E. GOLDTHORPE. *Department of Sociology, Makerere College*
Educated Africans: some Conceptual and Terminological Problems   145

Contents

VII Dr. L. BAECK. *Chargé de Cours, Université de Lovanium*
An Expenditure Study of the Congolese *Évolués* of Leopoldville, Belgian Congo ... 159

VIII M. R. DEVAUGES. *Office de la Recherche Scientifique et Technique d'Outre Mer, Brazzaville*
Mieux-Être et Promotion sociale chez les Salariés africains de Brazzaville ... 182

IX DR. V. PONS. *Department of Social Anthropology, University of Manchester*
Two Small Groups in Avenue 21: Some Aspects of the System of Social Relations in a Remote Corner of Stanleyville, Belgian Congo ... 205

X PROFESSOR A. W. SOUTHALL. *East African Institute of Social Research*
Kinship, Friendship, and the Network of Relations in Kisenyi, Kampala ... 217

XI DR. J. VAN VELSEN. *East African Institute of Social Research*
Labour Migration as a Positive Factor in the Continuity of Tonga Tribal Society ... 230

XII MR. R. G. ABRAHAMS. *East African Institute of Social Research*
Kahama Township, Western Province, Tanganyika ... 242

XIII M. R. GOUELLAIN. *Institut de Recherches Scientifiques du Cameroun, Douala*
Parenté et Affinités ethniques dans l'écologie du 'Grand Quartier' de New-Bell, Douala ... 254

XIV DR. D. G. BETTISON. *Rhodes-Livingstone Institute, Lusaka*
Changes in the Composition and Status of Kin Groups in Nyasaland and Northern Rhodesia ... 273

XV DR. D. MCCALL. *African Research and Studies Program, Boston*
Trade and the Role of Wife in a Modern West African Town ... 286

XVI DR. J. ROUCH. *Musée de l'Homme, Paris*
Second Generation Migrants in Ghana and the Ivory Coast ... 300

XVII	MISS A. IZZETT. *Federal Social Welfare Department, Lagos*	
	Family Life Among the Yoruba, in Lagos, Nigeria	305
XVIII	PROFESSOR J. CLYDE MITCHELL. *University College of Rhodesia and Nyasaland*	
	Social Change and the Stability of African Marriage in Northern Rhodesia	316
	INDEX	331

I. INTRODUCTORY SUMMARY

I. SOCIAL CHANGE, DEMOGRAPHY, AND EXTRINSIC FACTORS

Though much of Africa remains *terra incognita* from the sociological viewpoint, the results so far obtained require constant co-ordination if effort is not to be wasted. Many questions are unanswerable, both for lack of adequate data and lack of an appropriate framework of theory and relevant hypotheses. Yet the macroscopic picture has begun to emerge and it is already time to attempt an assessment of what the major changes mean in the social lives of African populations.

There is considerable documentation of the growth of towns, of the size of employed labour forces, the differentiation of incomes and the main directions of migration. What is much less accurately understood is the precise changes in the social relationships and roles of individuals which accompany these major events. There are too many catchwords: detribalization, the breakdown of traditional authority, the emergence of élites and of new political and economic forces, the emancipation of women and the rise of nationalism. The variety and contrasts of Africa are greater than ever before. There are both air-routes and foot-safaris, talking drums, newspapers and radios, doctors, lawyers and gangsters as well as lion men and witch doctors. It is difficult to find the less spectacular truth between the extremes.

Obviously the major centres of change are towns, mines, and plantations. But changes do not stop at town boundaries. What is the precise effect of these centres on the rest of Africa? All this can only be discovered by a study at the level of small groups, neighbourhoods and close networks of social relationships.

In what follows, reference to towns should be understood to include the other obvious population concentrations linked to mines and plantations, unless these are specifically excluded by the context.

Restriction of the study of change to towns and similar employment centres requires further modification. It is common to regard tribal Africa as timeless and unchanging. While there are senses in which this is true, it needs qualification. Recent research has revealed over and over again how fluid the traditional situation was. Most tribal boundaries lacked definition and the identification of tribes was highly relative. Despite the conditions of political insecurity, individuals and groups were constantly on the move, communities dissolving and crystallizing again in new patterns. Some tribes disappeared or were absorbed in larger units, others emerged as new entities through segmentation and incorporation of diverse elements. Communities with hereditary dynasties and stable boundaries were very much the exception. Dominant tribes such as Ashanti, Ganda, Lunda, Ngoni, or Hausa and Fulani gave a certain focus and a seeming unity to large areas but they were highly uncharacteristic and the apparent homogeneity and stability were an illusion. There was also slow change from hunting and gathering to agriculture, or between agriculture and pastoralism. But it is true that all these changes occurred within the limits of a largely subsistence economy and a kin-bound social structure. In this latter sense the new changes have been radical, however diverse the pre-existing conditions may have been. Social change within aboriginal Africa was on the whole change within systems of a certain type rather than change of systems, while there have obviously been most radical changes of system since the establishment of colonial rule. The factors in these new changes are adequately grouped under the closely linked headings of colonial rule and industrialization or participation in the exchange economy.

A third set of factors is involved in the missionary activities of the world religions, but these have always followed or inevitably brought in train the political and economic factors which seem paramount.

The case of Islam is somewhat different, for its carriers were not nationals of western industrialized states, as was the case with those who brought Christianity to the interior of Africa. A thousand years of Islamic influence on the East African coast certainly had the effect of breaking up such African societies as were unable to retreat before it, but led to no cumulative change. The extension of this influence inland in the nineteenth century, and from the Sudan into Uganda, proved a mere prelude to the more far-reaching changes brought about by European intervention.

The penetration of Islam across the Sahara into West Africa during the last seven centuries had much more profound effects. It was carried by invading groups which established the long series of conquest states ranging from early Bornu, Melle, and Songhai to the nineteenth-century emirates of the Fulani. They formed centres for further Islamic influence, but tended to inhibit rather than to encourage the type of change considered here.

Whether we look at the early Christian missions of the Portuguese, or at the more recent story of Christian missions in Nyasaland or Uganda, or equally at their absence beyond the traders' frontier in West Africa during the nineteenth century, it appears that missionaries found it virtually impossible to work outside the protection of a European Power or the support of armed force. Krapf who lived heroically and many others who died heroically in the missionary cause in East Africa and elsewhere found few indeed prepared to listen to their message until some ulterior motive had crept into the hearers' minds. Christian missions have thus been sometimes the forerunners, sometimes the followers of colonial government and frequently an enlightened and liberal controlling influence, but never permitted by events to have much lasting influence beyond the colonial frontiers.

Three broad spheres of change may therefore be distinguished: traditional change within substantially self-subsistent tribal systems, change in towns and centres of employment and contemporary changes in tribal systems no longer politically autonomous and now economically interlocked with the towns and employment centres. The first type of change does not concern us here and we shall concentrate mainly on the second and third.

But it is important to remember the extent of the first. Here again three type situations may be distinguished in contemporary tribal communities. There are those which have come to rely mainly on migrant labour, those which have successfully adopted cash cropping and those without either of these. In the latter case change is minimal and there is a conservative attitude towards the traditional tribal system. In the labour migrant tribes change is radical but is focused upon that part of their lives which members of the tribe spend away from home and there are even new pressures which have tended to entrench some aspects of traditional life.

It is probably in the successful cash cropping tribes that the most positive and important changes have occurred in the adaptation of tribal life to the entirely new political and economic context.

Numerous studies have been made of the adaptation of tribal political structure to modern local government institutions, of changes in customary law, and even of cash cropping and pastoral economies and of changes in the regulation of marriage and descent. But apart from generalizations about individualism, weakening of sanctions, secularization and commercialization, no clear picture has emerged of the trend of structural change within tribal communities at the fundamental level of family, neighbourhood, and small group relationships. So serious is this lack of detail and precision that many new features of kinship and marriage resulting from the general situation of colonial rule are looked upon as traditional not only by administrators and others outside the tribal system but also by most of those within. As one major example of this we may cite the case of bridewealth which is often regarded as a persistent conservative feature of tribal life, yet in its present form may to a considerable extent be a reaction to changed conditions. This misleading impression is partly due to the concentration of study on working out the mechanisms of traditional systems and partly to the difficulty of finding adequate concepts for handling these changes in structural terms. The main focus of the present studies, however, is on towns and centres of employment, while endeavouring to note the relevance of these changes for rural communities.

The purpose of this introduction, which brings together a number of main points emerging from the seminar discussions, is to set the stage for the study of social change at the local level by categorizing the main extrinsic factors of the situation within which changed social relationships occur, and to outline the most important new types of relationship and the norms which govern them. Some of the results of discussion are presented here, to be amplified by the material in the papers which follow.

Most of the Belgian, French, British, and Commonwealth territories have complete or sampling enumerations of population. The census *par rassemblage* in Portuguese territories is less satisfactory. Information on the dynamics of African population: fertility, mortality, and migration, is scanty and unreliable. Social anthropologists require an adequate framework of demographic data for intensive work. They can assist statisticians with pilot studies in developing efficient methods of inquiry and evaluating results. But their main contribution is to throw light on the conditions influencing demographic changes and the influence of demographic structure on other social phenomena.

Abstract formal analysis has shown that, in relatively stable populations not much affected by migration, the age structure is determined mainly by fertility, the expected variations in mortality being largely cancelled by consequent variations in rates of natural increase. Thus children make up a large proportion, and adults in productive ages a relatively low proportion, of any stable population with high fertility, regardless of its level of mortality.

Migration leads to abnormal sex ratios which affect family structure profoundly. As long as extended systems of kinship prevail, fertility rates are largely impervious to the influence of policy, but they may be consciously influenced in situations where the nuclear family becomes a more independent unit. The overall distribution of the African population, as determined by past conditions, is seriously out of step with present and potential economic opportunities. Hence migration coupled with the differential increase of various racial and ethnic groups leads to great but uneven pressure on housing and many other facilities in new population centres and so influences new patterns of social life.

Introductory Summary

Major international movements of labour migration in Africa are from the territories of the Western Sudan into Ghana and the Ivory Coast, from Ruanda-Urundi and neighbouring parts of Tanganyika into Uganda, of the Makua-Makonde-Mawia matrilineal peoples of north-eastern Portuguese East Africa into southern and coastal Tanganyika, and from south-western Tanganyika, Nyasaland, western and southern Portuguese East Africa into the industrial areas of Northern Rhodesia, Southern Rhodesia, and the Union of South Africa. Each of these movements involves some hundreds of thousands of persons annually, with adult males always predominating.

Other extrinsic factors which affect the form of social relationships in situations of modern change are: the nature of the link between a population centre and the surrounding rural or tribal area, the degree of ethnic diversity and differentiation of ethnic statuses, the diversity or uniformity of the regional culture and social structure, occupational characteristics, income levels and ranges, housing policy and administration, the degree of industrialization, and the strength of missions of the world religions.

Many of these factors are clearly interrelated and even overlapping. Their varying combinations can be assessed against the broad contrast between old established, slowly growing towns and new populations of mushroom growth. For ease of reference we shall refer to the former category as type A and the latter as type B. With those of type A must also be included many of the smaller towns, which are not necessarily old and which may have grown quite fast, but which have not attracted the major attention of government policy and have therefore sprung up in a rather haphazard or *laissez-faire* manner. They have also retained strong links with agriculture and the subsistence economy of the countryside. Not only African towns, but African territories as a whole, can be very largely grouped according to this distinction.

In the Union of South Africa, Southern and Northern Rhodesia, Kenya, and the Belgian Congo, most towns belong to type B. In Tanganyika, Uganda, the former territories of French Equatorial and British and French West Africa, most towns belong to type A. It will immediately be seen that the most industrialized territories

Social Change, Demography, and Extrinsic Factors 7

belong to type B and that this also means the territories with the largest white populations. Among those of type B it is some of the Belgian Congo towns which stand nearest to type A and among those of type A some Tanganyika centres stand nearest to type B.

Mining centres are affected differently from diversified towns. In some notable cases, mines have become the focus of development for towns in the full sense of centres providing general commercial and service facilities and varied employment opportunities not structurally contained entirely within a single giant industrial enterprise. This is a matter of degree and depends a good deal on the stage of development. It is obviously true of Johannesburg, of the Southern Rhodesian towns, where industry and mining is itself often considerably diversified, and of the main centres of the Northern Rhodesian Copperbelt and the Katanga region of the Belgian Congo. But smaller or newer mines, such as Williamson's diamond mine at Mwadui in Sukamaland, north-west Tanganyika, Kilembe copper mine in the Ruwenzori mountains of western Uganda, the scattered gold mines of Ghana, and other small mines in many territories, remain at present merely centres of concentrated employment rather than towns. The same is true of nearly all plantations.

Towns of type A are typically characterized by a more or less indigenous population core of considerable homogeneity. As a local tribe this provides a scale of status to which immigrants from a distance must conform and which may itself become further elaborated to include them. But there is a continuous gradation between short- and long-term migrants in relation to their economic status and distance from home, though local migrants are particularly important. Subsistence agriculture still plays a part in the life of these towns, since surrounding land is used for subsistence crops as well as commercial production, and town dwellers also have farms even at considerable distances to which they go and work and from which they obtain supplies.

Occupations are very diverse, in a setting which is predominantly clerical and commercial rather than industrial. Correspondingly, working groups are small and independent entrepreneurs numerous. There is also a continuous and very wide range of variations from wealthy proprietors of business, land, or property, and professional men down to poor dependants, casual workers, and beggars. Housing policy is marked by a permissive, *laissez-faire* attitude, accompanied by landlordism, extensive renting, and taking of lodgers. Uncontrolled residential patterns vary as much as the disposition and quality of housing, which ranges from imposing mansions to temporary hovels and overcrowded slums. The material standard of accommodation for the masses is very poor, but it is provided by spontaneous economic reaction to opportunity from within the African community as a whole, rather than artificially from outside it. It is in many ways better adapted to the needs of those it serves than more expensive accommodation, though much of it also falls below minimum standards of health and social amenity. While an extensive and corporate kinship structure rarely operates in these conditions, they are sufficiently flexible to permit some tribal or kinship concentration. Religious missions are often strongly represented, but rather as headquarters for rural and tribal operations than for anything very effective in town.

On the other hand, the newer centres of type B consist in the extreme case of a totally immigrant African population, which may be to a considerable extent of very distant origin. The break between town and country is sharp, and virtually excludes the subsistence basis of rural life. This may be because economic pressures have led to the capitalistic use of all land nearby, so that any subsistence or peasant population is excluded, or because Africans as such are legally prohibited from occupying it. Administrative control in towns of type B is close and appears to the immigrants to be exercised entirely by a dominant ethnic group of foreign origin and markedly different race. The African population is faced initially by a social vacuum without readily assimilable patterns or standards and this results in competition for status in non-traditional and extra-tribal terms. The occupational structure is based on clear distinctions between clerical, skilled, and unskilled workers and dominated by relatively few but large corporate organizations which are foreign to their African employees. African managerial, entrepreneurial, landlord, and professional roles are little developed and independent African economic activity is slight. Emergent class structure tends to follow the occupational structure closely but to be somewhat overshadowed by quasi-caste distinctions between different racial categories. The latter themselves have considerable differentiation in economic and political function which supports their social separation. Aspirations of the African population find expression in trade unions, and political parties, as well as tribal welfare associations. There are no traditional institutions to provide a focus. The main income levels, like occupations, are sharply distinct, but their overall range is not great. Clerks form the élite and are few in number.

The provision of housing is closely controlled and inflexible, being almost exclusively tied to large business concerns or to local and central government agencies. To obtain accommodation a person becomes classified as a family man or a bachelor and continued residence legally depends on proof of gainful employment. This puts the female population which these centres invariably attract in a highly anomalous position. Tribal or kinship concentrations are even less possible than in the older towns. Any regional diversities of culture and social structure tend to be at least temporarily overridden by the exigencies of a new existence in which they are irrelevant and their exponents in any case scattered and mixed. The activity of religious missions is bounded by the overall framework in its educational, welfare, and medical work, whereas in the older type of communities it may be a more positive factor in social change and the emergence of new groups and leaders.

Most towns in Northern and Southern Rhodesia and in the Kenya Highlands are surrounded by areas alienated to Europeans, so that Africans can only reside legally in the special areas set apart for them by municipal or other authorities. This system presupposes control of movement between town and country for its effective working. Urban authorities can only make squatting and *laissez-faire* settlement illegal if they assume some responsibility for the provision of housing. It is economically impossible to assume such responsibility without limiting the numbers to whom it applies. This was often given as the reason for attempting to control numbers, though many now consider the policy unsuccessful and the various techniques of control on movement in fact also serve security purposes which are irrelevant to housing.

The case of Southern Rhodesia is typical. Legislation restricts African residence in towns to land set aside for the purpose and to the duration of actual employment. Municipalities are also bound to provide housing for employed women. Gussman's case study of Bulawayo and comparable evidence from Salisbury indicate that this legislation set towns a hopeless task which they have been unable to carry.[1] Africans are forced to contravene the law by the mere fact of their residence, working women are forced to find accommodation in married or single men's quarters, and married couples are similarly forced to share with single men. Similar regulations exist in Northern Rhodesia but are reedport ineffective because of the absence of physical barriers to movement in and out of town. Illicit compounds run by European landholders relieve the sheer physical pressure on accommodation in towns like Lusaka, while on the Copperbelt the accommodation provided for mine employees is usually adequate in quantity to the numbers concerned. In Kenya the former system of registration, similar to that of Southern Rhodesia, has been abandoned and the present one specifically excludes data on employment and legally applies to all races though it has not been fully enforced. In Tanganyika compulsory registration has been rejected on grounds of cost and the impossibility of preventing evasion. The Belgian Congo also has a complex system aimed at least as much at preventing people from leaving rural areas as at preventing them from entering towns. This system has also been found to break down in the face of economic pressure especially in the larger cities such as Leopoldville. Uganda and the French and British west and equatorial African territories have not attempted to control movement by legislative or administrative methods.

Some population centres conform fairly closely to one or the other of these polar extremes, but most probably show mixed

[1] Gussman, B. W., *African Life in an Urban Area*, Bulawayo, 1952, Vol. I, p. 24.

features. Many West African towns show the characteristic features of type A. This is especially true of places like Oshogbo which have not been greatly transformed. On the other hand, in Ibadan traditional aspects have been modified by modern governmental functions and in Lagos the presence of the port and of large-scale modern commercial activity has led to a more mixed situation. The same is true, *mutatis mutandis*, of Dakar, Abidjan, Kumasi, Accra, Freetown, and many others. All these have large African populations, attracted by work in western economic enterprises but themselves engaging in considerable internal business activity on their own account and enjoying a good deal of autonomy in the arrangement of their way of life.

At the opposite end of the scale are most towns of the Central African Federation, where administrative control is close and nearly all housing is provided by large-scale agencies. Independent African economic enterprise is small, though in areas where there is local segregation of the African and non-African population, something of a protected market results, acting as a stimulus to African business within a restricted field. In Lusaka the unauthorized compounds in some ways resemble the slums of older towns, the chief difference being that the owners are white in the first case and black in the second. Since the Lusaka compounds are illegal, building of any quality or permanence is effectively discouraged, while the distinctive political, social, and ethnic status of landlord and tenant imparts a very special tone to their economic relationship.

The mining towns of the Belgian Congo are also characterized by extensive provision of institutional housing and the domination of African urban life by the giant enterprises which have caused it. Other Congo towns such as Stanleyville, Leopoldville, or Usumbura show a more varied pattern, with some of the housing built by the private initiative of Africans within an official siting plan and minimum building regulations. In Tanganyika towns, also, most Africans build their own houses according to minimum standards, movement is comparatively free and African petty trade flourishes. In Kenya towns, the main African residential areas are separate and housing is provided by local authorities to a large extent. In Uganda there is less official housing and more is left to private initiative.

Plantations exhibit both types of housing. In many cases there is a legal obligation to provide housing for employees, though this is sometimes commuted for cash or waived where insistence on conformity presents great difficulties. The oil-palm plantations in the Congo, Tanganyika sisal plantations, and Uganda sugar plantations provide estate housing for very large numbers of employees. But squatter settlements of uncontrolled type spring up around them in addition. In the Cameroons plantations most labour is self-housed, the estates being so sited that traditional African villages are dotted about between them. The squatters on European farms in Kenya build their own huts and there is usually an element of this wherever European family farms are found, as in the whole of Central Africa and in the Kivu and other highland areas of the Belgian Congo. Such farms constitute much smaller employment units than the mines and plantations previously considered, though there are many small plantations also. In such cases the social life of the employees depends a good deal on the personality of the individual farmer who controls their working existence as well as on the material provision made for them. The distinction between farm and plantation which we are using here is mainly one of scale, but also refers to the more varied crops associated with a farm by contrast with the frequent monoculture of plantations. It is conventional not to speak of sugar farms or of wheat plantations.

Where housing is officially provided it is usually of a higher apparent material standard, but the limitations of finance may lead to overall shortages and to very serious overcrowding. Where housing is left more to African private initiative, as in Enugu, Stanleyville, Dar-es-Salaam, or Tanga, its quantity may be relatively greater but its quality is often lower. Nevertheless, the stimulus and opportunity offered to African builders and property owners by the insatiable demand for low standard housing undoubtedly has an invigorating effect on African business as a whole and radically changes the socio-economic structure within which it operates. It means a much larger volume of capital and of entrepreneurial activity in numerous enterprises within the purely African sector, so that there is an earlier diversification of African economic activity in general. The price is paid in low quality of construction, sanitation, and general amenity. This price has been accepted in most West African towns and to some extent in Uganda and Nyasaland. The Congo and Tanganyika make provision for African building but control siting and design. Such a system may provide the optimum combination of freedom and control for African towns which are not traditional. Housing policies are often in practice determined by wider political rather than purely economic or planning considerations.

A reasonable classification is seen to emerge from the various combinations of the factors noted, and broad regional contrasts are valid. Exceptions can usually be accounted for by different local combinations of the same factors. For example, some mining towns in Ghana or Nigeria resemble the mining towns of Central Africa rather than the older towns of the West Coast, but the reasons for this are plain. We must now turn to the social relationships and the values which reinforce them within this varying framework of extrinsic factors.

II. NORMS AND STATUS SYMBOLS

The connexion between norms of conduct and patterns of social relationships is extremely intimate and becomes a crucial question in the study of social change. It is sometimes said that norm change must precede social change, but such a statement requires careful exploration. The concept of norms tends to exaggerate the consciousness of thought as the concept of structure exaggerates the regularity of action. In an ideal equilibrium society of great homogeneity where norm and action were perfectly attuned, without ambiguity or conflict, it would be necessary to assume that norm change must precede change in the pattern of action because otherwise any divergence in the latter would call forth the sanctions of the former and so restore the original equilibrium. Logical as this sounds, it involves some reification of norm and action as separable entities. Change will not occur unless a number of factors favour it, among which may be elements in the non-social environment. It may be at least as likely that, when some divergence occurs from a pre-established pattern of action, complementary norm change may be induced by it if other factors are in favour. Or the change in norm and action may be simultaneous. In the real world we are faced with a kaleidoscope of human activity, in which norm conflict and irregular action are ever present. Influenced by the same external factors, the minds of some persons may be engaged in working out attractive variations on old norms, while the spontaneous activity of others is giving expression to the same divergence.

Change in norms or in networks of social action does not necessarily imply new ideas or new actions, but only the approval of ideas and actions previously regarded as experimental and disreputable. Every real society consists of a core of orthodox norms and conforming actions round the margins of which continuous experiment goes on. It is from the margins of experiment that changing norms and actions emerge into sanctioned acceptance.

Even in stable situations, the assumption of homogeneity and

Norms and Status Symbols

invariability in norms or structure is an obvious over-simplification. To mention only one feature, social stratification immediately introduces a degree of difference, of opinion in the interpretation of norms, and of practice in the implementation of action. Even with the greatest consensus and solidarity, differences of age, of sex, of family size, not to speak of wealth or ethnic origin, make some variation and heterogeneity inseparable from society. It is not merely that norms vary in different parts of a social system, without any final arbiter of which version is right or wrong, but that they also operate at many different levels of generality. A group of people may be agreed upon a general principle in the light of which they elaborate the details of a particular application in various ways. Nor are most people highly consistent in securing complete compatibility between the varying sets of norms which activate them in different areas of their social life.

Without introducing any idea of social disorganization, inconsistency may be expected to appear in at least three different ways: as between different levels of generality from the universal to the particular in the statement of norms, between different social strata and between different areas of the social life of the same individuals. The more formal the structure of a social situation, the more unequivocal its norms may be and the more the actors in it are compelled to conform until the norms change. In general, the more fluid the network of relationships in a situation, the more equivocal or unformed is the accompanying set of norms.

Let us assume the by no means unheard of situation in which a factory is set up in the midst of an area of subsistence or cash-cropping peasant agriculture. It may well be that local people are not greatly attracted to factory employment and hence the labour force is largely composed of persons from other areas belonging to a number of different tribes. Such a situation in fact obtained in the cement factory at Tororo in Uganda. The framework of the work situation is determined by the employer and the outline of the roles involved is similarly defined. This much is tacitly accepted by the employee as part of the contract. He is taught new patterns of action required by the tasks to be achieved. No doubt he brings with him some presuppositions resulting from previous hearsay or experience of work situations which he rightly or wrongly thinks relevant. There is more certainty that the requisite actions, both in relation to objects and in relation to other persons, will be taught than that the appropriate norms will be effectively conveyed. The employee therefore finds himself, perhaps, operating simple types of equipment in conjunction with others, as he enters new networks of social relationships in the context of work. He is forced by circumstances and his economic motives into new relationships for which he is not necessarily equipped with any appropriate norms. No doubt he will intuitively experiment in testing out his previously acquired stock of norms, many of which may be quite unsuitable. As he is economically motivated to accept the new relationships we must assume that he adopts a flexible rather than a rigid approach to the adoption of new norms as required by the new situation. In such a case, therefore, the logical sequence is that the system of action is first learnt and the norms appropriate to it are acquired afterwards. Such norms are new to the actors concerned but may be similar to those acquired by others in similar situations. But undoubtedly many situations arise in changing Africa which are to some extent unprecedented. If such situations are repeated they are certain in time to give rise to sets of norms which are genuinely new, though no doubt only in the sense of slight modification.

Situations may be characterized by consensus of norms, or conflict of norms, or simple inadequacy or lack of norms. Social situations can, in a sense, lack norms though persons cannot. For sociology, norm equipment is part of the person by definition, so that it is carried into every situation. But the norms carried thus into a new situation by the actors may be largely incompatible with it and if it persists they will have to be dropped and new or modified norms developed and adopted in their place. These latter norms then belong to that situation and are part of its structure which was previously lacking or deficient. A course of action may be held to imply certain norms, even if they are not stated and the actors are unaware of them. Obviously social change involves a continuous stimulus and counter-stimulus between norm and action. The African tribesman acquires new wants as a result of structural changes which have already occurred within his society, such as the imposition of colonial rule and the collection of tax, or the establishment of new relationships with missionaries or traders. The new wants may drive him to work in a factory where, both at work and in his leisure time, he finds himself forced to enter into a whole series of new relationships in novel situations. As he and others repeat this sequence of action, new values grow up to govern the new relationships involved, though many conflicts remain. So norm and action go hand in hand, change in either requiring adjustment from the other if increasing conflict is to be avoided. Unless we define social change tautologically as identical with norm change, which seems unjustifiable, we must accept three possible types of change: norm change followed by behavioural change, behavioural change followed by norm change, and simultaneous change in behaviour and norms. Changes may occur in one situation which prepare the persons in it for another without them necessarily being aware of it. In many African rural communities where traditional trading was little developed (in contrast to West Africa where it has such a long history), markets have sprung up and women have become regular petty traders. Women have also begun to brew beer for sale instead of only for ceremonial occasions and they have begun to drink it themselves instead of depending on male favour. As we shall see later,[1] these changes, which involve both new norms and new relationships, have an important bearing on the position of women in towns, amounting to a kind of anticipatory urbanization.

Consensus of norms may commonly occur in social situations which have lasted for a long time without change, so that the forces which have maintained the persons concerned in relationship have also sufficed, in the absence of external disturbance, to produce an ironing out of differences and evolution of agreed norms. Conflict of norms arises from the disturbance of existing groups and from the bringing together into new groups of previously unrelated persons who from their accumulated stock of

[1] p. 46.

norms apply to the new situation some which are incompatible. Where situations are new and many of the persons brought together in them previously unrelated we must say that both structure and norms are relatively lacking. No doubt such persons have role relationships somewhere, as for example in their tribal homes, which have considerable stability and structure. They also possess an accumulated stock of norms relating to situations in which they were acted upon in reasonable consensus with others. But such role relationships and norms may provide little guidance in new situations. A new situation is of little social significance if it is ephemeral and is never repeated. If it is repeated it immediately falls into a pattern, more or less invariable, and gathers a structure of norms, more or less consistent. Until this happens, action is largely unpremeditated and lacking in appropriate norms. At this level sociology is powerless. But it is important to remember that many crucial situations in Africa approximate this state of normless action. Intensive observation must discern incipient norms and recurrent relationships within the flux, rather than dismiss such situations with qualitative blanket terms.

The phrase 'to pay lip service' clearly indicates the possibility of unobtrusive non-conformity in action under the cover of verbal recognition of the norms transgressed. When such transgression attains a certain frequency we have a minority group of non-conformists on the strength of which a modified norm may be advanced either as an alternative or a substitute for that already existing.

How fast can norms change? It is important to distinguish the rapidity of change in a system or a situation from the rapidity of change in persons. The two may coincide, but in the African context of change frequently do not. Wild young men may become respectable household heads at the age of forty. In the case of a migrant worker, leaving his tribal home and going to town for the first time, the shock must inevitably be great, however much he is prepared by the experiences of his fellows. He goes to town with certain fairly clear objectives. These objectives differ from those of rural tribal life and may even seem contradictory to them, but for the migrant worker they are complementary. To this extent, although he switches his objectives when he leaves home, this change is not unexpected, although it may be sudden. He gradually becomes aware of these objectives as he grows up in a rural community to which migrant labour has become an accompaniment. This latent awareness, therefore, is not sudden. But the switch of action patterns from the rural to the urban set of objectives is as rapid as the migrant's journey to town. These objectives, however, are only a part of the whole set of norms with which he is forced to operate in town and his adjustment to the whole urban set of norms must be sudden on his first arrival there. But this urban set of norms is part of a continuing situation which has evolved step by step although the entry of persons into it is so abrupt. So there are both gradual and sudden changes in the norms of migrant workers, while the set of norms operative in an urban situation changes gradually, picked up afresh by every migrant worker on arrival and reverting to latency for him each time he returns to the country. The impact of each migrant on the urban situation is infinitesimal yet this situation and its norms change under the collective impact of migrant workers, their objectives and the reactions which they set up in urban situation. It is only in the face of really sudden or catastrophic events and crises, usually of a political kind, that anything like sudden norm change can be forced upon a whole population or group. This may sometimes take the form of reversion to old sets of norms which have been overlaid. If such reversion is impossible an anomic situation will arise in which any appropriate patterns which can be borrowed from elsewhere are likely to be very rapidly adopted.

In type A towns like Oshogbo, Koforidua, or even Lagos, there is considerable continuity of norms between town and countryside, at least for the more stable urban groups of the local tribe. In type B towns like Salisbury, Gwelo, or Nairobi there is great discontinuity. Although migrants must, of course, be aware of the two sets of norms between which they oscillate, the two sets are indeed largely distinct, linked by the movement of persons between them. Within the same historical sequence change may proceed in irregular jolts. The impact of the Land Husbandry Act in Southern Rhodesia, or of land consolidation and villagization in Kikuyu, and of course the Buganda land settlement in an earlier period, are examples of fairly sudden externally induced change, specifically economic, but evoked by particular political circumstances. It may be suspected that, where such changes fit in with incipient aspirations, permitting them fuller expression than hitherto, changes in norms and social structure go fast and deep; but where this conjunction is absent, compulsory changes in the superficial pattern of relationships may be a veneer on an unchanged norm structure.

Pons's Stanleyville study (Pons, p. 205) provides clear examples of how closely incipient norms and concrete relationships go hand in hand in informal situations. People get to know one another and gradually turn into a more and more solidary group. Eventually they define the basis of their association, make rules and create offices. At the particular level, a new set of norms has come into being for them. But at a more general level they were feeling their way in the light of principles of which they must already have been at least vaguely aware. These principles themselves were new to them, but not new as principles, the main idea was borrowed from others and reinterpreted. Probably this would not have occurred until the moment at which the actual relationships of these people had reached a phase of development which made the borrowing and adaptation of the principles desirable. Thus the question as to whether norms or relationships came first becomes meaningless.

Norms are often symbolically expressed. At this point they may represent aspirations rather than hard and fast rules of conduct. Most frequently they are oriented towards considerations of status and class. Fashions of dress, manners of eating, material possessions and housing, certain types of verbal expression, as well as actual social relationships, especially formal associations in their rules and the number and form of their offices, all indicate not only the place of people in a system of stratification but, particularly in a mobile situation, the direction of their aims. They will adopt what seem to them the ostentatious symbols of a status to which they aspire, but by their economic limitations, by misunderstanding and the necessity to fit borrowed elements into the existing role structure in which they find themselves, they are forced to modify and reinterpret all along. They also find themselves committed to the acceptance of certain types of behaviour consistent with their aspirations, and the rejection of other types.

Misunderstandings and mistakes may occur in the initial transfer of objects or usages from one culture to another, in the sense that the original borrower may not in fact have fully understood the place of such features in the culture from which he borrowed them. But these errors are of little significance. The objects are fitted into a new functional nexus. Their new use may be regarded as misguided or ridiculous by members of the culture from which they were borrowed. But for those into whose culture the new objects are adopted the new use is just as appropriate and proper as was the old in its context. To drink beer out of the spout of a teapot is as sensible as turning a beer gourd into a lamp-stand.

The desire for valuable and useful objects has nothing necessarily symbolic about it, nor any connexion with status. But this symbolic link is proved when the object is desired for its appearance rather than its use, as in the case of the broken wireless or gramophone, the sunglasses without lenses and the shirt with no back, or the unused parlour. Similarly, the relative prestige of occupations largely depends on the solid estimation of concomitant differences in wealth and power, but the latter two factors are not alone decisive and leave room for considerable play.

In all situations of economic change, social mobility tends to be increased. Thus women aim at raising their status by marriage, and in this are guided by various status symbols. In Lagos the government servant used to provide the type of the wealthy man. Now it is said that the government servant's wealth is all show; his car was bought on a government loan, his rent is deducted at source and his actual salary cheque is small, so government servants are disparagingly referred to as 'senior debtors' and rich businessmen with plenty of ready money are preferred. Lawyers and doctors who are both educated and wealthy constitute the cream. Girls from one-roomed homes want to get 'a room and a parlour' when they marry and to live on tinned food and bread instead of on traditional diet. For men also a good house is now a better symbol of urban prosperity than a plurality of wives. Two storeys are better than one and a man will justify his inability to maintain his children by saying that all his money has gone on building. Formerly the old educated families of Lagos formed a fairly stable élite but now anyone who can spend lavishly on entertaining is accepted in any society.

There is an unavoidable conflict for women, because the dutiful wife of a stable marriage wins the respect of her husband and general high esteem, yet her jural status may be even lower than it is in the rural community. She loses the influence which comes from the vital agricultural and domestic roles which can no longer be performed in town. The high status goal of grandmotherhood is likely to be beyond her reach because her children may scatter or she herself retire to the country before it can be attained. On the other hand, the free-lance woman may forfeit respectability and general esteem, yet can undoubtedly win an economic and jural status as an independent business woman and property owner which is not open to her respectable sister.

Education is recognized as the main avenue to wealth in Lagos and young men will study throughout the night to get their General Certificate of Education. For similar reasons there is tremendous pressure to get an overseas education and boys stow away in order to get to England. Because many Christian families have an objectively higher standard of living than Muslims, the religion of the latter usually implies a lower status than Christianity and reluctance to intermarry is partly due to this. Great confidence is still retained in sacrifices, magic, and medicine to affect the boss and get promotion, or to impede the advancement of others. The Aladura separatist churches are socially inferior, but their leaders and prophets are much consulted in secret by orthodox Christians claiming higher status.

Symbols also permit the vicarious enjoyment in fantasy of status which in reality is out of reach. This appears in the adoption of formal European titles and behaviour and in the emphasis on smart western clothes by those in occupations below the white-collar level, for whom such clothes seem at first sight inappropriate. An interesting recent phenomenon of the same kind is the adoption of Ghana styles of dress for political celebrations in many other British African territories, with the implication that the clothes worn carry with them something of the achievement of Ghana in winning independence.

The norms for a new situation may be carried over from a traditional context, but more frequently are borrowed from western contexts which lend them prestige. Some of the norms of Yoruba traditional crafts were carried over into western forms of production. But there is a vast amount of borrowing of behaviour from district commissioners, missionaries, courts, and every dominant western institution which has been imported to Africa. Yoruba men and women have rejected arranged marriages and adopted the western romantic view of the individual marriage contract, which was consistent though it brought its own conflicts. The Ibo have also rejected arranged marriages but without accepting the romantic norm pattern, so that many are left without valid criteria for use in choosing a mate, because the old norms in this respect are incompatible with rejection of lineage authority and isolation of the nuclear family. Another frequent adjustment reported from Oshogbo, Accra and for higher status families all over tropical Africa is that whereby a man has an official or show wife for European contexts and a traditional wife, mistress, or concubine behind the scenes for informal tribal contexts. In some cases urban courts may assist through their judgements in redefining applicable roles, reconciling conflicts, and importing new norms from elsewhere.

Interpretation of the status gained in modern contexts by particular tribes in terms of special characteristics of their traditional structure is full of pitfalls. For a special sequence of historical circumstances seems to provide a sounder explanation. The intermediate experience of a tribe between its present adaptation and its past traditional structure is of great importance. The Tonga of Nyasaland were so placed that they received mission education before their neighbours and so got the early clerical jobs and now dominate the trade unions. Here the influence of traditional structure seems too indirect to be relevant. The Tutsi have exercised extreme political dominance in the traditional hierarchical systems of Ruanda and Urundi. But, on the other hand, when they become employees in Leopoldville, they aim first at acquiring a servant when their means permit, instead of going first for bicycles, radios, and other consumption goods like their fellow Africans. By contrast, the Kongo who do not bother with servants in Leopoldville, which is in their tribal area so that they have no difficulty in getting help from relatives, try to have servants when they are working 2,000 miles away at Usumbura in the country of the Tutsi. The difference seems to be that the Tutsi value servants as indices of status as well as for utility, both in their home town of Usumbura and when far away, but the Kongo only do so when far away from the help of relatives. Similarly, in Kampala wealthy Ganda employ servants of other tribes or quite unrelated Ganda, because it would usually be shameful and embarrassing for status reasons to employ a relative. But wealthy Luo, with an egalitarian traditional system and very strong agnatic ties which transcend modern status differences, employ servants who are usually relatives. For a young Luo does not mind assisting a relative informally, but would often be ashamed of open employment as a servant by a member of his own tribe.

That which represents the aspirations of one people may be regarded as an obstruction by another in apparently similar circumstances. Thus in Ghana the long established policy of using vernacular languages in the first years of schooling, which educationists have considered to be generally beneficial to the child, is being reversed on the ground that it is unfavourable to progress and prevents full participation in the outer world. Meanwhile in neighbouring French Togo, where school instruction is wholly in French, the introduction of teaching in vernacular languages is being considered on the ground that the use of French alone tends to destroy native culture.

The study of norms and of symbols of status or prestige demands the techniques of sampling and attitude questioning. But it must be complemented by intensive observation of the small group relationships in which norms and symbols find expression.

III. SMALL GROUPS AND SOCIAL NETWORKS

Work on small groups has two important aspects. Most obviously, it concerns social groups which are small in size, but also constitutes a special approach to the study of face-to-face relationships in small clusters within larger populations which seem to lack corporate structures except as a wide impersonal framework. The object is both to study small groups for their own sake and to see how the wider corporate structures impinge upon those who compose them, that is, how continuous chains and interlocking networks of role relationships link the members of small groups to the structures of the wider society and the persons who play key roles in them. The small groups themselves are not necessarily the units of analysis and in many situations there may seem to be few if any coherent small groups at first sight. The object of study then is to discover the type and the channels of interaction between persons, and the extent of regularities which give a minimum of order and coherence to social life in communities which have no clear structure of discrete groups. The emphasis is first on relationships within a group or network, which is the most neglected field of study. Small groups in this sense are, of course, quite distinct from the artificial small groups which have been studied in laboratory situations. Although they are very fluid and therefore in some ways more difficult to study, there may sometimes be more stability in the pattern of small group relations during periods of rapid change in which more formal structures are swept away. Tribal norms also survive to some extent in the domestic situation when they have become inoperative in wider contexts.

The effect of this approach is to enlarge the field of positive knowledge by defining, or approaching a definition of situations hitherto regarded as presenting an unstructured fluidity which defied positive analysis. This approach also stresses social relationships as the small-scale framework of this type of structure. Relationships are seen as reflecting and interacting with sets of norms. Even highly fluid and rapidly changing situations are reduced to variations on a finite number of types of interaction and directions of change, rather than dismissed by qualitative assessments of chaos, disorganization, or breakdown of norms, which fail to penetrate sufficiently beyond general impressions to the actions of the persons concerned.

This is not to deny the fact that some social structures serve the needs and problems of persons currently involved in them better or worse than others, but emphasizes the fact that disorganization is usually a very relative term, sometimes denoting little more than a change from one pattern of relationships to another. Suggestions of anomie must be pressed home to the actual quality of the relationships held to justify them.

The dictum that to study a small group you have to get close to it must be followed. The form these small groups take varies enormously. Serious problems of selection and sampling arise. There may be ephemeral clusters, perhaps resembling a more stable nucleus round which evanescent particles revolve, there may be cliques, gangs, neighbourhoods, or emergent interest groups which begin to acquire a recognizable associational structure. The initial problem of selection and definition of the unit of study is solved at the lowest level by starting with any person as a potential nucleus for a network of relationships. This method inevitably leads to the discovery that some persons play a more active, positive, and important part as nuclei than others, and field work is justifiably concentrated upon them as nodal points in the structure. It enables the field worker to penetrate the sphere usually dealt with by the novelist, in following individual ambitions yet doing so objectively and seeing them against the background of a recurrent pattern of activity.

The problem of sampling and of representativeness is a real one, for we are dealing with data which lie on the margin of the quantifiable. The first point to make is that small group analysis of the type under discussion gives knowledge of the fabric of society which statistical sampling on a basis of formal question and interview alone can never provide. The alternative at this level is not between representative or unrepresentative data but between some knowledge or none. The statistical status of information on small group relationships is inevitably ambiguous at first, but its intrinsic reliability will increase as more work is done. There is no need for statistical studies and those which go beyond the present limits of the quantifiable to remain in separate compartments as is sometimes the case. Some intercalibration is possible. The data available on persons intensively studied in informal or small group relationships ought to include all that a sample survey would yield and a great deal more. The material is both quantitative and qualitative, but this distinction is relative and changing in that improved techniques should bring more qualitative material within the field of quantitative statement. In any case, intensive studies will include, and go beyond, the usual quantifiable data on age, sex, ethnic status, kinship and family composition, occupation and income, education, religion, associational membership, and any other such objective criteria thought to be relevant. Ideally, the distribution of these factors among the subjects of intensive study should be related to their average distribution in the population as a whole and in particular relevant categories of it, as revealed by sampling and interview. The degree of representativeness of the persons intensively studied will then be known and gaps if possible filled. The result is that all the further qualitative data obtained by intensive studies will refer to a sample of known representativeness in terms of the major quantifiable criteria, although the sample was not randomly drawn. This is what is meant here by intercalibration. Quantifiable factors can be controlled for representativeness just as well in small group studies as in extensive sample surveys, provided both kinds of work are done. But the former work also penetrates deeper than the level of these conventional factors and knowledge of the distribution and frequency of characteristics at this deeper level must await the accumulation of work and the slow refinement of analysis.

In some cases, informal networks of social relations form the interstitial links between families, kin groups, neighbourhoods, factories, and local authorities. They provide contexts for the induction of strangers into new communities. But this interstitial region may also be occupied by more clear-cut groups and associations, serving various functions and changing in this respect over time. They may provide kinship surrogates for persons accustomed in their rural homes to widely ramifying kinship systems which cannot be reproduced in towns and employment centres.

Beer bars are a ubiquitous context of informal networks, assuming various forms depending on the degree of control enforced or the extent of actual suppression attempted. They appear with some of the same social attributes in situations as diverse and distant as the Cameroons Plantations, Stanleyville, and Kampala. They tend to provide an atmosphere which is, in a sense, impersonal yet at the same time informal and potentially intimate. The context is not restricted by the relatively rigid norms of tribal life; there is at least initial anonymity, a clean slate on which the new arrival can begin to write his urban destiny on the basis of individually achieved rather than ascribed status. Apart from assisting in the induction of newcomers, such places tend to provide attractive neutral ground for the commencement of love affairs and the transactions of thieves and receivers. For all these reasons those who run them form important fixed points in the network of the most informal and fleeting relationships.

Thus, intensive study of small-scale relationships also provides a means of exploring the interstitial limbo in the more formal structure of society. The more formal the structure, the less extensive and significant is the limbo. It is at its maximum in many African towns because the formal structure is so wide or alien that it leaves great gaps in the social life of masses of the people. It is of long-term importance in towns which continue to depend on a large population of temporary migrants and it is of transitional importance for both towns and individuals moving on to a more formally structured existence.

The more formal structures which may supervene are of a very varied associational type. There are the purely social clubs for chatting, dancing, drinking, and all kinds of recreation, and there are the widespread mutual benefit associations, frequently focused especially on such matters as saving, repatriating destitutes, and providing for burial expenses. For the more educated, wealthy, and sophisticated, who usually also become the more permanent town dwellers, there are more specific interest groups and professional associations.

But outside such élites small group relationships seem to afford rather vague and general satisfactions, in some cases replacing and in others supplementing the stronger kinship and local units of tribal life. Where formal organization is attempted it seems very much concerned with the allocation of status. Youth groups round Lagos, though easier for welfare agencies to run if large, tend to collapse if their membership exceeds about thirty, apparently because when they are smaller the chance of office bearing is greater. It is more important to be than to do and a large group defeats its object. Proliferation of titles and offices is very common. Associations in Freetown are reported with more than half their members in titled office. Similar evidence from East and Central Africa suggests that this element is general to Africans in towns. The titles and sometimes the smart clothes which have to be worn further indicate that these organizations give their members a vicarious participation, through fantasy, in the prestige-bearing European or western style social structure which in real life lies beyond their reach.

The study of small groups is focused mainly upon face-to-face relationships. It has been suggested that such relationships may usefully be distinguished as structural, categorical, or egocentric according to the basis upon which persons intuitively classify one another on meeting. Face-to-face relationships of a structural type are aspects of roles defined within the structure of an institution. Thus, though people meet face to face either in the family or in the factory their relationship in these contexts is structural in this sense. Categorical relationships are those in which persons meet in an informal context yet without knowing one another very well, and consequently begin to act on the basis of intuitively assigning one another to various type categories as an empirical approach towards appropriate behaviour. Egocentric relations are those in which people know one another sufficiently intimately as persons to base their mutual expectations of one another's behaviour directly on this personal knowledge. Good examples of categorical and egocentric relationships are given from two small groups in a Stanleyville street.[1]

It is important to note that, in the new situations, networks of face-to-face relationships spring up without the conventional bases of kinship or neighbourhood which are so all-embracing in traditional African society. But although the full nexus of kinship and tribal obligations is often purposely evaded by town dwellers, kinship and tribal bonds are constantly drawn upon and turned to new uses. We also have to consider how much the family, which is the small face-to-face group *par excellence*, contributes to the situation in towns.

[1] See Pons's paper.

IV. KINSHIP, TRIBALISM, AND FAMILY AUTHORITY

Reference is frequently made to the breakdown of African kinship in towns and this, like the description of their general social situation as disorganized, can be a misleading over-simplification. The adoption of more appropriate methods for discerning what regularities exist has demonstrated that, however radical the changes and however repugnant to Western values their concomitants, it is rare to find complete breakdown, anomie, or total lack of system. Social life continues and its rules must be discovered.

The most general statement that can be made is that in the new situations the scope of kinship rights and duties has narrowed and become more uncertain and the body of kin included in them become reduced. In these situations the total contribution of kinship relations to the social structure is relatively less than in tribal subsistence communities, especially by comparison with relationships of more specialized economic, recreational, or other associational type.

The new situations are unfavourable to the corporate kin groups which are so important in many tribal systems. The extreme development of corporate kin groups in the shape of large localized lineages can never be reproduced in the new fast-growing towns. But it is important to remember that even in Lagos, Oshogbo, Oyo, and in other Yoruba towns, there is a high degree of correspondence between compounds and localized lineages. A lineage may number as many as a thousand persons, but the larger lineages segment and the compounds which correspond to the segments are scattered about the town.[1] It will also be remembered that in the capital towns of the Tswana, some of them holding many thousands of people, localized lineages provide the core of wards which make up the town.[2] These are extreme cases of the accommodation of localized lineages to an

[1] P. C. Lloyd, 'The Yoruba Lineage', *Africa*, XXV, 1955, No. 5.
[2] I. Schapera, *A Handbook of Tswana Law and Custom*, p. 9 ff., 2nd edition, Oxford, 1955.

urban setting. Elsewhere, in towns which have grown more rapidly from nothing by immigration and constitute a sharper break with rural life, the corporate localized lineages of tribal communities find little reflection.

The fundamental difference of most African kinship in towns is that, where a large part of the African urban population retains rural roots and returns to the countryside at the end of its working life or before, the range of kin provided for any town dweller is essentially incomplete. Many of the key positions in the kinship system to which he was reared remain vacant in the town. The collection of relatives with whom he is able to establish and maintain kinship in the urban context is miscellaneous and haphazard. This leads to improvising. The elaborate distinctions of traditional kinship categories are no longer viable because the functional connexion between them is destroyed by the absence of vital components. The grandparental generation may be completely lacking. There may be a father's sister in town but no mother's brother. Because the range of kin presented in the urban population is incomplete, the individual is left to cast about and pin obligations of kinship on to whom he can while himself endeavouring to evade them when it seems worthwhile. Most of the rituals of kinship cannot be performed for this reason, or only in a truncated form which severely weakens their contribution to solidarity.

The reason why kinship obligations can be more easily evaded in town is not merely the frequently high mobility, as a result of which particular kin are constantly disappearing from the urban scene, but the restriction in the scope of kinship already noted. The significance of kinship in the economic field becomes slight because, although relatives help one another to find jobs, it is rare to find brothers or other close kin working as servants in the same house, in a factory at the same bench, or in a mine at the same rock face. But even if they did, they would be working within a system regulated by persons unaware of their kinship and by rules which deny its relevance. The solidarity which obtains where relatives must rely on one another for the production of their food is absent. In the political field, too, kinship loses much of its relevance. In tribal systems, the extent to which political roles are subsumed in or linked to those of kinship varies greatly, but is always more than is usual in town. Although kinsmen in town rely on one another for some degree of mutual aid and security where possible, African urban populations are bound to recognize the predominant part played in its maintenance of order by the interlocking network of large-scale economic and political institutions, including those of local government and the police, even where these are not conceded full legitimacy by them. It is only in some of the West African towns that Africans are found in charge of the main institutions of law and order. But many innovations are occurring in this field, as in the appointment of African burgomasters in the Congo and the appointment of the first African Mayor of Kampala. Where African townsfolk have organized spontaneously for political ends it is the concept of tribe rather than kinship which provides the only traditional integrating factor.

It is the domestic field which still provides the main scope for kinship in town. This too is limited where single men form a large element in the population and where irregular unions are a frequent substitute for traditional marriages. The extrinsic factors of urban administration and housing policy exert strong influence here. Where most housing is officially provided, movement to town restricted and independent employment rare, there are usually large numbers of single men, frequent irregular unions, and the more stable families are restricted to the nuclear type. Where movement into town is unrestricted, housing built by African private enterprise and independent employment frequent, the situation is altogether more favourable to family life and even extended families and larger groups of kin may be found. Salisbury, Gwelo, the Copperbelt, Katanga, Nairobi, Mombasa, and most plantations are obvious examples of the first situation: Dar-es-Salaam, Kampala, Blantyre, Leopoldville, Brazzaville, Douala, Lagos, and most West African towns of the second. It corresponds to the distinction between towns of type A and type B.

In New-Bell, Douala, quite large family groups have succeeded in establishing themselves, by a remarkable adaptation of the traditional residence pattern, whereby complex star-shaped dwellings represent the rural multi-hut system. This is especially characteristic of the Bamileke but also of many other tribes in the Cameroons region. Family clusters occupying from five to twenty huts spring up on this basis. The occupants have some sense of common descent and the immigrant feels he has some claim to become a partly or wholly dependent lodger with any kinsman however distant. A distinction may be made here between lodgers who live with the family free and tenants who pay for board and lodging.

It is probable that in the plantation situation kinship clusters have more chance of survival than in more diversified urban contexts. Plantations usually show a strong concentration of particular tribes, making likely the existence of many kinship links among close neighbours. But the labour force of most plantations is very unstable, with a high percentage of bachelors, so that kinship links are distorted and rather limited to those between men of working age. Plantation existence may constitute only an interlude, though perhaps an oft-repeated one, in lives still firmly embedded in the fuller kinship systems of rural tribal communities.

Whatever the emphasis on descent and residence in the kinship system to which a person is reared, when he goes to town he is forced into a situational approach. The precise distinctions of numerous traditional kinship categories tend to be replaced by a vague sense of mutual obligation attaching to general kinship as such. Although there is some continuity in that newcomers are usually assisted by relatives in their initial introduction to town life, the available circle of kin upon whom they can call is constantly changing. Therefore each person has to discover and establish his own set of urban kinship relationships, rather than simply growing up into a known and pre-existing network. Urban kinship tends to have this in common with tribal bilateral kinship, that the relevant circle of kinsfolk varies for almost every individual and that each is offered or can discover various possibilities which he proceeds to select and manipulate. This does not mean that certain relationships, such as that of a man with his wife's brother, do not retain something of their traditional tone. It does mean that the classificatory extension of kinship categories of superordination and subordination is unlikely to apply, for the sanctions to authority are absent. What is most required in town is recognition of the diffuse obligation to assist one another in need, where and when possible. This may explain why the urban recognition of common kinship fades almost imperceptibly into that of common ethnic origin between those of the same tribe. There is a tendency to extend the concept of brotherhood metaphorically to all fellow tribesmen. Though corporate kin groups fail to survive, new corporate associations based on tribal affiliation may be created.

Tribalism offers benefits of an obvious but less specific kind than kinship. Attachment in terms of common language and culture gives comfort in the midst of a highly segmental intertribal field. Urban is thus different from rural tribalism, one of its main functions being to classify the multitude of Africans of heterogeneous origin and so provide a basis for the emergence of new groupings to meet new demands.[3] It takes its place as one of a number of possible classifications, no longer the overwhelmingly predominant one, the others being common occupation, similar wealth and status, or like leisure interests. This form of urban tribalism is a category of interaction within a wider system, not the corporate and largely closed structure of social relationships provided by a tribe in its traditional area.

It is therefore not surprising that few new kinship terms or categories have emerged. The adoption of 'bere' and 'anti' by the Yoruba may result more from peculiarities of their kinship system,[4] with its unusual paucity of categories, than from any adjustment to town life. Urban conditions encourage concentration on the nuclear kinship categories, but understood in a more diffuse sense than traditionally attached to them. Examples of metaphorical or symbolic extension of kinship are not only the application of the concept of brotherhood to all members of a tribe, but also such features as lodgers calling their landlady

[3] See Gluckman's paper.
[4] William B. Schwab, 'The Terminology of Kinship and Marriage among the Yoruba', *Africa*, XXVIII, 1958, No. 4, Oct. 1958, p. 301 ff.

'mother'. One of the furthest extensions of the idiom of kinship recorded, is that of the *goumbe* youth societies of Ghana and the Ivory Coast, which take over the function of kin groups in relation to their members, acting as families between which marriages take place and providing a domestic grant to enable new couples to set up their menages.[5] Furthermore, the use of a *lingua franca* by members of a number of different tribes forces them to ignore the finer points of distinction in their kinship systems and to be satisfied, at least in inter-tribal dealings, with the lowest common factor in the main kin concepts on which there may be general agreement.

The urban situations most inimical to the development of local kin groups are probably those associated with the maintenance of strong rural ties. Evidence from Central Africa indicates that, even where migrant workers or entire families spend the whole working lives of their adult members in towns or mines, they maintain *in absentia* the most detailed interest and long-range participation in home tribal affairs through writing letters, sending money, and passing news constantly among themselves.[6] This is because they recognize that, however long they stay away to work, their tribal home still offers the only viable family home especially for security in old age. Though they become townsmen, they remain all the time tribesmen at a distance. The urban phase of their existence is economically essential to them, and may fulfil other ambitions as well, but all the time they ensure that their place is still kept warm for them in what is still their home. In Leopoldville, when a scheme was started for Africans to acquire plots of land by secure title, even very sophisticated *évolués* refused to take it up anywhere except in their own tribal areas. In this way economic development strengthened neo-tribalism by encouraging the picking up of old links. In Ghana political leaders have been known to save up to buy cocoa land and put illiterate relatives in charge of it. Here again primarily economic opportunities serve to strengthen tribal structure in a new way.

It is interesting to contrast this with the migration from Ruanda-Urundi into Uganda, where many migrants become per-

[5] See Rouch's paper.   [6] See van Velsen's paper.

manent residents, but, significantly, not in towns but by increasingly complete absorption into the rural community.[7] In the case of the great migration from the savannah areas of West Africa into the forest zones of the Ivory Coast and Ghana close links are retained with the original tribal groups, as in Central Africa, and settlement in the south is only temporary.[8]

The children of West African migrants from the north by coastal women are often caught in the conflict of patrilineal and matrilineal claims. Their fathers are patrilineal and usually Islamic, while their mothers may be matrilineal. Each parent attempts to abscond with the child and bind it to his or her tribe. Some children are torn from their allegiance to either and have become a distinct and rootless group in the coastal towns with its own emerging associational life.

Evidence from the Copperbelt, from Dar-es-Salaam, and from Sierra Leone shows how tribal headmen or representatives have been important in the early stages of urban settlement but later were eclipsed. On the Copperbelt the formal way in is through tribal elders, but in Salisbury through friendly societies, usually of twenty to thirty tribesmen, which also act as burial societies. Immigrants later tend to join groups with a more specific focus, such as friendship at work or common religion. Similarly, immigrants to Freetown come under the patronage of tribal headmen or notables and join voluntary associations with special interests later, entry to certain élite associations being the most difficult of all. Tribal associations are reported from East, West, and Central Africa. They mark a stage in which immigrant workers have become sufficiently used to town life to be able to organize themselves effectively in that context, yet on the basis of interest fundamentally centred in the countryside, indicating that they reject any irrevocable commitment to the town. The Zongo Volunteer Group in Kumasi, originally formed to self-police the strangers' quarter, became a tool of political factions and played a violent part which caused its suppression, after which it assumed the form of a yam trading organization. Tribal associations often exhibit

[7] A. I. Richards, *Economic Development and Tribal Change*, pp. 267, 274, 279, 285.
[8] See Jean Rouch's paper, also R. Mansell Prothero, 'Migratory Labour from North-Western Nigeria', *Africa*, XXVII, 1957, No. 3, p. 251.

the same need for status satisfaction through proliferation of flamboyant office titles as we have already noted in the case of small groups.

There is considerable literature on tribal associations, which goes far beyond the scope of the present discussion. We have remarked that three phases may be seen, the first in which the stake of most Africans in town is too fleeting for effective tribal associations to be formed, but in which both kinship and tribal bonds are seized upon situationally for mutual aid; the second phase in which tribal associations are formed for general welfare purposes, and the third phase in which Africans begin to move beyond a tribal basis to form associations for common interests and to express similar achieved status, cutting across tribal lines. Where towns are closely associated with a locally dominant tribe, such as the Yoruba in Lagos, the Zaramo in Dar-es-Salaam, or the Ganda in Kampala, specifically tribal associations are not found among its members because the tribal structure is sufficiently elaborate and adaptable to provide alternative channels for social relationships. Thus in Kampala, there is a strong Luo Union of immigrants from Kenya, a Banyarwanda Barundi Association of those from Ruanda-Urundi, and embryonic organizations of some Uganda tribes such as the Toro, but no tribal associations of the Ganda as such, for they are already organized in many special purpose institutions. Many West African tribes, such as the Yoruba, Ibo, or Temne, already show an elaboration of associational structures not usually regarded as characteristic of tribal life. This may be linked with the traditional concentration of population in some areas or with the generally greater diversity of the traditional tribal economy. These are two factors which tend to reinforce each other.

Another adaptation of tribalism to modern life is the *utani* or joking relationship of Tanganyika tribes, the origin of which remains somewhat obscure. In Tanganyika there is a long and continuous history of labour migration from the time of slave caravans to that of employment in the sisal estates and the main coastal towns. Definite routes of migration became established and *utani* provided a basis for mutually beneficial links between members of the different tribes involved in each route. In Dar-es-Salaam these tribes originally formed tribal quarters on the outskirts of the town in the direction from which they had come, but these have since become largely dispersed. The Bemba, Ila, Tonga, Ngoni, Ndebele, Lozi, Bisa, and Yao also have joking relationships in the towns of Northern Rhodesia. Mitchell relates this specifically to the co-existence of traditional tribal hostilities and enforced peaceful association in industrial areas.[9] No such relationships exist in Southern Rhodesia, while tribal burying and friendly societies are much stronger and long lasting in the towns of Southern than of Northern Rhodesia.

The phenomenon sometimes called 'supertribalism' is reported both from West Africa, among the immigrants from the northern savannah tribes such as the Songhai, Djerma, Mossi, and their neighbours, and from Northern Rhodesia, where the Chewa, Nsenga, Kunda, and other people from the Eastern Province are thought of as 'Ngoni' by the Bemba and Northern Province peoples, while all the quite varied peoples from Nyasaland are lumped together as 'Nyasa' and the Eastern Province people for their part consider the Lungu, Tabwa, Lunda, and Bemba of the Northern Province as all Bemba. Of course, this is rather a matter of external classification than of self-identification. Similarly, in Tanganyika people insist on calling even Nilotic speakers 'Ganda' if they come from Uganda. But it is reported that, in Accra, Catholic immigrants from Haute Volta become Muslims, because as foreigners they have more in common with the mass of Muslims from the north than with any other group. They even remain nominal Muslims when they go home.

Just as possible kinship bonds are put to use in a highly selective way, so the tribal category itself becomes in town one of many possible special interests to which appeal may be made when a basis for common action is sought. Thus in Mombasa about one-third of the dock labour belongs to the trade union and about 90% of the union's membership is Luo. Here trade union leaders were able to use the appeal to tribalism in gaining union support,

[9] J. C. Mitchell, *The Kalela Dance*, Rhodes-Livingstone Papers No. 27, Manchester, 1956, p. 35.

because of the large number of Luo who happen to work in the docks. But other special interests in Mombasa have had to cross tribal and racial boundaries. The printers' union links African and Asian members. The Ratepayers' Association brings together Europeans, Asians, Arabs, and Coloureds. On the other hand, even a wealthy Ismaili is likely to have closer face-to-face relationships with poor Ismailis than with members of any other ethnic group who belong to his own economic level. Times of crisis and violence tend to throw people back on racial and ethnic lines, where skin colour is the most obtrusive categorical label in superficial relationships and the traditional solidarity of ethnic and kinship groups goes deeper than newer special interests. Where the human material to be organized includes large numbers of one tribe, especially when they are also away from their tribal home, the tribal card is probably still the strongest one to play.

In relation to housing members of the same tribe tend to cluster together where circumstances permit, but often they cannot. Where there is control of movement as in Central Africa and where there are long waiting lists for institutionally provided housing, the first applicant to qualify gets the accommodation and anything like tribal neighbourhoods is impossible. This is generally true of officially provided quarters all over Africa. But where there is less congestion and waiting for accommodation, and a more *laissez-faire* attitude towards the provision of housing, certain tribes often become associated with particular quarters of the town. In Greater Kampala there are many tribal quarters of this kind, associated with Toro, Rwanda, Luo, Nyambo, Haya, Acholi, and other tribes. They are in no sense exclusive and have no formal basis. The same tribe has several small clusters in different places. Similar situations no doubt obtain in the stranger's quarters of West African towns. It was also true of the early development of Dar-es-Salaam. In Mombasa it is reported that in the more *laissez-faire* housing areas the Luo tribal family is able to maintain customary rules such as separate accommodation for each wife and for adolescent children of each sex. In crowded institutional housing this is impossible. The two major variables are thus the type of housing, which may inhibit both tribal clustering and the observation of customary kinship rules, and the degree of integration with town life, which tends to give increasing importance to non-tribal interests as a basis of association, especially in the case of the economically more successful.

Everywhere tribal bonds have been put to new uses, dropping features of the close-knit traditional structure which become hampering and inappropriate, evolving new types of interpersonal relationship and associational organization. The more stable and sophisticated may transcend tribal bonds and tribal language altogether, in favour of new specialized roles and institutions, but this is a slow process which has only just begun.

Within this context of kinship and tribalism we must examine the changes which have taken place in the authority structure of the family. There is a very general assumption that family authority is weakened, but it is a much more difficult matter to state with precision the changes that have taken place and to explain just where and how kin groups and families impose discipline on their members. The first question is the extent to which the family itself exists in the new situations. Once again the same contrast obtains between West Africa and other regions. In the west family life is firmly established in both the old and the new towns. Modern pressures are, of course, stronger than in the countryside, but for large numbers of people there is no sharp distinction between family life in town and neighbouring rural areas. This can be seen in the case of the Yoruba family in the new town of Lagos, in more traditional towns like Oshogbo and in rural families. The same is true of Akan family life both in Accra, Koforidua, and the countryside. But there are also large immigrant populations in the west, such as those involved in the great labour migration from the north already referred to. Though they form a smaller percentage of the total population, their condition resembles that of migrant labour in East and Central Africa in its disproportion of the sexes, high mobility, lack of family life, and failure to achieve full integration in an urban existence. This is the prevalent situation in most large African employment centres, as has been described.

The labour migrant is not entirely cut off from family and kin, because he almost invariably moves along kinship channels in establishing himself in town. But the factor which determines kinship relations here is the need for mutual assistance. Kinship supplies little discipline or authority, yet it is a potent influence. The influence of a kinsman in town depends less on his tribal status and more on the length of his residence in town, his economic success and his housing situation, all of which determine his ability to help. For the temporary migrant, therefore, the influence of tribe, kin, and family is diffuse and situational. There is give and take of money, food, lodging, and information on available jobs, because each realizes that he himself may alternate between the positions of helper and helped. Common kinship and tribal origin therefore constitutes a general recognition of the obligation to help and the claim to be helped in turn. It does not include the more specific aspects of kinship in joint ownership of property and observance of tribal custom. A man recognizes this strong general bond with other members of his family and kin in town, a weaker version with fellow tribesmen and even in some circumstances a faint reflection with all Africans as such but little or none towards the urban community, if such is considered to exist. Friendship becomes a major alternative to kinship and the kinship obligations of temporary migrants are rather similar to the diffuse and general recognition of obligations between friends. For those who stay longer, neighbourhood, similar economic status, common place of work, and other joint interests of an achieved kind begin to rival the claims of common descent.

But kinship and family remain of tremendous latent importance. The vast majority of those who go to towns still expect to return to tribal homes in old age. The full nexus of tribal rights and obligations which binds them at home is in abeyance rather than broken. It retains their ultimate allegiance, yet is little use for maintaining order and harmony in urban relationships.[10]

The aged return to the country. The women who come to town in the wake of the labour migration seem in a number of areas to be less fertile than the average, though more valid proof of this is urgently required. Such children as are borne by them

[10] For elaboration see van Velsen.

are very frequently sent to the country for their upbringing. The discipline imposed by the exigencies of rearing children, as well as the influence of elders, is lacking.

If this is the prevailing condition of the less stable elements of urban populations, what can be said of the more permanent? Here there are families, there is a network of kinship and also considerable continuity with tribal life. There is still the general factor that reliance on kinship is less because the number of roles alternative to those of kinship in every sphere is so much greater. Long-term family life is more characteristic of the towns of type A. Families of long standing are also found in the Congo towns, on the Copperbelt, and in cases like the wealthier Ganda of Kampala, the Yao of Blantyre-Limbe, the Zaramo of Dar-es-Salaam, and the Swahili elements of East African towns. Except in the Congo and the Copperbelt, permanent African family life in town is associated rather closely with the local tribe in whose territory the town grew. It does therefore reflect the joint influence of tribal structure and specialized urban roles.

It is the diversification of economic roles that seems to contain the most crucial complex of factors, closely linked with education and the influence of new ideas. The varied economic opportunities of towns, though these differ in expectation and actuality, provide alternatives or escapes to adolescents as well as to adults, and of course to women as well as men. Again, it is important not to lose sight of the continuing strength of family and kinship and to analyse their precise modes of expression. It is sometimes the strength and not the weakness of these which leads to results which are widely deplored. African workers are notoriously prone to absent themselves from work, or disappear from their jobs altogether, in order to attend to family affairs in their tribal homes usually characterized as weddings and funerals. Employers do not always realize that, as long as an employee cannot foresee a permanent urban career, followed by retirement in town on conditions as favourable as he thinks, rightly or wrongly, that he will be able to obtain in his tribal home, he is bound to insist on maintaining his stake in the latter. In order to achieve this there are many obligations on which he cannot afford to default, among them attendance on kinship occasions when absence would be construed as lack of solidarity, disloyalty, withdrawal of membership, and even ill will or witchcraft. In this way the migrant labour system itself enforces a tenacious attachment to certain symbolic expressions of kinship or tribal obligation and solidarity.

It is inevitable that the urban and rural contexts should be manipulated by those who oscillate between them, and played off against one another to the best advantage. Family, kin, and tribe can effectively disrupt a person's urban employment obligations. Yet the latter also offers an escape to any who find the former too irksome. In this way new forces penetrate deeply into the countryside. Parents usually complain of children flouting their authority, yet enlightened families are often frustrated by parental conservatism, while in other cases the parents themselves abandon control. The Toro of Uganda have established a tradition of domestic employment in Kampala and there is much complaint of Toro girls evading family control and bringing dishonour to the tribe. Yet a Toro father will himself send his adolescent daughter to fend for herself in town alone.

Nowhere does the urban family have the almost absolute authority within its own sphere which it once possessed in many tribal settings. Its sphere has narrowed and the alternatives have multiplied. The process is more properly represented as one of role differentiation and diversification than one of breakdown.[11] In western countries the state and many institutions within it have gradually adopted specialized responsibility for matters which once lay entirely within the competence of the family. In Africa much of this development occurs for some people with the startling rapidity of their own transition from rural to urban life. For all it has been compressed within the short term of little more than half a century. It is inevitable and cannot be deplored. But the rapidity may have a shock effect which undesirably weakens the whole sense of responsibility of families for the socialization of their younger members. While the latter find many new opportunities which can also be turned into escapes from the irksome

[11] Cf. Talcott Parsons and Robert F. Bales, *Family, Socialization and Interaction Process*, Glencoe, 1955, pp. 1–8, where a similar point is made in relation to recent changes in American family structure.

authority of older kin, parents and older kin may be tempted to throw up their hands in horror at the younger generation and, finding themselves deprived of some old powers, to abandon all. In the course of time there should be a greater intuitive discernment of the changes which have occurred, a realization and acceptance of the more restricted familial sphere and a more positive performance of the duties which remain.

V. THE POSITION OF WOMEN AND THE STABILITY OF MARRIAGE

So far we have made little distinction between the effect of towns on men and women except to note inequality of numbers. The traditional status of African women has been thought to depend on their economic contribution to the family, or on whether the emphasis is bilateral or strongly on the father's or mother's side in matters of descent, paternity, affiliation, and residence rules. The factors have not yet been fully analysed and much more comparative study is required. Meanwhile, new forces have led to a much greater range of variation in the roles and status of women, as well as to a radical contrast between their position in towns and in traditional rural life.

It is the newer population centres where the population is least settled which show the most abnormal numerical preponderance of men over women. There is plenty of documentation for this. Extreme preponderance is found in Salisbury with more than seven men to every woman and in Nairobi with five men per woman. The Southern Cameroons plantations are another case and most large plantations elsewhere such as those of sisal in Tanganyika or sugar in Uganda. Ratios of around twice as many men as women are also found on the Rhodesian Copperbelt, in Mombasa, Kampala (Kibuga), and Brazzaville (Poto Poto). In Dar-es-Salaam and in Elisabethville the inequality is less, the latter case being a striking tribute to the Congo policy of stabilization and family housing. In Stanleyville and in Freetown men only slightly outnumber women and in the many older and more slowly growing West African towns with indigenous roots the ratio is near to that of the general population.

Ardener shows convincingly that certain obvious results flow from this fundamental demographic factor alone. Not only does it create a high demand for women on the part of men, but their scarcity value enables women to secure much higher standards of living by entering into irregular unions with a number of men. This temptation is almost irresistible for women who find themselves in poverty-stricken marriages, overworked or maltreated by their husbands, perhaps in many cases with the additional reproach of barrenness. There are strong but patchy indications of the low fertility of women in town, particularly those in the lower income groups and those who lead independent lives. This may result directly from the urban activities of African women, or from the special attraction which towns exert on women from the countryside who find that they are barren. These two sets of factors have not yet been distinguished. In East Africa the children of town women are often kept by relatives in the countryside. This is often a convenient adaptation of the custom in a number of tribes whereby children were reared by senior female kin, who even had the right to claim them.

The systematic use of contraceptives is undoubtedly still very rare, though quinine, alcoholic spirits, and native medicines are doubtless used in this connexion or as abortifacients. Barrenness is still an irreparable stigma on a woman in the eyes of men. As is well known, many husbands seek proof of fertility before committing themselves to marriage. Where premarital pregnancy carries a social stigma and illegitimate children are not well provided for by the family system, girls are faced with an insoluble dilemma. They are forced to risk pregnancy because without it they may fail to get a husband. Yet if pregnancy occurs at an inconvenient moment for the lover, as for example while he is still in school or without funds to maintain her, it may itself be sufficient cause for him to abandon the girl. Undoubtedly many prostitutes ardently desire children and are often forced into their profession because barrenness disqualifies them for marriage. The social prestige of monogamy has made this worse, for a polygynist could tolerate one barren wife among several, but it is much more essential for a man to ensure that his one official wife is fertile. Barrenness is obviously convenient to a prostitute and tends to perpetuate the profession because its members are thereby largely disqualified from becoming wives. But it is only one of many causes. Of 70 prostitutes interviewed in Accra, 31 in fact had children.[1] It has been suggested that independent women do not

[1] Ione Acquah, *Accra Survey*, London, 1958, p. 73.

at first welcome the encumbrance of children in town, but later aim at the security brought by stable marriage and children. This may be generally true, but many special local factors affect it and more comparative data are required.

The proportions of the sexes in adults is a crude indicator. Preponderance of men over women implies that many of the former cannot be living in stable unions, but equality of numbers is no proof of marriage stability, for many women may be living singly or in irregular unions. Women have followed men to town, but in smaller numbers and for rather different reasons. Men have come to town as a result of administrative encouragement or pressure, as the only way of raising money to pay taxes and for other ends, partly because it has become habitual and finally because there is increasing recognition that towns are the centres of economic progress. In most towns, women of the neighbouring tribes form a much higher proportion of the total female population than men do of the male. In Kampala, Ganda women were 57% of all women and Ganda men only 26% of all men in the suburb of Kisenyi and in that of Mulago Ganda women were 64% and men only 37%. In Jinja, the local Soga women were 31% of all women and Soga men only 18% of all men. In Dar-es-Salaam Zaramo women were 45% of all women, Zaramo men 33% of all men. In Kahama 32% of the men were from outside Unyamwezi but only 21% of the women. On the Copperbelt, women from Ndola District were 13% of all women, men 9·5% of all men. In Livingstone, the local Toka, Tonga, and Leya tribes provided 23% of the women and 15% of the men.

One simple explanation of this would be that local men get drawn more fully into the life of a town than those who are distant and they are also most likely to have their wives with them. But also for various reasons more men than women are drawn away from rural areas, not to their nearest town, but to other places of employment. This affects many men employed by government departments and other large agencies. Men also develop special attachments to particular types of employment even when they are very distant, as in the case of men from Central Africa travelling to mines in the south, whereas most towns pro-

The Position of Women and the Stability of Marriage 49

vide the same type of attraction for women and there is less likelihood of them going on their own anywhere but to the nearest large town. Exceptions to this are certain tribes whose women have a pre-eminent reputation for beauty and sexual attraction, such as the Haya of Tanganyika, the Nandi of Kenya, the Bua of the Congo, and the Baoule of the Ivory Coast. These may be unusual in travelling to centres far from home. When an attempt was made to prevent Haya women leaving their home district by bus or by the Lake Victoria steamer they chartered a plane to Nairobi. In areas further from any town it is always the men who begin to leave home first. The result is that the male urban population is more varied ethnically than the female. There are not only the local women married to local men who tend to be a more stable element in the town population than the rest, but there are the other local women drawn into town to cater for the needs of the men from more distant areas who have not brought their own wives.

In this connexion it is also interesting to note the strikingly different impact on men and women of the labour migration from Ruanda-Urundi into Uganda. While there were far fewer women than men involved, the number of months stayed by a woman in the course of her first two visits to Uganda averaged 48 months on one migration route and 50 months on another, whereas the corresponding figures for men were only 8 months and 14 months.[2] Furthermore on these two routes, 86% and 98% of the women expressed the intention of settling in Buganda, whereas the corresponding proportions of men were only 28% and 34%.[3] This strengthens the impression that when women leave home and their tribal subsistence life, whether their goal is town, plantation, or even new settlement in a more prosperous cash-cropping area, they leave home far more definitively than do the men. This is partly to state the obvious: that only men who have become confirmed migrants, or have decided to leave home for good, bring their wives to join them.

It is important in principle to distinguish between women

[2] A. I. Richards, *Economic Development and Tribal Change*, Cambridge, 1953, p. 265.
[3] ibid., p. 267.

who come to town because their husbands feel sufficiently well established to bring their wives to join them and those women who come to town independently and to escape male dominance. In practice these categories are somewhat blurred and do not represent the whole picture. Some women who come independently settle down to marriage later on and some who come with or to join husbands break away from them afterwards. A more important fact is that many men who come to town without wives bring young female relatives to cook for them. Here there may be a blend of some young girls' desire to escape from home to the excitements of town with traditional obedience to male kinsmen. One typical sequence of events is that a man brings his young sister to town and they start a common menage. He then takes a temporary wife and tension arises between her and his sister. Eventually the young girl leaves to find a job or a temporary male protector and so embarks upon the characteristic life of the unattached woman in town.

In considering the economic roles of women in towns it is again necessary to distinguish those who come with husbands and remain in unions which are relatively stable from those who come in various ways to fend for themselves.

In West Africa, town women of nearly all categories are great marketers and petty traders, but elsewhere this activity is newer and much less extensive. In the more strictly controlled towns and mine compounds, where least room is left for individual initiative, the role of women as wives is divested of most of its rural economic importance without any substitute. This is another aspect of the whole situation which results in men trying to leave their wives at home to maintain their rural domestic economy while they are in town. Illicit brewing and various forms of prostitution may provide the only economic opportunities readily available to the ordinary town woman to fill the vacuum left by the loss of her rural tasks.

This tends to make the status of such town women either negative or disreputable. In the lower income groups the physical and cultural context of urban home life makes domestic fulfilment difficult. It is only in the higher paid élite groups that house pride

The Position of Women and the Stability of Marriage

becomes a viable proposition in terms of the type of housing available, or the cost of any refinement and personal expression in decoration, furnishing and fittings, and the likely education of the wife which enables her to interest herself in urban life at this level.

Husbands, and even to a less extent lovers, disapprove of independent activity by women outside the home, feeling that it will lead to liaisons with other men. In West Africa there are distinct parallels in the widespread association of market women with prostitution.[4] But it is remarkable that in the West petty trading is recognized as a reputable and predominant feminine activity at almost every level of status. There are some signs of a gradation from West to East in this. In East Africa there is a great tendency to regard all urban women as sexually loose, especially any who work, or appear well dressed. This prejudice is extended by the general populace even to highly educated girls attempting to enter professions.

In Leopoldville it is said that the husbands of women traders are of low status and in Ghana men of very high status do not like their wives to trade, at least not openly in street or market. Shopkeeping is more respectable. Although it is a matter of degree, there is obviously far greater acceptance of independent activity by urban women in the West than elsewhere and this is closely linked to the other characteristics of West African towns both old and new: the greater stability of the population, the relative numerical equality of the sexes, and the general permissiveness of the urban régime. But women living singly, or without legal husbands, and in economic independence are one of the most striking characteristics of African towns in contrast to rural areas. In Koforidua 70% of women were traders and 25% of them were living singly. In Stanleyville 30·3% of women over sixteen years old were living singly or in concubinage. In Kahama 22% of household heads were female compared with 2% in the surrounding countryside. In the Kampala suburbs of Kisenyi and Mulago 23% and 34% respectively of household heads were female. The repayment of bridewealth by women themselves to secure freedom

[4] Nadel, *A Black Byzantium*, Oxford, 1942, pp. 152, 333.

is reported from a number of areas including the Bakweri of the Cameroons.

We must now discuss the wider conflict of values and ideals which bears upon the changing position of women. Africa remains a continent of polygamy. Polygyny is the undoubted goal of men in rural society, though comparatively few reach it until their later years. This is a built-in value for societies based on patrilineal descent groups. Expansion of the descent group is a positive good and in patrilineal systems polygyny improves a man's chances of numerous progeny, although the number of children per woman is often less in polygyny than in monogyny.

Economic change has undermined the traditional basis of the compound polygynous family in towns and other employment centres, but the early results of this have been that the same norms and values have found expression in new forms. The usual male reaction has been either to practise successive monogamy instead, which is certainly polygynous from the diachronic point of view, or to combine official monogamy with concubinage. Only small numbers of men in the élites strongly influenced by Christian belief set a positive value on the strict observance of monogamy. We are therefore justified in assuming that most Africans still consider that sexual access to a plurality of women is a male right. Islam supports this and Christian teaching has made little headway against it.

Traditional evaluations of premarital chastity and of the exclusiveness of a husband's sexual rights varied greatly, but a high valuation of premarital chastity in women is certainly very widespread and insistence on the husband's exclusive rights of sexual access even more so. Both Islamic and Christian teaching has supported this view and men have tended to adopt it even where it was not traditional. The parallel insistence, in the name of Christianity and western civilization, on the emancipation and equal rights of women is in flat contradiction of the male view outlined above, though this is rarely recognized by western opinion. The vast majority of African women remain subject to the modified sanctions of rural tribal life and are not vocal about changes in their status or rights *vis-à-vis* men. Of those who have to some extent emerged from tribal life, there is a section of the small élite which is strongly influenced by Christian teaching, and interprets equality ideally to mean premarital chastity followed by permanent monogamy for both men and women. Much larger numbers of women outside tribal life tend rather to demand for themselves the same standards of sexual behaviour as they see practised by most men. If the latter obtain sexual access to numerous women, both before and after marriage, women as a whole see no reason to restrain themselves from complementary behaviour. Even in the schools established by the Anglican Mission in Uganda it has been shown that sexual experience among adolescent boys and girls is very widespread.[5]

We thus have an asymmetrical situation. In general, traditional male values persist in only slightly modified form, strengthened by Islam and to an increasing extent condoned by western secular opinion, while Christian orthodoxy has made little headway against them. The impact of female criticism of male behaviour is slight because of the political dominance of men. But male criticism of laxity in female behaviour carries considerable weight, backed by traditional values, Islamic and Christian teaching, and even by the small élite of women themselves. This gives definition to the view that there is a serious conflict over the whole social position of women, their sexual, marital, and legal rights, which has no counterpart in the case of men. The movement for the emancipation of women occurs at two levels. Among the élite it is led by the most respectable and sincere women, often deeply imbued with Christian values. At this level it has not made much impact yet, because it assumes a scale of values which is implicitly rejected by the majority of men, yet at the same time inhibits the women themselves. It is quite different at the ordinary level of the masses, where women who move out of traditional contexts simply assert themselves in a practical manner, rejecting in their own lives the traditionally held male standards for women, choosing their own mates, and supporting themselves independently, but refraining from participation in any public debate or campaign about the rights of women.

---

[5] See John V. Taylor, *The Growth of the Church in Buganda*, London, 1958, p. 281.

Introductory Summary

The long tradition of independent marketing and petty trade by West African women with their own capital provides them with a much stronger basis for adjustment to an emancipated status than is available elsewhere. Yet in West Africa there are many tensions in this sphere.

The situation of Yoruba women in Lagos provides an important example. The Yoruba family compounds, which correspond to the segments of agnatic lineages, have a firm footing in the town with their own land and compound buildings which give solid expression to their stable urban position over a number of generations. It is difficult to avoid the conclusion that this urban lineage land and property exerts a very powerful influence in maintaining a degree of familial authority and control over female members. It forms a potential source of capital for further business operations and so secures further corporate influence over individual action. The lineage can thus prevent even a highly educated couple from sending their daughter to school in England. Women dare not forfeit the approval of their compound because it is still able to provide for them if their husbands prove unsatisfactory. This leads to a vicious circle in which wives are not prepared to commit themselves to their husbands and husbands refuse to maintain their wives. Yet an ambitious woman is able to establish her own household on the strength of her independent earnings. She is able to accept the attentions of men without coming under their power as husbands. She can even arrange the marriages of her dependants and may try to break up a daughter's marriage to secure for her another husband who will advantage her more, or influence a daughter to make money out of lovers instead of entering a long-term union.

On the other hand, the balance between corporate group and individual as well as that between man and woman has changed. Men do their own courting instead of leaving it to their seniors and girls aim to better themselves by marrying better educated and wealthy men. There is a considerable amount of quarrelling and even violence between Yoruba couples. Husbands may beat their wives but wives are also quite strong enough to fight their husbands and tear their clothes off them, trying to degrade them

The Position of Women and the Stability of Marriage 55

before their fellows and at their place of work. Either partner may spite the other by refusing sexual intercourse. A man may either deny paternity of his child or on the other hand try violently to abduct it from its mother, while equally a mother may deny her husband's or lover's paternity of her child and hawk it round to some other man whom she favours for the moment.

At first sight there appears to be something of a contradiction here. It is said that Yoruba women are able to make men bid for them in spite of the fact that they appear to have no economic value for their husbands or lovers. The only hold that many women have appears to be the attraction of their sexual services. During the period of courtship and cohabitation prior to pregnancy they maximize their demands for money and gifts. If pregnancy and childbirth supervene they often fall back upon their family and lineage for the long two-year period of lactation. This deprives the man of his main objective in the relationship and he frequently seeks satisfaction elsewhere. In the absence of pregnancy, a woman frequently transfers her favours in order to raise money and gifts from a new partner and may even be encouraged in so doing by senior female relatives. This is a major source of trading capital, yet the profits of trade go to the woman, be she mistress or wife, and not to the male provider. On the man's side, the traditional obligation to clothe and feed a wife has broken down, so that in Lagos at any rate even a highly educated and respectable wife has no secure right to such provision. The apparent strength of the woman's position may come partly from the artificial shortage which is created by the constant withdrawal of women for two-year periods of suckling. Pregnancy and childbirth may initiate a period of stability for a new family. But even if it does not, instead of the woman being left in a very weak bargaining position, quite apart from dishonour and real hardship, she is often able to turn the situation to her advantage. Her family and lineage is both near at hand and able to support her and she may even welcome the opportunity to withdraw from one relationship and prepare for another. Little social stigma attaches to pregnancy or the birth of children outside legitimate marriage and thus women are freed from one of the greatest limitations which usually besets them when attempting economic and social independence. The difference between the corporate rights and interests of the lineage and family towards offspring and the attitudes of individual parents towards them, is probably most important for the balance of incentives in the system. The crucial fact is that both these sets of interests are physically situated in the same place, whereas in most towns outside West Africa the problems of men and women in mating and procreation occur in contexts far removed from the corporate kin or family groups which might provide solutions. Excluding the special features of a particular tribal structure, the Yoruba case is of extreme relevance. But much more detailed study is required, differentiating social and economic levels in relation to different types of family situation and varying stability in connubial relationships. Parallels may be expected wherever the local tribe has enjoyed some continuous, corporate, and propertied existence in an urban area for several generations, and where, consequently, there is also an almost even numerical balance between the sexes. This applies not only to the old Yoruba agricultural towns, to the Ibo of Onitsha, the Edo of Benin, and the Ashanti of Kumasi, but to very many towns of type A where some degree of continuity has been possible, at least for the better off and well-established families.

In towns of type B throughout the east and south we find a situation dominated by the unequal numbers of men and women, the pressure to promiscuity, the lack of family continuity or security in town, and the somewhat empty role of the wife, who is deprived of her traditional economic pursuits while brewing and prostitution offer the only tempting opportunities. These factors are woven into an elaborate syndrome. Normal economic opportunities for women are restricted or illicit. Men tend to leave their wives in the country. There is a tremendous demand for the sexual services of the scarce women in town. Irresistible pressure carries the latter into irregular liaisons, brewing, and petty trade, which seem at first to offer even to the poorest woman emancipation from male-dominated tribal social systems. Such illicit activities are particularly suited to women in town, partly because they compensate for the loss of their other roles and partly because all

The Position of Women and the Stability of Marriage

women even if single are virtually forced to live with men to obtain lodging and in order to claim the status of wives to avoid being turned out of town. Men who bring their wives to town have an endless struggle to preserve them unscathed in the frustrating idleness of inadequate accommodation, while men without wives struggle equally hard for the favours of unattached women and the wives of others. This leads inevitably to general lack of respect for urban women as a whole, preference for marrying country girls and so to perpetuation of the whole cycle.

In type B towns the position of women is both equivocal and strategic for the system as a whole. While the married woman finds herself deprived of many of her rural economic and domestic tasks, her status and influence being reduced in accordance with the lower value of her contribution, the free-lance woman may actually have to make a less radical adjustment to urban life than a man. This is partly because changes in the rural areas from which women come anticipate urban conditions in some respects and partly because many urban women do not fully have to come to terms with the foreign-dominated structure of town life in respect of wholly new types of work depending on new technical skills, rigid hours of work, complex organization of interdependent tasks, and manipulation of specifically defined relationships with persons of wholly foreign culture. Of course, these problems are met to a lesser extent by the minority of women who become factory operatives, seamstresses, or domestic servants.

The brewing and selling of beer, petty trade, and informal prostitution provide a familiar link between widespread changes in the countryside and the life of urban women. In very many tribal areas where beer was rarely drunk except on ritual occasions and where it was primarily reserved to older men, beer is now brewed constantly for sale, often by unmarried girls for pin-money, and is drunk by young men, women, and girls indiscriminately. In many areas near towns irregular sexual liaisons are becoming more and more common, accustoming girls in this respect to the prevalent patterns of town life. Petty trading, though not equal to the West African level, is now almost universal and provides another special link between rural and urban living for women. Consonant with and reinforcing these factors is the special position of women in town as nodal points in social networks. Women who stay for a number of years in town, passing through a series of temporary unions, maintaining themselves independently when necessary by brewing, trading, and informal prostitution, or acquiring and renting accommodation, may make a much more fundamental contribution than is implied in these particular services. They provide a refuge from the impersonality of urban and industrial life. They offer an essentially generalized context of relationships which may be a welcome escape from the strain of strict working hours and narrowly defined segmental roles. It may be that they enable many to achieve egocentric relationships as a relief from the categorical and structural relations which predominate in town.

There are many paradoxes here. We are saying that women stay in town longer than men, yet represent aspects of life which are nearer to the countryside. Women may also gain in economic and jural status while losing honour and respect, or vice versa. A woman may want respectability, education, a well-paid job, and then a faithful husband and the solace of children. Many of these are at present almost incompatible. By the time a girl has had a lengthy education and training for a career, she has passed the normal age of marriage in most African societies, and becomes a bad risk in the eyes of many potential husbands. If she wins a husband of her own class, she may find her society wedding followed by a gradual decline into a polygynous situation, and her legal status becomes a handicap in tying her to a husband who no longer loves her and wants to remove her out of the way of his subsequent attachments.

The changes in the roles of women in modern African contexts are partly to be seen as reactions from highly diverse cultural backgrounds to the basically common political and economic forces now operative throughout the continent. But they also draw attention to certain fundamental features of the place of women in human society, inviting comparison at the deepest level with the analysis which has been made of recent changes in the American family, as perhaps the most extreme example of changes occurring generally in western countries. The common ground here is the crucially expressive element in the role of women by contrast with the primarily instrumental contribution of men.[6] The present position of women, which is so unsatisfactory from many points of view, seems likely to continue unchanged as long as the basic situation responsible for it still obtains. As the core of stable and prosperous African townsfolk increases the social effects may be less harmful, but the example of Lagos[7] shows that the factors which make for instability and tension in the position of women in the family are by no means confined to the lower income groups, to those whose stay in town is short, or even to situations in which men far outnumber women.

The stability of marriage clearly reflects one highly important aspect of the position of women and profoundly affects the type of authority and discipline which is found in the family. The broad distinction lies between subsistence societies, in which the marital roles of spouses are deeply embedded in a widely ramifying system of formally structured kinship relationships, and all other social situations, in which the isolation of the spouses and of nuclear families is greater, so that both interpersonal and non-sociological factors have more influence.

Within the subsistence context, this problem has been the subject of considerable study in recent years, the results of which are stated with great clarity by Mitchell.[8] Certain types of social structure transfer all possible jural rights over married women to their husbands' groups more completely than others. This depends partly on the extent to which kin groups are corporate and partly on what type of descent is stressed. A distinction is made between uxorial rights over a woman's domestic and sexual services as a wife and genetricial rights over her children as mother. It is suggested that the stability of marriage in the simple sense of its duration, is greatest in patrilineal societies with corporate groups which acquire genetricial rights, least in matrilineal societies with

---

[6] Cf. Morris Zelditch, Jr., in *Family, Socialization and Interaction Process*, by Talco Parsons and Robert F. Bales, Glencoe, 1955, pp. 309-15.
[7] See Izzett's paper.
[8] See Mitchell's paper.

corporate groups which never transfer genetricial rights, or bilateral societies in which these rights are irrelevant; while patrilineal or matrilineal societies in which genetricial rights are only acquired by individuals occupy an intermediate position. Much of the evidence on marriage fails to attain the degree of refinement required to test this hypothesis, but most of what there is supports it. The most serious criticisms of previous formulations would appear to have been adequately met.[9]

Joint ownership or interest in property such as land, cattle, and housing is usually a factor which gives particular strength to the influence of corporate descent groups. Kin groups are closely bound together by their rights and obligations in management and disposal. Some doubt remains as to whether such rights may sometimes conflict with those of a genetricial or uxorial kind. Where an agnatic group enjoys genetricial rights in its wives as well as corporate rights in land and house property the case is clear. But the property-owning group may retain the genetricial rights in its daughters and only transfer uxorial rights to those who marry them, as in the case of the Ganda and Soga. This threatens to pull the wife back to her natal lineage instead of binding her irrevocably in a jural sense to that of her husband. These features are often symbolized in the extent to which a wife is actually considered to be absorbed into a kind of membership of her husband's lineage while that of her natal lineage lapses, but much more comparative evidence is required. It is the point at issue in the comparison of the Asian systems of the Kachin, Gauri, and Lakher, where differences in rights over the person of the wife, as distinct from merely genetricial or uxorial rights, seem to be of the greatest importance.[10]

Matrilineal systems in which genetricial rights are not transferred at marriage favour divorce in this respect because neither marriage nor divorce affects the prior pattern of these rights. In Africa a male kinsman is almost invariably warden of the property, even when it passes through women. Consequently, male property

[9] E. R. Leach, 'Aspects of Bridewealth and Marriage Stability among the Kachin and Lakher', *Man*, April 1957, p. 59. L. A. Fallers, 'Some Determinants of Marriage Stability in Busoga: A Reformulation of Gluckman's Hypothesis', *Africa*, XXVII, pp. 106-21.
[10] E. R. Leach, op. cit.

like genetricial rights lies with the natal lineage and divorce causes no disturbance. But where property is not only transmitted matrilineally, but actually held by women, as in parts of Malaya,[11] it may be difficult for a man to extricate himself without serious loss from a marriage to which he is committed. Here it is the personal interests of the husband which make for stability. Precisely similar situations may now arise in Africa. For example, in Kampala an Indian Muslim may marry an African woman in order to acquire through her rights to land from which he would otherwise be legally debarred. The marriage tends to be stable, because the husband cannot afford to lose the investment in which he is involved. Although the woman's property rights are secure, she too stands to gain from the stronger financial resources of a husband who may be running a profitable business and therefore she favours the continuance of the marriage. Such decisive property rights of women are rare in traditional Africa and are one of the striking characteristics of the new towns. Women so fortunately placed are usually reluctant to commit themselves irrevocably to a husband, or indeed formally to a husband at all. In this new situation it appears that the jural structure is of lesser importance, because it can be evaded through irregular unions and through high mobility, so that the mutual interests of spouses are more important determinants both of the type of unions into which they enter and of their stability.

Ownership of property by a woman may tie her husband to her but on the other hand gives her greater freedom of manœuvre. Whether such unions are stable depends on the particular balance of forces on the husband's and on the wife's side. Structural elements may often be associated with opposite effects in different circumstances. Thus marriage by exchange is reported from one part of Africa as being associated with high divorce and from another as preventing it because of the difficulty of unscrambling two couples simultaneously. Obviously, wife exchange must have quite different meanings in these two situations, depending on the whole complex of property transactions, and rights and obligations

---

[11] M G. Swift, 'A Note on the Durability of Malay Marriages', *Man*, Oct. 1958, No. 208.

of individuals and groups associated with it. Incontrovertibly a system must be one which does not attach value to deep personal bonds between man and wife, when circumstances beyond their control may at any time tear them apart. But this is true of most traditional African kinship systems and reinforces the point that such unions are maintained by the structural position assigned to them rather than by the personal attachment of the spouses.

Undoubtedly many independent variables are operative. Traditional Africa appears to have had sufficient homogeneity for the hypothesis on uxorial and genetricial rights to apply effectively in most cases because the allocation of other significant rights follows the same pattern. This is less and less the case in changed situations. The challenge to the jural supremacy of the male is probably the most important factor here. The various institutional arrangements in terms of which traditional marriage systems can be analysed from this point of view are simply not reproduced in the new situations. Patrilineal and matrilineal descent, cross cousin marriage, marriage by exchange, bride wealth, fraternal succession, corporate lineages, all either cease to operate in town or become modified and variable almost beyond recognition.

Tribal elders may tell the urban Zulu that he should be happy to hear that his wife has borne him a child in the reserve, even if he was not the genitor. But the Zulu woman who goes to town herself, is hardly operating within this structure at all as long as she remains there. Her husband's agnates may not know of the children she bears, nor be able to gain control of them if they do. Though recognizing that tribal institutions adapt and retain remarkable vigour in the migrant labour situation, and that Africans in town try to keep their fingers on the pulse of rural tribal life and have very definite aims for their own long-term place in it, we must still accept the fact that urban men and women mate and reproduce outside the tribal structure. Many may revert to their proper place in it eventually, but much happens in the meantime and others never do.

Where marriage is virtually indissoluble wives may yet in fact leave their husbands and both live with and bear children by other men. From the point of view of the continuing structure it is fundamental that such marriages do remain jurally valid and such wives' offspring remain the children of their mothers' husbands and members of their descent groups, wherever and by whomsoever they may have been begotten. But in situations of change, where new causal factors enter, there may be a significant rise in the proportion of jurally valid marriages in which the wife is actually cohabiting with and bearing children to someone else. Undoubtedly this influences both norms and social relationships. Furthermore, increasing numbers of urban women are living in longer or shorter unions which never attain the jural status of marriage and to which this whole hypothesis therefore does not apply. In a relatively unchanging society the jural quality of a union may be most important to the structure, but in situations of rapid change the actual social relationships in which a union is manifested may be more significant. It is therefore necessary both to collect further evidence adequate to document the marriage stability hypothesis and also to discover the relative frequency of regular and irregular unions in changing situations.

A mere statement of the jural position may be quite misleading, as in the case of Italy and Spain where legal divorce is impossible. At the same time, there is a tendency to assume almost complete stability in the jural systems of subsistence societies, whereas in advanced legal systems laws may change radically, as has been the case with English divorce law over the last hundred years. Where the family is set firmly in the context of corporate descent groups, the jural stability of marriage is important, even if the rate of actual separation is very high. But where the nuclear family is becoming isolated, as in America and to a lesser extent in other western countries, the stability of social relationships becomes in many ways more important than their jural status. This may well be increasingly the case in many African towns, more especially in those of type B. The impact of external factors even on the jural situation was amply demonstrated when divorce rates in many countries nearly doubled after World War II and then fell slowly back almost to their pre-war level.

In Northern Rhodesia it appears that there is little difference in the stability of urban and rural marriages.[12] This may be because the traditional marriage of most of the tribes concerned is of the low stability type and consequently allows for the new urban pressures. There is no information on the extent of irregular unions. Yoruba social structure is of the type we should expect to be associated with stable marriage, yet in Lagos unions seem to be very unstable. This may be because in town the jural basis of marriage has itself changed or because unions are not marriages in a jural sense. Traditional Ganda marriage was of the intermediate type, in which limited genetricial rights were acquired by individuals. The main effect of modern change has probably been to increase the proportion of irregular unions in Kampala and other towns, rather than to change the jural basis of marriage. Another corollary of this hypothesis has been that, contrary to frequent popular belief, high bridewealth is not a cause of stable marriage, and vice versa, but is made possible as an expression of those structural features which ensure stable marriage. We may hazard the further hypothesis that the more the traditional kinship structure favours instability of marriage, the less change will be found in this respect in the marriages which take place in town and possibly also the lower will be the proportion of irregular unions.

It is appropriate and desirable that sociologists should concentrate on those aspects of marriage stability which are to any extent determined by the systematic features of a social structure, independently of the particular idiosyncratic personal relationships and circumstances of spouses. But the extent to which such determination in fact obtains must be made clear. Evidently it may be quite overborne in many situations of rapid change and high mobility where systematic regularities are at a minimum.

The Bakweri of the Cameroons Plantations are an example of this.[13] Their descent system is double unilineal and they insist that marriage was stable. Their tribal lands are dominated by the plantations which lie adjacent to them or even surround them, and they are outnumbered two to one by the immigrants whom the planatations have in various ways attracted. Thus the traditional

[12] Mitchell, J. Clyde, 'Aspects of African Marriage on the Copperbelt of Northern Rhodesia', *Human Problems in British Central Africa*, XXII, Sept. 1957, pp. 9–11.
[13] See paper by Ardener, p. 83.

system of the Bakweri is to some extent irrelevant, being punctured through and through by new external factors. An attempt was made to limit bridewealth, on the assumption that its exorbitant level, resulting from immigration and substantial money incomes, prevented young men from marrying and forced them to promiscuity and adultery, but the effect seems to have been to increase instability by making it easier for bridewealth to be repaid and a marriage broken. It was found that 63% of all legitimate unions completed had ended in divorce, not taking separation into account, while one in six women were in illegitimate unions. This situation is taken to reflect an overwhelming demographic inequality, with twice as many men as women in the area as a whole, including both plantations and tribal areas.

Even if bridewealth is to be regarded as the reflection and reinforcement of a particular traditional structure rather than its cause, it may in return become a causal factor in a changed situation. The Luo of Kenya live in corporate patrilineages and transfer genetricial rights over women to the husband's group. They also pay high bridewealth. This régime had political implications in the past, since wives were highly incorporated into the solidary local lineages of their husbands and it was on the number of their sons that the power of the lineage ultimately depended. The political significance is minimal today, though many of the values attaching to it remain. But the economic significance is much greater. Many relationships have acquired a commercial interest which they never had before. Undoubtedly fathers and brothers struggle more greedily for high bridewealth now that it is easily translatable into money terms. New factors enter into the assessment of bridewealth such as the length and expense of a girl's upbringing and her level of education. Crude virginity tests may be abandoned as barbarous, but the general respectability and good breeding of a girl is still crucial. The average amount of bridewealth paid is very large in relation to the possible earnings of the average man, so that the amount of bridewealth received on its daughters by a lineage segment still directly determines the ability of its sons to marry. This joint economic interest and dependence of the lineage on bridewealth inevitably provides a strong incentive for men to keep a strict watch over their sisters and daughters. The care exercised over girls until they marry is, of course, different from the protection of marriages once made. Once bridewealth is paid the incentive is weaker. But in fact the payment of bridewealth tends to drag on, so that the concern of men for the property aspects of the marriages of their sisters and daughters becomes perpetuated. Most importantly, this concern maintains the solidarity of the lineage and with it the whole system of group control over property and genetricial rights which is unfavourable to divorce. The stress on the importance of children to the lineage also remains. Thus we find few independent Luo women. Not many wives accompany Luo labour migrants to Kampala and those who do are found in stable marriages. The Luo Union in Kampala has often been strong enough to repatriate women who break loose from this system.

The influence of education, wealth, and status on marriage stability is still very little understood. The new factors making for instability are rather obvious but their precise incidence of interrelation requires further detailed analysis. Disproportion of the sexes accentuates women's efforts to escape from tribal restrictions by throwing men into a deeper conflict of interests. The same men demand varied sexual opportunities while despising those who provide them and insisting that their wives should stay at home.

The purpose of this introduction and of the papers which follow is to throw light on different key aspects of small-scale relationships in situations of modern change. It is at this level that the influence on African society of the factors of demography, kinship, tribalism and migrant labour, marriage and sexual relations, friendship and new forms of more specialized associational life can most objectively be observed and analysed.

II. SPECIAL STUDIES

I. ANTHROPOLOGICAL PROBLEMS ARISING FROM THE AFRICAN INDUSTRIAL REVOLUTION

M. GLUCKMAN

In this paper I summarize some of the results which have emerged from the work of the Rhodes-Livingstone Institute staff of anthropologists through the last twenty years. This work has covered both urban and tribal situations. I limit my discussion to our own researches in Northern Rhodesia and Nyasaland, but I want to pay tribute to the stimulus and help we have received from the analyses of our colleagues in other regions. Inevitably, we have depended mainly on scholars working in South Africa, and here I acknowledge particularly the studies of Professor Schapera in Bechuanaland and Dr. Hellmann in Johannesburg.

Perhaps out of the tradition of anthropology, we have been interested largely in the problem of why tribalism persists, both in tribal areas and in towns, in spite of the industrial revolution which has produced such great social changes. Our main argument is that in the rural areas membership of a tribe involves participation in a working political system, and sharing of domestic life with kinsfolk; and that this continued participation is based on present economic and social demands, and not merely on conservatism. On the other hand, tribalism in towns is a different phenomenon entirely. It is primarily here a means of classifying the multitude of Africans of heterogeneous origin who live together in the towns, and this classification is the basis on which a number of new African groupings, such as burial and mutual help societies, are formed to meet the demands of urban life. In both rural and urban areas, these affiliations to fellow-tribesmen have to be analysed as they operate alongside new forms of association, such as Christian sects, political pressure groups, and economic groups. These new associations are clearly more important in the towns than in the rural areas. Persisting loyalty to a tribe therefore operates for a man in two quite distinct situations, and to a large extent he can keep these spheres of activity separate.

Two important, and to some extent opposed, methodological principles have influenced our approach. The first is the standard rule of anthropological research that one must collect data by direct observation of a restricted field of social life, and that these data primarily determine the lines of one's analysis. This entails an emphasis in analysis on actual social situations which have been observed—law cases, the boycott of a butcher's shop, a trade union meeting, a tribal dance in the town, the activities of married couples in the urban setting, and so forth; and it requires that we cast away any preconceptions deriving from our knowledge that most of the urban dwellers come from a tribal home, until we have analysed these social situations as the precipitates of a particular type of social field. The second principle arises from a general orientation in sociological analysis. This is the assumption, which is confirmed by empirical observation, that in the new Central African towns we are dealing with a system, though not of course a perfect system with a closed, repetitive pattern. Urban life exhibits sufficient regularities for us to extract systematic interconnexions which we can arrange to exhibit a structure, and we can study how this structure changes. Since we are examining a structure of social relations, we know that it has to be analysed in terms of roles; and that these roles will themselves influence the behaviour of the occupants of the roles, whatever their origin and their personal differences of temperament. In terms of this orientation, we should expect the fact that tribal Africans live in a town and participate in the activities of industry, commerce, and general urbanism, to exert dominant pressure on their behaviour. Hence the starting-point of our analysis of tribalism in the towns is not that it is manifested by tribesmen, but that it is manifested by townsmen. The African newly arrived from his rural home to work in a mine, is first of all a miner (and possibly resembles miners everywhere). Secondarily he is a tribesman; and his adherence to tribalism has to be interpreted in an urban setting.[1] Here the general orientation of an analysis based on our view of social system is supported by the field data which dominate our field notebooks.

All this seems obvious to me, and I know the approach is well validated in sociological literature. But it has to be stressed again and again, for it is fundamentally important and it has been overlooked in past researches which have thus been vitiated. Even much present research is vitiated thus. We can understand easily that practical men, dealing with the Africans who flock into the new towns, and who know that these Africans have just left tribal homes, should think of them as the same individuals who a few days ago were tribesmen. What is more surprising is that this approach dominated the thinking of a generation of anthropologists who first tackled the study of urban Africans, and that it still influences present-day students of the urban situation. The tradition of anthropology is still 'tribalistic', and with it goes a tendency to make the tribe and the tribesman the starting-point of analysis. Hence anthropologists have tended—if I put it oversuccinctly—to think in terms of 'detribalization', as if this were a slow, long-time process.[2] On the contrary, it seems to me apparent that the moment an African crosses his tribal boundary to go to the town, he is 'detribalized', out of the political control of the tribe. And in the town, the basic materials by which he lives are different: he walks on different ground, eats food at different hours and maybe different food at that. He comes under different political authorities, and associates with different fellows. He works with different tools in a different system of organization.

In short, this patent set of observations, as well as our theoretical orientation, should lead us to view the Africans in urban areas as acting primarily within a field whose structure is determined by the urban, industrial setting. An African townsman is a townsman, an African miner is a miner. We may anticipate that as soon as Africans assemble in towns and engage in industrial work, they

[1] See Gluckman, 1945.
[2] See essays in Mair, 1938 (here only I. Schapera and M. Fortes took the point of view I am representing). The view I am criticizing emerged clearly in Malinowski, 1946; cf. my critical essay, *An Analysis of the Sociological Theories of Bronislaw Malinowski* (1948).

will begin to form social relationships appropriate to their new situation: they will try to combine to better their conditions in trade unions, and associations of law-breakers will emerge as well as friendly and burial societies, and so forth. Of course, these Africans continue to be influenced by many factors arising outside of the urban situation: the rapid growth of the towns and their own inexperience of towns, the constant movement of African labourers between tribe and town and between towns and the tribal culture and life from which they come, as well as customary linkages and hostilities between different tribes. But even these tribal influences operate now in an urban milieu, and not in a rural milieu. The urbanized African is outside the tribe, but not beyond the influence of the tribe. Correspondingly, when a man returns from the towns into the political area of his tribe he is tribalized again—de-urbanized—though not beyond the influence of the towns.

I have given this introduction to emphasize the methodological principles which underlie the researches of my colleagues in urban areas. Now I shall examine shortly some of these researches, before passing to some corresponding points in research in the tribal areas. I deal with two recent books, Professor J. C. Mitchell's study of *The Kalela Dance* which is performed on the Northern Rhodesian Copperbelt[3] and Dr. A. L. Epstein's book on the Copperbelt town of Luanshya, *Politics in an Urban African Community*.[4]

One of Epstein's main themes is how, during the growth of a copper-mining town, typical urban associations and industrial groupings ousted European attempts to work with authorities based on tribal affiliations. When the copper-mine at Luanshya was established in the early 1930's, Europeans provided managerial staff and skilled working force: the heavy labour was performed by thousands of Africans from tribes spread over British, Belgian, and Portuguese territories. The mine, like many industrial enterprises in Europe's industrial revolution, had to provide both order and some social services for this heterogeneous population. Gov-

[3] 1956.
[4] 1958. See also his publications on the work of African Urban Courts, cited in his bibliography.

ernment's resources were not adequate for these tasks, and in any case European and African mineworkers dwelt on the private property of the mine. The Africans were housed in a compound under a Compound Manager. He was responsible for the housing, part of the feeding, and some welfare work for the Africans, for dealing with their working conditions and complaints, and for maintaining order among them and settling their quarrels. Faced with thousands of Africans of different tribes, the mine officials, reasonably enough, thought that it would be wise to deal with them through representatives of the tribes as groups. Therefore the Compound Manager instituted a system of Tribal Elders, who were elected, and given special robes and special houses. He planned that the mine management could communicate with its African labourers through the Elders, while the Elders in turn would inform the management of the wishes and complaints of their tribesmen. In addition, the Elders would look after the welfare of newcomers, involved in the ceaseless drift of men within a system of migrant labour. Finally, the Elders came to judge the small disputes that arose between men, and between men and their wives. The people themselves welcomed this institution; and a similar system was established in Luanshya Municipal Location, which had grown up distinct from the mine's compound.

Most of the Elders, chosen by the Africans themselves, were fairly closely related to the royal families of the tribes concerned. The authority system of the tribes was projected into the urban, industrial sphere.

This system of administration worked fairly well until, in 1935, there were major disturbances throughout the copper-mining towns. These disturbances arose out of African demands for better pay and working conditions. A strike began on two other mines, and the Compound Manager at Luanshya asked his Tribal Elders what would happen there. They assured him that there would be no disturbances. The Manager asked the Elders to go among the miners and calm them, but one of the Elders, a senior man, was driven away from a meeting, and accused of being in league with the Europeans. A mob stormed the Compound

Office, and the Elders had to seek sanctuary within it. Clearly they had neither influence nor power within the strike situation. Yet after the disturbances, the Elders resumed their previous role. By 1937 there were some forty accredited Elders on the mine, and Epstein says (p. 36) that 'the system of Tribal Elders operated satisfactorily in the main, and was appreciated by the mass of the people'.

I have time only to touch on Epstein's analysis of the background to this development. He stresses the tribal background of the Elders—their frequent affiliation with the families of chiefs, their knowledge of tribal customs and values, their skill in adjudicating in disputes, and so forth. Yet, in a way paradoxically, they came simultaneously to be associated with the European mine management. During the strike they were driven away as in league with the Europeans. Two important elements in their position have therefore to be stressed. First, as tribal representatives, whose authority was based on the political system of the tribe, they had no connexion with the situations in which African miners worked in the mine itself. Here the workers were organized in departments and gangs within which tribal affiliation was irrelevant; and it was in this situation that common interests had brought the miners to joint action in the strike. This was industrial action, in which tribal allegiances, and hence the Elders, lacked all influence. But, secondly, in the administrative system the Elders had become representatives of the mine itself, in dealing with its workers, and hence when those workers came into dispute with the mine, they regarded the Elders as enemies. When the strike had ended, the Elders could resume their former role.

This position changed slowly until a second series of strikes broke out on the Copperbelt in 1940. There were disturbances, with shooting of miners, at Nkana mine, but none at Luanshya. At Mufulira, a strike committee of seventeen men was set up to negotiate with the management. At all mines, the authority of the Elders was rejected, and the strike committee at Mufulira was the beginnings of a new régime which was to oust tribal affiliation as a basis for handling industrial matters among African miners. For after the war, the British Government (now a Labour Government) sent out trained trade unionists to help Africans form trade unions. The development of trade unionism was present among the Africans themselves, but it was now encouraged by Government policy. Eventually, the African Mineworkers Union emerged as a powerful, organized, industrial union throughout the mining towns of Northern Rhodesia, negotiating with management. As its last step on the way to power, the Union insisted that the Tribal Elders system be abolished, for the trade union leaders saw the Elders as a threat to their own authority, and as a means which the mine might use to oppose them. An overwhelming vote of the miners approved of this abolition. The trade union had finally ousted the formal organized power of tribal representatives from the industrial field, though later I will describe how tribal affiliation continued to influence trade union politics.

In the Municipal Compound developments were not so clear-cut. Epstein suggests that the monolithic structure of the mine with its centralized power over the working, residential, etc., lives of the workers, provoked the response of a monolithic African trade union, also catering for many aspects of the miners' lives. The Municipal Compound, on the other hand, is inhabited by Africans employed in many trades and by many employers. But there similar developments have occurred, in that Government's attempt to work with institutions based on tribal affiliations has been opposed by the emergence of associations from life in the town.

Epstein goes on to point out that the dominance of the trade union did not eliminate tribal allegiances within the industrial field. To some extent, these allegiances have ceased to be so significant in industrial matters where the Africans are opposed in their interests to the European mine officials. But tribal affiliation is still important in matters between Africans. Thus elections within the union for official posts in the union have to some extent been fought on tribal lines: for example, other tribes complained that the leadership was dominated by the Bemba tribes; and tribalism entered into other activities.

Nevertheless even here it is not straight tribal hostility and loyalty that are operating. During the early years of the mine, the posts open for educated and semi-skilled Africans were largely taken by Nyasalanders and Barotse. Bemba, who are the most powerful tribe near the mine, filled many minor authoritative posts. Hence while many Africans see the struggle for leadership on the mine in tribal terms, this covers a struggle between groups of different skill.[5] After the firm consolidation of the trade union's power, a dispute began with the mines and the European trade union not only for better pay for Africans, but also for the opening to Africans of better-paid posts demanding higher skill. Hence the issue emerged, whether the union was to press for a few highly paid openings for a few well-educated Africans, or for much better all-round opportunities for the mass of relatively unskilled labourers. Out of this struggle, a new and militant leadership, more representative of the labourers, won many union elections. The struggle reached its climax when the mine management opened new skills to Africans and put them on a monthly salary, instead of payment by ticket of work done. It also insisted that they join a new and separate union, formed by salaried Africans and led by a Barotse. The old union came out on strike against this move; and eventually the Government, holding that this was a political strike, arrested 62 trade union leaders and deported them to their tribal areas.

The significance for us of this strike is that it brought into the open the emergence within the African urban population of affiliations based on what we can call 'class principles'. The African union, after its victory, has been split by a division of interests between component categories with independent interests. This division on 'class' lines has what Epstein calls a 'pervasive' effect spreading into many institutions. Professor Mitchell has examined the effect of this situation on the activities of a popular dance-team on the Copperbelt, in his analysis of *The Kalela Dance*. It is danced by teams of Africans who come from single tribes. During their dances they mock other tribes, by alleging that these have, among many unpleasant habits, loose, and even perverted, sexual lives. Thus on the surface the dance proclaims proudly the virtues of the team's own tribe, and derides

[5] See also McCulloch, 1956.

other tribes. Yet the members of the derided tribes attend the performance and laugh as loudly as any at the salacious wit against themselves. Mitchell was struck by the fact that, despite this surface of tribal competitiveness, the dancers had named their hierarchy of officials after the hierarchies of British or civil dignity. Moreover, the dancers did not wear tribal dress: instead they were dressed in smart and clean European clothes, and they had to maintain their tidiness and smartness throughout the dancing. This was insisted on, although the dancers themselves were mostly unskilled, and poorly educated, labourers. He interprets the dance as reflecting the aspirations of all Africans for a European way of life, or civilization, and he shows from other data how the values implicit here form a prestige scale for all Africans. But, he argues, these unskilled labourers are not striving through the dance to participate in the European part of Central African society: this is cut off from them by the colour-bar. They are striving in the dance to associate themselves with the new African élite. While in political activity the Africans may combine against the Europeans, internally they are differentiated on a class scale, which people are striving to ascend.

Yet the dancing-team is a tribal team, deriding other tribes. Its actions have therefore also to be related to a persisting significance of tribal allegiances in the towns. Here Mitchell works out that tribalism in the town operates as a primary mode of classifying the heterogeneous masses of people, whom a man meets, into manageable categories. With his fellow-tribesmen he can converse, and he shares their customs and way of life. In practice, Mitchell discovered that there was far less tribal inter-marriage in the towns than is usually assumed, so that a man marries the sisters and daughters of his fellow-tribesmen. More than this, by the use of social distance scales, Mitchell found that all the many tribes in the towns were grouped into several limited categories by other Africans, and that specific institutionalized modes of behaviour had developed between various tribal categories. Thus he discovered that joking relationships between tribes in this region had developed in modern times, and were not, as previously thought, traditional. Mitchell thus stresses that tribes in towns form categories by which people group one another, and this categorization determines a lot of action in casual as well as intimate relationships. Both he and Epstein stress that in domestic situations, where as we have seen most marriages occur within tribes, tribal custom and practice are effective, though much modified by the demands of the urban situation.

In some towns in Central and South Africa, but not on the Copperbelt, membership of a tribe has become the basis for forming various kinds of associations.

These studies show that we can find plenty of systematic regularities in the new African towns. These regularities are obvious in that people live and go about their business within the towns in relative security and absence of fear. Hence clearly there is some kind of working, integrated social system in these towns. But the social system must not be thought of as rigid, tight, closed, or self-consistent. The social field of the towns consists of many semi-independent areas of life, where people associate for specific purposes: to run a home and raise children, to be entertained with friends, to work and improve status, to achieve political objectives, etc. Different principles of organization may be effective in the various areas of relations. Hence a trade union can oust Tribal Elders, and with them tribal authority from the town, without affecting tribalism as a category or even loyalty to a tribal chief in other situations. I would stress, too, that this situation is not confined to Africans. Tribalism acts, though not as strongly, in British towns: for in these Scots and Welsh and Irish, French, Jews, Lebanese, Africans, have their own associations, and their domestic life is ruled by their own national customs. But all may unite in political parties and in trade unions or employers' federations. Tribalism in the Central African towns is, in sharper form, the tribalism of all towns.

These urban studies emphasize that tribal association in these towns does not dominate political life. Tribalism is not an organized set of political relations. Here modern urban tribalism differs radically from tribalism in the rural areas. In the rural areas, under British rule, each tribe is an organized political unit, with a complex internal structure. At its head, in Central Africa at least, there is usually a traditional chief, with a traditional council of elders, and a system of villages and other political units. For here it has been Government policy to rule through the tribal organization. Government has thus lent its powerful support to the continued working of the African political systems, as systems. We may also say that continuing, and in the sociological sense conservative, loyalty to chiefs has been important here. Moreover, since the new industrial and urban political associations develop in the towns, they only affect tribal allegiances indirectly. But we also consider that the tribal system in the rural areas serves new needs of tremendous importance to the modern African.

In order to earn the money we all know them to require, Africans in Northern Rhodesia mostly go out to work, for longer or shorter periods, in mines and other labour centres. (I have not space to deal with events in tribes which have gone in for cash-cropping or -fishing.) But they consider they have little security in their life in the towns. It is difficult for them to rear their children as they would like there; till recently they could not own houses, and few now can do so; there is no provision for unemployment; sickness and accident compensation may not exist and are always low; there is little provision for the old. The insecurity of town employment for each personally is great, and they remember the years of great depression when mines closed down, and thousands of African workers (indeed like American workers) had to return to the land. In this situation, they look for security to their tribal homes: ever-present needs in the modern total field where they make their living, as well as sentiment, tie them to the rural areas.[6]

These tribesmen are therefore earning their living in two widely separated areas, and ultimately they feel that their main security lies in the tribal land—and objectively this seems to be true. Hence Watson says of the Mambwe that they raid the towns for money from their rural base. The success of tribes in achieving the required deployment of their men on two labour fronts varies according to a complex of variables I cannot here examine. But

---

[6] The two works which stress this problem most for the region are: Watson, 1958 and Gluckman, 1943.

all tribes do turn in the end to their right to land, for ultimate support.

Land here is not an individual item of land which a man owns for himself and by himself. For he secures his rights to land in two ways. First, as a citizen of the tribe he is entitled to some arable and building land, and to the use of public pasturage, fishing waters, and wild products. Secondly, in all tribes except those who shift their gardens widely and have an abundance of land, he gets rights to land from membership of a village and a group of kinsfolk. That is, a man's right to land in the tribal home depends on his accepting membership of a tribe, with all its obligations. This right of every subject, while he is a subject, to land, is jealously safeguarded. I examined the development of land-holding in all the Central and Southern African tribes, and found that in no case, as land got scarcer and more valuable, had chiefs expropriated to themselves an unreasonable quantity of land. Instead, they had in various tribes, as pressure on land increased, steadily legislated to safeguard the fundamental right of every tribesman to some land. The first step by the chief was to take power to commandeer land allocated to a subject which he was not using, for distribution to the landless. Then—in a developmental series—the chief took power to take over for the landless, land which had lain fallow for a certain period: the cycle of soil degradation has here begun. The final step was to restrict each family to a limited area of garden land. People get around these laws by various devices, but the trend of development in the view of both the leaders and the mass of the tribesmen is clear. Every man who is a member of the tribe has a right to live and support his family on the tribal land.

I am sure that honest fellow-feeling and sympathy and justice have contributed to this legislation. But in addition those who remain behind have an interest in the work of those who go away to the towns, for these bring home the money which the people require. In a way, those who stay at home hold the land as security for support in money from those who go out to work. And those who go out to work pass money to those who remain, in payment for this security. So that they get security by their continued allegiance to the tribe, for they hold land from the chief in return for loyalty and support. Hence they adhere to their chiefs; and as they adhere to their chiefs, they accept with the chiefs, for the rural areas, the organized system of tribal political relations. Very few tribesmen wish to overturn the tribal political system as such, though new interest groups, and new élites, in the tribes may struggle for power in tribal councils. With acceptance of the tribal political system goes acceptance of many customs and observances built into that system.

In tribes where land is worked in co-operating groups of kindred, or where kin organize their departures to town so that some remain at home to work the land and care for dependants, security in holding of land also involves acceptance of kinship obligations, and with these of many parts of the tribal culture. I cannot elaborate this theme, for lack of space.

We see, in short, that tribalism persists in the rural areas because of Government support, and because the tie to tribal land is of the utmost importance to a man. With this tie goes acceptance of the tribal political system with its culture, and of its smaller constituent units with their culture. In short, tribalism in the rural areas consists of participation in a highly organized system of social relations, based strongly on the chief's rights as trustee for his people over the tribal land. Tribalism in the towns is not such an organized system of political and other social relations. It is an important basis for grouping people in categories, and it is most important in social life. Associations form between fellow-tribesmen, and tribal loyalties and hostilities may influence the working of urban-type groups. But here specific urban and industrial groups have developed, and ousted attempts by Europeans to transplant African tribal authority systems to deal with urban-industrial problems. Class linkages are also beginning to pervade the life and culture of the new towns. In all these respects, Central African towns differ only in degree from any town, anywhere in the world probably. In crisis, common interests arising from industrial and urban association seem steadily to overcome tribal ties and divisions.

I want to stress that I am here summarizing studies in British

Central Africa. In other territories, British, South African, Belgian, French, or Portuguese, developments may have been very different. And we must assume in our analysis the presence of a powerful body of European settlers. In West Africa, again, things have been different; and once independence from colonial rule is established, the position of chiefs in the total political situation varies radically.

I hope my description and analysis are clear enough within the space allowed me, and you will accept that I have not had a chance to qualify my argument or to state some of the complications. Perhaps I can then briefly summarize the main methodological problems which I think arise:

1. The starting-point for analysis of urbanization must be an urban system of relations, in which the tribal origins of the population may even be regarded as of secondary interest. The comparative background for these analyses is urban sociology in general. We have to start with a theory about urban social systems; but these social systems are to be seen as made up of loose, semi-independent, to some extent isolated, sub-systems. Field data have to be collected with this view in mind, and over-concentration on the ethnic origins of the people may sidetrack observation of the critically important events. Because towns are occupied by members of many tribes, the role of tribal affiliation is prominent in inter-tribal contexts. I believe that the specifically anthropological contribution to our understanding of this process of urbanization is the interpretation of detailed records of complex social situations, such as Mitchell made of the Kalela dance, and Epstein of a butcher-shop boycott. Anthropologists may be able to assume the existence of certain important urban sub-systems; transport, management of enterprises, police, administration, sewage collection, etc. The validation of facts and generalizations in the urban areas requires complex quantitative research, of the kind done by Mitchell for our region. But the interpretation of what is measured depends on having the correct systematic view of the area of urban life.

2. If the developments in an urban area are to be examined, a good method is the analysis of the system at certain critical points,

where disturbances and struggles provide social situations which exhibit the arrangement of alignments, and which show trends of development. This requires an analysis through time, which I consider far more satisfactory than an analysis of 'functional' aspects. Both Mitchell and Epstein have adopted this method.

3. Our examination of town and rural areas shows that it is possible for men to dichotomize their actions in separate spheres, and this may be an important contribution to the working of the embracing social field. But knowledge of the total field may be necessary to analyse the areas within it, as we have seen in examining the continued adherence of men to their tribal chiefs. Here long-term developments may have to be surveyed over a whole region: it is important to be aware that all Central and Southern African tribes have stressed the rights of all subjects to some land.

4. Within the working of the total field, it is possible to close areas for analysis, and neglect the complexity of important events and institutions which effect social life in the selected area. Thus Epstein did not have to analyse the internal working of mine management to make sense of political developments in the African population of Luanshya; the tribal systems can be analysed without examining in detail the urban areas, though their presence must be taken into account throughout the analysis.

REFERENCES

Epstein, A. L.	1958.	*Politics in an Urban African Community*. Manchester University Press for the Rhodes-Livingstone Institute.
Gluckman, M.	1943.	*Essays on Loẓi Land and Royal Property*. Rhodes-Livingstone Paper, No. 10.
	1945.	'Seven-Year Research Plan of the Rhodes-Livingstone Institute'. *Human Problems in British Central Africa: The Rhodes-Livingstone Journal*, No. 4, December.
	1948.	*An Analysis of the Sociological Theories of Bronislaw Malinowski*. Rhodes-Livingstone Paper, No. 16.
Mair, L. P. (ed.)	1938.	*Methods of Study of Culture Contact in Africa*. International African Institute, Memorandum XV.
Malinowski, B.	1946.	*The Dynamics of Culture Change*. Yale University Press

McCulloch, M.	1956.	*A Social Survey of the African Population of Livingstone.* Rhodes-Livingstone Paper, No. 26.
Mitchell, J. C.	1956.	*The Kalela Dance.* Rhodes-Livingstone Paper, No. 27.
Watson, W.	1958.	*Tribal Cohesion in a Money Economy.* Manchester University Press for the Rhodes-Livingstone Institute.

II. SOCIAL AND DEMOGRAPHIC PROBLEMS OF THE SOUTHERN CAMEROONS PLANTATION AREA

EDWIN ARDENER

This paper describes a social situation in which many problems typically associated with urbanization arise, without the existence of any single urban centre of important size. This is a feature of the plantation economy of the area, which is characterized by a large number of moderately sized settlements (camps and 'stranger' or squatter villages), scattered over a wide area. The result is not urbanization, but the area is dominated by what have come to be known as 'urban values', and has for practical purposes one commercial and industrial focus.

INTRODUCTION

The divisions of the former German Cameroons are a little confusing and need explanation. The primary division is into the French and British spheres. The French-administered part is a compact block of territory, but the British section consists of a narrow strip broken in two to the north and south of the Northern Nigerian town of Yola. For administrative purposes the smaller northern strip and the northern part of the southern strip are administered with Northern Nigeria and so far have elected to remain so. The southern part of the southern strip is known as the Southern Cameroons, which, since 1954, has been a separate unit in the Federation of Nigeria and now has its own legislature and Premier. This paper is primarily concerned with the coastal area of the Southern Cameroons, which was in German hands from 1884 to 1914, although at Victoria there was a famous British missionary settlement from 1858 to 1887. The indigenous population of the area is a group of closely related Bantu-speaking tribes, just within the north-western limits of the linguistic family. The largest of these (some 16,000 people) is generally known as the Bakweri, the name used by the neighbouring Duala people, who were the first interpreters. They call themselves *Vakpe*, which by dropping the Bantu prefix may be rendered *Kpe*. In this paper, however, the common form of the name is retained. The political unit was generally no larger than the village, in which the 'chief' or village-head was descended patrilineally from the founder of the village. Their environment was and remains the lower slopes of the Cameroon Mountain, a relatively isolated volcanic block rising (in some places straight from the coast) to a height of 13,350 feet. The soils are extremely fertile and immediately attracted planters with experience of the Portuguese island of Sao Thomé, which has a similar geological history.

The first plantations began in 1885, on the coast, within a year of the establishment of the German protectorate, alienation of land being at first by purchase from the village-heads and elders. The main block of Bakweri on the mountain were not subdued until 1894, after having defeated a previous German expedition. The conquest was followed by the rapid alienation of land to individuals and companies, the re-siting and reorganization of villages, and the grouping of many of them into reserves. By the time of the First World War about 410 square miles of land had been alienated for plantations, mostly of cocoa, rubber, and oil-palms. It was discovered very quickly that the mountain tribes were not numerous enough to supply the labour needed for the plantations, and men from Togoland and then from the hinterland of the protectorate were brought in, at first by direct recruitment. Much of the immigration that began under this stimulus found its way eventually into the native areas close to the bigger plantations. By the time the British administration became responsible for this area under League of Nations Mandate, the immigration of 'strangers' into many of the indigenous areas had become a problem and, despite later expansions of the German reserves, it has remained one up to the present day.

Between the wars the plantations were bought back by German companies, and during the depression there was an important change in their principal crop from cocoa to bananas, which have remained ever since the most characteristic product of the planta-

Social and Demographic Problems of Southern Cameroons 85

tions and are now the chief export of the Southern Cameroons. After the last war, with a few exceptions the plantations were vested in the Cameroons Development Corporation, a body whose net profits now go to the Southern Cameroons government. In 1952 or 1953 it would have been true to say that the plantations were the only important economic producers of the Southern Cameroons. Since about that date, however, there has been a startling expansion of co-operative banana production in the coastal area. The Bakweri Co-operative Union of Farmers, only founded in 1952, was expected in 1958 to export $1\frac{1}{2}$ million stems, valued at £1 million. At the same time the timber extraction industry has also grown in the area. One of the perennial problems of the Southern Cameroons has been to even up development in the territory and there has been encouragement of native export crops and some plantation development of coffee and tea in the hinterland, away from the main coastal plantation area. Nevertheless, in 1958 the Cameroons Development Corporation (C.D.C.) is still the main employer in the territory (with about 18,000 men), and the plantation area is still the chief, and for some tribes the only, outlet for migration in the Southern Cameroons. It also attracts workers from neighbouring parts of Nigeria and the French Cameroons. In the main plantation area (Victoria Division) the largest settlements are: Victoria with a population of 8,000, Tiko with 5,300, and Buea, the administrative capital of the Southern Cameroons, with 3,000. These are census figures for 1953, but even allowing for increases since that date they are adequate to show that urbanization, even by African standards, has barely begun.

In 1953–55 the former West African Institute of Social and Economic Research organized a team study of the effects of the plantation economy from three points of view: the effects on the working population (by means of sociological and economic studies in the plantations themselves), on the areas from which migrants come (this included two field studies), and on the inhabitants of the plantation area (including a field study of the Bakweri). A book embodying this research is in the press at the moment. In addition, we have since 1956 been engaged on a marriage stability and fertility investigation in the plantation area which is also to be published soon. This paper is not, therefore, a detailed report or description of these studies, which will soon be available, but a selection of a few of their findings. At the end of this paper there is a summary of the different samples used in the statistical investigations.

THE POPULATION OF VICTORIA DIVISION

The population of Victoria Division is 85,500. This is almost entirely African. Europeans, all of whom are employed or the dependants of employed persons, and none of whom are settlers, have numbered only about three or four hundred in recent years, and indeed do not number more than nine hundred in the Southern Cameroons as a whole, whose total population is about 750,000. There is no Asian commercial element: no Indians and (this is uncharacteristic of the rest of the Federation of Nigeria) no Lebanese. On the other hand there is a large-scale African immigration into the Division of over 66,000 persons compared with a total indigenous population in the order of 18,000. About half of these immigrants reside in camps on plantation lands, where the majority of the adult males living there are employed. The other half are living on native lands, sometimes in such concentrations as to outnumber the indigenous inhabitants by ten to one. Since about 1955 it seems likely that the proportions of immigrants living in native areas has increased to more than half of the whole, as a result of a decline in the plantation labour force, combined with the new economic opportunities in the native areas.[1]

The Division as a whole contains almost twice as many males as females. In the plantations, the proportion of males is of the order of 70% of the population, and in the native areas 60% (sex ratios respectively of 233 and 150 males per 100 females). Since the indigenous population living on the plantations amounts to only about 7% of the total living there, the lack of females in

[1] In this paper the terms 'native' and 'indigenous' are used in their literal senses, in contradistinction to 'stranger' or 'immigrant'. In contradistinction to 'European', the term 'African' is used.

Social and Demographic Problems of Southern Cameroons 87

the camps is primarily due to the structure of the immigrant population in which, as is common, there is a high proportion of unmarried adult males. The major part of the shortage of females in the native areas also occurs where immigrants grossly outnumber the indigenous population. The primary factor therefore in the shortage of females in the Division as a whole, both in plantation and native areas, is the predominance of males in the immigrant population. In addition, there has been an apparent decline in the village populations of the Division in this century. Comparison between enumerations in 1903, 1928, and 1953 in rural Bakweri areas show a steady decline of about 23% in the first twenty-five years and of 17% in the second. When it is remembered that the common bias in early enumerations is towards underestimation these figures alone have some significance. There is other evidence, however: one of the original German reserves is now empty of indigenous inhabitants, one virtually empty (one inhabitant), and one nearly so; while many villages have small, sometimes ludicrously small, populations (one has only three inhabitants). In the absence of any considerable urbanization, and since the number of indigenous workers on the estates has rarely reached or exceeded 1,000, migration alone seems unlikely to account for this. High mortality doubtless played a part in early years. Low fertility also seems to have played a role. In a fertility survey we conducted in 1957, the data suggested that the net reproduction rate has in the last thirty years been below replacement level, although it may very recently have risen to just above unity.

THE POPULATION ON THE PLANTATIONS

The surveys of the plantation population undertaken by the team showed that about half the Cameroons Development Corporation labour force, which has been between 25,000 and 18,000 men in recent years, was supplied by 10 of about 80 to 100 labour-supplying tribes. In 1958 64% came from the Southern Cameroons territory, 31% from the rest of Nigeria, and 5% from the French Cameroons. The great majority of the Corporation's labour, on the evidence of the two samples used by the team (which corroborate each other) was under 25 years old (80%), and illiterate (78%). Nearly three-quarters had at least one wife with them in the plantations (74%). More than half the children claimed by the workers (62%) lived on the plantations, the majority of these (70%) being under 7 years of age and over half being male. For every 100 workers, married and unmarried, there were up to 110 dependants (wives and children) living in the plantation area. One-eighth of the workers admitted to having dependants other than wives and children living with them. The more highly paid the worker, the more dependants tended to be with him.

The provenance of a worker was an important determining factor in the data. Generally speaking the highest proportions of married workers and the highest proportions of dependants in the plantation area occurred among workers from the areas which have had longest and closest contact with the plantation economy. Workers from the up-country Divisions of the Southern Cameroons were less likely to have attended school, to be Christians, or to be married (monogamously or polygamously), and were likely to have fewer dependants in the plantation area although some tribes formed exceptions to the general rule. French Cameroons workers formed a well-defined group and tended to be considerably older than the average and to be well established in plantation work. A high proportion of them were married, and they had the highest proportion with more than one wife, although 90% of them claimed to be Christians. Most of their wives were with them, and many married men were betrothed again. They had the highest ratio of dependants (wives and children) in the area per worker (182 per 100 workers—compared with the average of about 110). French Cameroons migrants were also the only ones to show a tendency to permanent settlement. Nigerian workers, on the other hand, tended to be younger than average, and to have low proportions of married men, combined with higher than average proportions of men who had been to school, as well as the highest proportion who had finished primary school or beyond. About 90% claimed to be

Christians, and about half were betrothed. They had lower than average proportions of dependants.

Where workers were married they tended to bring their wives with them, no matter how far their home areas were from the plantations. Of the quarter of married men who had a wife at home the great majority claimed to have left her there because of the high cost of living in the plantation area. On the sample evidence, the Corporation's plantation population, comprising workers and their wives and children with them, contained a majority of males (63%), which is less than the figure for the total population of all plantations including those not operated by C.D.C. (70% males). The most important conclusion yielded by the data from the point of view of the sex ratio in the plantation area, especially in Victoria Division, was that the considerable excess of males on the plantations themselves was due primarily to the numbers of bachelors, and only to a tiny extent to the failure of married men to bring their wives to the plantations.

Migration, whether to the plantations or to the native areas, is, as far as can be determined, almost never permanent. The term 'detribalization' cannot be applied in its narrowest sense to the Southern Cameroons. The only migrants who may be considered 'settled' are a thousand or two French Cameroons men who have merged into the life of the plantation area.[2] On the other hand, a degree of community of feeling beyond the tribe has grown up between Southern Cameroons men in the plantation area. This has been helped by the small populations of ethnic groups (the largest in the Southern Cameroons has less than 60,000 members, most less than 15,000), and by a striking number of languages and dialects. No one tribe has been able to dominate the plantation labour force or the immigrant body as a whole. The common medium of communication is Cameroons Pidgin English which is widely understood all over the Southern Cameroons, as well as in the French administered sphere and on the neighbouring Spanish island of Fernando Po. In the plantation area, Pidgin English is the first language of many immigrant

---

[2] After this paper was written one such migrant previously assumed to be settled has returned home, after nearly forty years in the Victoria area.

children, and, in rare cases, the only language in which they are fluent.

Immigrants who come to work for the plantations live, as has been said, in plantation camps. There is a tendency for certain tribes to be more numerously represented in certain estates, but camps never contain men from only one area, and even working gangs are usually of mixed origin. Men were asked in our surveys whether they would prefer to live in camps or work in gangs with only men of their own tribes, so far as might be practicable. About 80% of those questioned rejected the idea. Part of the novelty and interest of plantation work is the contact with men of other areas and the opportunity to escape from too close supervision from fellow-tribesmen. On the other hand, migrants are rarely far from a group from their own area, with whom they are often members of a 'tribal union' or 'youth league'. This type of association is highly characteristic of Nigerian migrants and especially perhaps of Ibo (who form the largest single ethnic group on the plantations), but not quite to such an organized degree among Cameroonians. On the plantations no immigrant group has a complete monopoly of a trade or type of work. On the other hand many are rarely, and some never, found (as yet) outside the unskilled and semi-skilled categories. The higher grades of work are occupied by men of tribes which have been longest in contact with the plantation system, or have longest had opportunity for education at home. 70% of the artisan grade (trade-tested men) come from 10 tribes, the largest number from the Bakweri of the plantation area and the second largest from Nigerian Ibo immigrants. In the clerical grade Bakweri and Ibo are again numerous. In these upper grades, however, there has been a slow but progressive increase over the years in the numbers of ethnic groups represented. In this context it may be noted that it is in unskilled and semi-skilled labour that Southern Cameroons sources have been most deficient, and it is this gap that migration from Nigeria has primarily to fill, not, as some Southern Cameroons people imagine, primarily a deficiency in the higher grades. In plantation work as a whole there is no dominant ethnic group socially and economically, although broadly it may be said that Nigerians and Bakweri have higher status than men from some undeveloped areas. The success of Nigerians has tended to be resented by Southern Cameroons men, but less so since the region acquired a measure of internal autonomy, and fear of political dominance has been reduced. Europeans are confined to the senior grades, in which there are also increasing numbers of Africans. Nigerian immigrants are at some disadvantage here compared with Cameroons men, owing to the policy of 'Cameroonization'.

POPULATION LIVING IN NATIVE AREAS

Half of the total immigration into the Division, it will be remembered, goes into the native areas. This fell into the following categories from our estimates of 1955: plantation workers without houses on the estates, and dependants of workers farming in the native areas (8,000–10,000 persons), other employees and dependants (2,000), traders, craftsmen, and dependants (6,000–8,000), and subsistence and commercial farmers (4,000–6,000), fishermen and dependants (7,000), and an indefinable floating population of 2,000 or more. Since 1955 total immigration has not changed greatly, but now fewer immigrants are plantation workers and their dependants, while more are in the 'other employed' category and among the export farmers. Immigration to native areas is partly a reaction to the increased economic needs created by the presence of the plantation labour force, which the small indigenous population would be unable to satisfy alone. Immigration may perhaps be said to produce 'working immigrants' and 'supporting immigrants', although the personnel of these two groups interchange.

In the native areas the relationship between the indigenous people and immigrants is of three broad types. At one extreme there are the blocks of villages in which immigrants are rare. In these, immigrants are assimilated to the life of the village, and in such areas they are generally engaged in subsistence agriculture. Such men are likely to be long-established migrants. Then come the numerous villages on or near a main road or close to a plantation in which there is a 'stranger quarter', outside the fence that normally surrounds the native village. The stranger quarter does not always come under the direct control of the village elders, and there are usually prominent immigrants who act as elders of the stranger quarter in case of minor disputes. In the larger stranger quarters some tribal contingents have their own 'headmen' (as the 'Ibo headman' or the 'Yaunde headman') who represent their groups in disputes with others. In more than minor cases both natives and immigrants have recourse to the local Native Court, in which the bench is entirely indigenous, or, in one area, with a single 'stranger' member. In the third form of the relationship between native and immigrant, the native village has no 'stranger quarter'. Its fence has long since vanished and there is a sprawling, congested, often slum-like, settlement in which some few houses are occupied by a dwindling number of natives, and the rest by immigrants. All the smaller reserves which are surrounded by plantation lands are to some extent in this condition. A small segment of the scattered Balong tribe which lives in Victoria Division now numbers only 300 persons and was outnumbered by ten to one until recently; since 1957 an influx of timber workers must have increased the ratio still more.

THE BAKWERI

The kinship system of the indigenous Bakweri is one of double descent. Villages contain numbers of small patrilineages which are the land-owning groups and whose senior men are the elders. The village head is selected by the elders from the senior lineage. Villages are small: none contains more than 1,000 people, many less than 50; lineages are all small. Certain medico-magical rites, chiefly concerned with fertility, are matrilineage matters, the custodian of one of the medicines being the informal head of the matrilineage. The matrilineages were however always of subsidiary importance in indigenous political and economic life. The decline in the village populations has led to the thinning out of genealogies and has had effects on the practical working

Social and Demographic Problems of Southern Cameroons 93

of the kinship system. For example, in Bakweri land inheritance, in the absence of sons of the deceased, land should go to the closest male relative in the agnatic line. In practice the nearest male patrilineal heir is now often so distant that a daughter may inherit in default. Sometimes the next heir is her own daughter. Women could not own land indigenously, and if such cases had arisen in old Bakweri custom, daughters would have been regarded as carrying on the patrilineal line and holding land in trust for eventual male descendants. In the last year or two, sales of land by women have however occurred, even though these transactions have no customary standing, and are also of doubtful legality, under the protective legislation which is in force. The interplay here of demographic and sociological factors is interesting. It might perhaps be maintained that the pre-existence of a double-descent system would make inheritance by women easily acceptable. On the other hand the matrilineages were, and remain, active only in the ritual sphere. In addition, as I have pointed out elsewhere, inheritance by daughters is here not matrilineal inheritance, but an extension from patrilineal inheritance.[3]

There are cruder and more direct effects of demographic factors on Bakweri society. The sex ratio in the plantation area being what it is, the temptation has existed for sixty years for indigenous women to leave or avoid married life in the villages in order to live as concubines of immigrants or as prostitutes. The 'stranger quarters' and the immigrant settlements contain numbers of these women, but they are also found in the villages themselves. The frequency of divorce is high. From our recent figures 63% of all legitimate unions ever completed by a sample of 1,062 village women, and 40% of all legitimate unions ever contracted, had ended in divorce. There were 683 divorces per 1,000 women. This ignores separations which, at the time of the survey, had not resulted in the repayment of bridewealth, the criterion of divorce. Bakweri bridewealth is now a payment of from £30 to £50. Fifty years ago payment was in goats, and repayment at divorce would be made by a woman's father to her

[3] 1956, pp. 74–75.

husband. A woman would not normally have been able to collect livestock to refund her own bridewealth without male help, and this, together with penalties for adultery, was an obstacle to divorce. Now, however, a woman is in a position to gather money from prostitution sufficient to repay her bridewealth herself. Payment is also made into the Native Court, which repays the husband directly, without the need to involve her father. The chief ground for divorce given by women is lack of proper maintenance by the husband: but this has become little more than a cliché. Husbands may divorce their wives for adultery or on other grounds, but in practice it is the women who precipitate divorce by running away. Only 2·3% of the divorced unions reported from our sample of women ended at the husband's direct initiative, that is, by his actually driving out the wife. Among Bakweri women, frequent divorces, interspersed with periods of concubinage and prostitution, have become as much a habit of life as labour migration has become to the men of other tribes. One in six of women in extant unions in our sample were in illegitimate unions, about equally divided between concubines and true prostitutes. 26% of those of this group of women who were aged between 30 and 34 years were in illegitimate unions, and 11% in prostitution alone. The peaks of the incidence of concubinage, prostitution, divorce, and of childlessness broadly coincided among the women of this age-group and it seems very likely that the low fertility of previous years is directly related to marital instability.

The instability of Bakweri marriage has some theoretical interest, in view of the correlations put forward by Gluckman and Mitchell between types of descent system and the degree of marital stability. Although double unilineal systems have not been considered by them, it would seem that, genetricial rights among the Bakweri being vested in the patrilineage, their scheme posits a high degree of stability. It would be valuable to know how stable Bakweri marriages were before 1884. Unfortunately, no reliable data are available, although it is generally maintained by the Bakweri that marriages were long-lasting. This cannot be easily proved, although it is unlikely that they were as un-

Social and Demographic Problems of Southern Cameroons 95

stable as they are now. In the present situation, to attempt any correlation with the descent system, while ignoring the effects of immigration and the unbalanced sex ratio, would be largely valueless.

CONCLUSION

This paper has illustrated how problems frequently labelled 'urban' may arise, even in an acute form, in what may be considered a largely 'rural' area. The processes at work may therefore be regarded as independent of the size or degree of nucleation of settlements. The distinctions commonly made between 'old' or 'indigenous' towns, on the one hand, and, 'new' or 'European' towns, on the other, seem to recognize the same principle. Life in Victoria Division may have more in common with that in a new Copperbelt town than has life in an old Yoruba town. Indeed, a plantation economy on the Cameroons scale may have more intensive social repercussions than one based on coal-mining has had at Enugu in Eastern Nigeria, without encouraging the growth of any single large town. Rather, each village or plantation housing-estate tends to become a miniature town, a miniature slum, or a miniature suburb. The actual area of farming land available in rural areas adjacent to or surrounded by plantations may be proportionately less than that available in the hinterland of a large town, and may not be as efficiently workable. By their very nature, extensive plantations cannot be easily established in areas of dense pre-existing population, and a plantation economy may tend even more than most to lack a local reservoir of labour, and to rely on immigrant workers.

The nucleation of population into large towns is suited to many modern commercial and industrial needs, but not one necessary or desirable for all. The sociological aspects of African urbanization most often discussed are directly related less to the size of the population unit, than to certain well-known characteristics of the population itself. Among these may be mentioned: a high turnover by immigration and emigration, special age structures and sex ratios resulting from the selectivity of this migration, a heterogeneous ethnic origin, and a high proportion of persons in wage- or salary-earning employment. These characteristics may be modified or emphasized by forms of settlement prescribed by employers or municipalities, but in free operation they tend to produce the sort of settlement pattern of which 'stranger village' and urban slum are two varieties. Where there are population aggregates, even very large ones, without these characteristics, the sociological aspects are of a different kind. The significant distinction is not therefore between 'rural' and 'urban', but something other, definable, as has been indicated, in special demographic and economic terms.

REFERENCES

Published

Great Britain: Colonial Office — *Reports . . . to the United Nations on the Cameroons under British Administration.* (Annual.)

Nigeria — 1954. *Census, 1953.* Bulletins No. 2 (Bamenda Province) and No. 5 (Cameroons Province).

Ardener, E. — 1956. *Coastal Bantu of the Cameroons.* London: International African Institute.

Warmington, W. A. — 1958. 'Saving and Indebtedness among Cameroons Plantation Workers'. *Africa,* Vol. XXVIII, No. 4.

Unpublished

The work of the West African (subsequently Nigerian) Institute of Social and Economic Research from 1953 to the present is soon to be published and provides the following kind of statistical data, as well as descriptive material.

1. A random sample of the Cameroons Development Corporation labour force of about 3% (661 men interviewed), 1954 (W. A. Warmington). Provides data on a wide range of labour topics as well as some demographic data.

2. A sample of labour camps of the C.D.C. labour force: about 7% of the labour force (1,711 men interviewed), 1954 (E. and S. Ardener). Demographic data, attitudes to migration, and other material.

3. An enumeration of the labour force (about 25,000 men) to elicit tribal affiliation, January 1955. This is brought up to date up to January 1958 (E. and S. Ardener). Data on differences in employment grades between the different ethnic groups. Index of extent of migration. Analysis of trends of labour supply.

4. An examination of the original sheets of the 1953 census to elicit unpublished data. An examination of German records to compare previous enumerations (E. Ardener).

5. A field study of migration from Banyang tribe of Southern Cameroons, 1953-4 (M. J. Ruel). Analysis of tax figures and anthropological documentation.

6. A field study of migration from Esu tribe of Southern Cameroons. Enumeration of migrants (data for population of 2,847) and anthropological documentations (E. and S. Ardener).

7. A field study of Bakweri tribe of Southern Cameroons (1953–5) followed (1956–8) by a survey of fertility and marriage stability (E. Ardener). Sample of 1,062 women: the female Bakweri population of marriageable age of five villages and probably a quarter of the adult female population of the tribe. Various fertility data, and data concerning divorce, concubinage, and prostitution.

Data from 1 to 6 are published in a work entitled *Plantation and Village in the Cameroons* (Oxford University Press for Nigerian Institute of Social and Economic Research, 1960). Data from 7 is to be separately published.

III. MOMBASA—A MODERN COLONIAL MUNICIPALITY

GORDON WILSON

Mombasa Municipality is divided into four geographical areas. The Island of Mombasa is usually the area meant when one talks about 'Mombasa'; it is $5\frac{1}{2}$ square miles and contains over 70% of the municipal population. There are three mainland areas each of which has roughly the same population, but with a much higher percentage of local coastal people than the Island. The Island contains the Provincial Government Offices (Coast Province), the Mombasa District Administrative Headquarters, the port of the Old Town, and Kilindini Harbour, which is the largest in East Africa. The railways have extensive marshalling yards and other installations on the Island, to service the port, accounting for one-fifth of its area. Private enterprise has built extensive warehouse facilities in and around the railway yards to handle import and export goods and commodities for up-country customers. One in three working Africans is directly

CENSUS MOMBASA MUNICIPALITY, FINAL FIGURES 1958

	Africans	Asians	Arabs	Goans	Europeans	Others[1]	Total
Total Island	54,353	25,068	14,540	1,815	3,074	4,139	102,989
North Mainland	11,361	498	3,192	27	912	176	16,166
West Mainland	9,587	90	819	17	183	42	10,738
South Mainland	14,553	223	470		230	18	15,494
Totals	89,854	25,879	19,021	1,859	4,399	4,375	145,387
′ % of total	61·8%	17·8%	13·1%	1·3%	3·0%	3·0%	100·0%
″ % on Island	60·5%	97·0%	76·4%	99·8%	70·0%	94·6%	70·8%

′ % of total means the percentage of the total population by ethnic community.
″ % on Island means the percentage of that community which is on the Island.

[1] The largest component of the category 'Others' is persons of mixed and sometimes unknown ancestry. Then there are fairly large numbers of Seychelles and Somali, with a few Chinese and Japanese.

connected with the port, railway, or 'go-down' services, while four out of five Africans work on the Island.

The population of the Island and other mainland areas is shown in the table opposite for August 1958.

It can be seen from the table that there are six ethnic or racial divisions in the population of Mombasa. Historically there were Africans on the coast who became loyal and trusted servants to the immigrant Arabs who have had contact with this area since at least one millennium B.C. *The Periplus of the Erythraean Sea*,[1] an account by a Greek sailor of about A.D. 80 described the flourishing Arab trade in ivory and slaves. The beginning of Arab permanent settlement is thought to be documented in the 'Chronicles of Kilwa'[2] in the tenth century A.D. The history of their trade and settlement since is well documented and presents a picture of war, trade, settlement and resettlement, periods of wealth and power, with others of bitter defeats and suffering.

The first Europeans to enter the scene came at the same time as the opening of Asia to European imperialism in the fifteenth century. Vasco de Gama called at Mombasa and Malindi in 1498.

Western dominance did not become permanent until the nineteenth century when the British made a treaty with the Sultan of Zanzibar. It was not until the Imperial British East Africa Company was chartered in 1888 that development began in earnest, and even then the motive was to open a trade route to Uganda. In 1895 European settlement in Kenya was assured as the funds were available to complete the 'Uganda' railway which was to link Mombasa to Kisumu and Kampala. The British opened the Mombasa Club in 1896, and moved it to its present site in 1897.

With the railway came the engineers, banks, hotels, stores, and traders from Britain, Ceylon, India, Germany, and Persia. Kilindini Harbour, the place of deep water, soon replaced the Old Dhow Harbour and by 1926 the first deep-water berths were opened. The need for labour on the railways brought the first large-scale Asian immigration. Goa was to provide the human material for Government clerks and office workers.

The Asians have had a much longer contact with the Coast than

[1] Basiles, 1912.   [2] Strong, 1895.

the period of the immigrant railway labour. The Ismaili community dates from its first settlement at Bagamoyo in 1815, a town which was to become the German capital of Tanganyika. Mombasa pioneers, of this community, arrived in numbers in 1900.

The Dawoodi-Bohra Muslims settled in Zanzibar in 1748 while the first settlement in Mombasa was in 1880. Today theirs is one of the largest and wealthiest Asian communities in Mombasa. There were members of the Muslim Bhadala community well established in Zanzibar as early as 1705. The dhow trade was their speciality and there is ample evidence that it has existed for more than a thousand years. Other communities also claim early contact, but the above examples suffice to indicate that the early pattern of settlement was trade and commerce. Railway labour added to the numbers, but was a secondary migration.

The following table gives the present breakdown of the Asian community by ethnic group and population.

THE ASIAN COMMUNITIES OF MOMBASA

Goan: listed as 'Goan': 1,859
listed as 'Asian': 208
Total: 2,067

Mohammedan		*Hindu*	
Ismailia	2,548	Sikh	2,698
Dawoodi-Bhora	2,142	Oshwal Vanik	2,948
Memon	1,725	Navnat Vanik	1,591
Ithna-Shri	1,161	Patel	2,396
Bhadala	1,010	Lohana	892
Lohar	618	Brahmins	726
Surti Khalifa	505	Arya Samaji	623
Khumbar	340	Vanza	543
Kokani	259	Bhatia	271
Samatri	168	Goldsmith	233
Baluchi	453	Parsi	259
Others	293	Sindhi	168
		Maharashtra	52
		Rajput Dhobi	647
		Others	420
Total	11,222	Total	14,467

Total Asian: 25,897

The Asian community is divided first into two major divisions, the Muslims and non-Muslims, each with representation on Local and Central Government bodies. The religious division became important politically after the partition of India. The Muslim community has had more political unity than the Hindu in recent years. The Sikh section of the latter has pressed for separate political representation for many years.

Each of the above Hindu communities has its own form of worship, temples, and community organizations. Many groups have their own schools. Among the Muslims the majority have their own mosques, but co-operate more directly in education and the provision of schools.

It can be said sociologically that the above represent closed ethnic groups juxtaposed within each of the two major religious divisions. Each prefers to marry endogamously and exceptions are not only rare, but generally condemned. The group which has changed most in its adaptation to Western culture is the Ismailia community under the leadership of the late H.H. the Aga Khan.

The European community is divided into groups by occupation. The largest group is commercial. Its members are transient, take little interest in local or other politics, are on short contract terms, and mostly employed by companies with a head office in Europe concerned primarily in producing dividends for individuals who have never seen East Africa.

The next is the civil servant of Central Government, the East Africa High Commission, and Local Government. This is a large group too, but one which provides a higher percentage of potential settlers than the first described. Moreover, its members are better educated, on the average, and have a clearer understanding of the political and social problems of the country than the former.

The third group could be called 'settlers'; many are in the agricultural sense, while others are in the purely commercial or professional fields. This group is most active in local politics and in such groups of voluntary association as welfare organizations, church committees, sports clubs, societies, fraternal organizations, etc.

There were two types of Africans on the Coast prior to European ascendancy. The indigenous coastal tribes provided the porters, servants, and frequently wives for the immigrant Arabs. These tribes have maintained a degree of insularity to Arab and Western cultures which is quite astonishing. They have changed little in spite of the long and intimate contact. Giriama women, for example, still go about half naked only a few miles from Mombasa, while the majority of the Digo and Nyika are still pagan.

The other African group was the slaves. These were up-country Africans taken in organized raiding parties to provide labour for the extensive Arab coconut plantations on the coast and for trade with Arabia, Persia, and India. In 1824 Lieutenant Owen of the Royal Navy made the first covenant with local Arabs on the issue of slavery. Lieutenant Reitz was left to carry out the terms of the covenant and the first settlement of freed Africans was formed. Other settlements followed with the arrival of the first missionaries, Krapf and Rebmann of the English Church Mission Society in 1846. A third group of Africans came at the turn of the century with the railway.

Up-country Africans began to migrate to the Coast as the railway reached their tribal areas. First the Taita and Kamba and, by 1910, there were large numbers of Kikuyu working in the Port. The Luo and Bantu Kavirondo (Baluhya) began arriving in large numbers during the recent war. They became a majority

PLACE OF ORIGIN OF MOMBASA LABOUR

Adult males

	1952[1] %	1958[2] %	%
Coast / Taita	38·0	19·8 / 13·3	33·1
Kamba	26·0	22·5	
Kikuyu, Embu, Meru	12·0	2·8	
Joluo / Baluhya	16·0	20·0 / 10·9	30·9
Other Kenya	4·0	3·9	
Uganda / Tanganyika / Others	6·0	1·6 / 4·6 / 0·6	6·0
Total population	30,755	40,462	

[1] Evidence submitted to Royal Commission (1952).
[2] Mombasa Survey Census, 1956–8.

during the recent Mau Mau Emergency as the Kikuyu, Embu, and Meru, by then well established, were restricted in movement or sent back to the African Land Unit in Central Province. The table opposite illustrates the change in ethnic distribution brought about by the Emergency.

The ethnic groupings in the population of Mombasa have also changed dramatically in the past ten years as shown in the following table:

POPULATION OF MOMBASA

	Booker–Deverell 1947	%	Mombasa Survey 1957	%
Europeans	1,750	1·7	4,399[1]	3·0
Africans	56,000	55·0	89,854	60·5
Asians			25,879	17·8
Arabs			19,021	13·1
Goans			1,375	1·3
Others	43,000	43·3	4,375	3·0
Total	101,000		145,387	

[1] This figure includes European children who were away at school at the time of the survey.

The trend in the African population is towards a more 'urbanized' pattern as the ratios of women and children to men have changed. More Africans are bringing their families to the town. This is shown in the table below:

AFRICAN POPULATION MOMBASA[1]

	Booker–Deverell 1947	%	Mombasa Survey 1957	%
Men	27,500	49·1	40,471	45·1
Women	14,000	25·0	24,650	27·4
Children	14,500	25·9	24,742	27·5
Total	56,000	100·0	89,854	100·0

[1] Taxpayers in Mombasa District in 1957 were 35,517 of whom 30,527 were on the Island and 4,990 off (District Commissioner's Report for 1957). The District is much larger than the Municipality, but the population is not very much greater when the total males are compared. Children were considered as 1–15 years. Juveniles of 16–18 years do not pay tax unless they are employed as adults.

The pattern of work has also changed in the past ten years and even more dramatically during the past two years. We stated earlier that large numbers of Africans are engaged in working the Port of Mombasa and the go-downs of the private companies. Much of this work is piece work. The following table illustrates the change in pattern of the number of shifts worked by Africans who work on a 'casual' basis. In 1946 and 1956 it can be seen that they worked to a 'target' wage of 12 shifts per month in the former year and 18 shifts in the latter. The target had moved higher. In 1958, however, the average worker was working 26 shifts which is nearly his full capacity.[3]

This change in attitude is directly connected to the political and social revolution which is taking place among urban Africans today. It is the first time in the history of East Africa that educated Africans, at least educated to the point where they can read and write in English and Swahili, are unable to secure employment in 'white-collar' jobs. These men are forced to work as labourers and therefore are able to communicate directly with this large illiterate group by reading the political speeches, manifestos, etc., reported in the vernacular and English press. The press has given a good deal of space to this type of 'news' in the past two years. The illiterate African was uninformed, uninterested and oblivious to political demagoguery, nationalism, 'freedom', or political personalities as recently as two years ago. Today he is keenly aware even if his understanding is still hopelessly inadequate.

The political awakening has brought a concomitant demand for the fruits of 'progress'. Some classes of labour are able, by their own efforts, to achieve more by working harder. The table which follows proves that this has happened.

There has been a revolution in expectancy. The level of aspiration of the average worker has gone beyond the level of that which can be secured by his wages and therefore he is restless, sensitive, emotional, and ready to react at the slightest provocation or encouragement to riot, strike, or lay down tools. Three recent strikes in Mombasa were not for higher wages, but for the removal of supervisors, one Asian, one African, and one European, who were alleged to have 'abused' them verbally.

[3] A shift is an eight-hour working period. There are three shifts per day, with an hour's break some time during the shift when it is convenient in terms of the work which is being done.

WORKING PATTERN, CASUAL PORT LABOUR, MOMBASA

Shifts worked	Nov. 1946 Casual %	1956 Steve. %	1956 Shore %	July 1958 Steve. %	July 1958 Shore %
35 over		3·6	3·1	9·4	
30–34		10·5	9·6	31·3	35·4
25–29		25·4	22·9	39·3	52·8
20–24 over 20	12	22·6	23·9	18·5	14·2
Less 20	86	38·5	32·8	0·8	1·4

Wage rates have been raised far beyond what Government has decided is an adequate statutory minimum wage pegged to a cost-of-living formula.[4] Moreover, Booker and Deverell found that the minimum wage in 1947 was the 'most common' wage while today it is earned by a minority of Mombasa labour. In 1958 the statutory minimum merely acts as a net to protect the African, usually the new arrival or juvenile, from earning less than a legal minimum which is adequate to provide his basic needs of clothing, food, and housing.

WAGES 1947–58, % INCREASE

	1947	1958	% Increase
Minimum (statutory) plus housing	39/00	108/00	177·0
Minor employees only: Railway, Govt., Municipal	40/50	108/00	167·0
Kenya landing and shipping (monthly)	54/50	152/25	180·0
Daily shorehandling (casuals)	2/00	7/10	255·0
Daily stevedoring (casuals)	2/50	7/60	204·0
Average wage (unskilled)	38/50	139/00	261·0
Domestic servants (median wage) not including housing or rations	40/00	123/00	207·5
Complete budget (Deverell)	38/59	97/86	153·6
Complete budget (Carpenter)	43/50	108/00	150·6

It can be seen from the above that the complete budget, including rent, clothing, etc., of Deverell on the one hand and

---

[4] The cost-of-living formula and statutory minimum wage was adopted as a result of the Carpenter Report, 'Report of the Committee on African Wages', Government Printer, 1954, parts of which were made law in Sessional Paper No. 21 of 1954. Carpenter draws heavily on a series of professional studies by Professor Leo Silberman, Professor Thornton-White, Professor Batson, Mr. Phillips, Mr. Booker, Miss Deverell, and Miss Mary Parker. The report was considered a liberal and adequate study which dealt fully with its terms of reference.

Carpenter on the other, has increased by 150%. Wages in the same period have increased by between 167% and 261%. The 'real' wages, even at the statutory minimum provide more now than they could have provided ten years ago. Moreover, there are other hidden benefits not revealed by the table.

In the first place housing is of a higher standard and less crowded than it was ten years ago. Secondly there are numerous supervised canteens and eating houses which provide adequate and low cost meals. More firms provide subsidized staff housing than formerly or pay a housing allowance in lieu. Central Government, High Commission, and Local Government provide free and adequate housing for all minor employees or an allowance of 21*s*. in lieu. Free milk is provided for children at African schools and highly subsidized nursery schools are provided for African children to enable women to work.

The following tables show the comparison of housing facilities in Mombasa. The table ends with 'over 80' and most remaining Africans fall into this category. Asians and Europeans each have 10% in the over 200 category and 5% in the over 400.

Kinship is the basis of an average African's security in the towns as he moves from the tribal context to the urban setting. Initially he is housed, fed, clothed, and frequently found employment by a real or classificatory kinsman. The burden he creates on his host stretches the family budget to breaking point and

COMPARISON OF HOUSING FACILITIES, MOMBASA ISLAND ONLY

Square feet per Adult Equivalent: 50 square feet Health Minimum By %

Ethnic group	00–20	21–30	31–40	41–50	51–60	61–70	71–80	Over 80
African (private)	2·6	6·5	9·4	10·2	12·6	8·0	9·5	41·2
Arab-Swahili	2·0	5·4	9·0	10·6	9·6	8·0	9·3	46·1
Asian	1·7	4·4	8·5	9·9	10·5	8·6	9·9	46·5
Goan	1·6	2·7	5·0	7·4	11·6	6·6	6·6	58·5
Europeans	—	—	3·6	1·8	1·8	5·5	7·3	80·0
Mixed and others	5·4	11·9	13·4	15·6	11·5	5·4	6·5	30·3
Total all groups	2·1	2·5	9·1	10·3	11·3	8·3	9·8	46·6

Mombasa—A Modern Colonial Municipality

DEGREE OF OVERCROWDING, MOMBASA ISLAND

	Overcrowding by health standard %	Seriously overcrowded %
African	28·7	18·5
African Institutional	24·3	12·6
Arab-Swahili	27·0	16·4
Asian	24·5	14·6
Goan	16·7	9·3
European	5·4	3·6
Mixed and others	46·3	30·7
All ethnic groups	24·0	13·7

AFRICAN HOUSING PROVIDED BY INSTITUTIONS

Ethnic group	00–20	21–30	31–40	41–50	51–60	61–70	71–80	Over 80
Municipality	1·6	5·6	8·4	10·2	25·8	31·6	7·2	9·6
Railways	2·3	6·8	10·2	18·0	33·3	18·4	6·2	4·8
Central Govt.	—	1·2	8·0	10·4	20·0	28·6	18·8	13·0
Private employer	—	—	6·4	8·2	18·6	30·0	27·0	9·8
African Institutional total above	1·0	3·4	8·2	11·7	24·5	27·2	14·8	9·2

often family harmony. If he is fortunate enough to secure employment in the first few weeks, all goes well; he is able to repay his relative for hospitality and to establish himself with a room or to share a room with another 'single' man. The term 'single' is used advisedly because the majority of unattached males have a legal, dependent wife, child or children back in the tribal land units.

AFRICAN HEADS OF HOUSEHOLD: DOMICILE OF WIFE

Wife with husband:	46·0%	i.e. Spends more time with
Wife in location (tribal land unit)	39·8%	i.e. Spends more time away or never been to Mombasa
Visits regularly	5·2%	i.e. Equal time away and with
Wife elsewhere	7·7%	i.e. Wife deserted, returned to parents, works away, etc.
One wife with	1·3%	i.e. Polygamous unions

The table above illustrates that there are nearly as many Africans who have their wives in the tribal land units as there are with a wife in the town. A high percentage of Africans send a regular contribution to their village either to a wife or to a parent. This is shown in the following table:

EXTERNAL EXPENDITURE

Wages	% who spend on education	% who send money home
s. s.		
0 to 93	10·0	50·0
94 to 120	18·2	50·0
121 to 150	27·6	83·8
151 to 200	30·8	57·6
201 to 300	23·6	72·7
301 to 400	50·0	92·0
401 to 500	50·0	87·5
Over 500s.	72·0	66·7

The percentage who state that they send money home regularly increases by the amount earned. The next table shows the amount sent monthly by % of the sample and the amount, by % of the sample, spent annually on education.

AMOUNT SPENT IN SHILLINGS

Amount in shillings	Monthly % who remit regularly to home	Annually % who spend on education
None	31·0	67·7
1–10	16·0	0·6
11–20	14·8	4·7
21–30	11·2	2·4
31–40	7·6	2·4
41–50	9·0	0·6
51–60	3·6	0·6
61–70	1·8	1·0
71–80	2·8	1·0
Over 100	2·3	16·7

Note that 16·7% (the last figure in the third column) of those who spend on education are committed in excess of 100s. per annum. Nearly all were financing a child or relative at secondary school.

The family and kinship obligations of the tribal community in the rural area are directly reflected in the pattern of expenditure in the urban area. Moreover, these obligations are directly enforced through regular visits of relatives who come specifically

Mombasa—A Modern Colonial Municipality 109

to 'dun' the urban African for cash contributions to the whole range of his ritual, ceremonial, and kinship obligations as well as the modern demands of taxes, education, clothing, fines, and medical expenses.

These demands are usually met by the urban working African because his status is still intrinsically bound to the tribal culture. The vast majority of urban Africans in Kenya continue to marry in much the same way and are bound by the same conventions as their rural brothers. It is essential for them to maintain family and lineage ties to ensure a favourable marriage in the future or to ensure the stability of a marriage already contracted and consummated, but not financially free of obligations.

Temporary liaisons are frequent in the urban areas, but intertribal marriages are still exceptions to the rule of traditional marriages within the tribal group. Moreover, every African maintains an interest in land back in his location on which he hopes to establish his permanent home and family. He is loath, therefore, to behave in a way which would alienate the affections of his close kin-group upon which, in the final analysis, he is dependent to establish his rights to land, cattle, eldership, or, in other words, his security in old age.

The urban environment is a serious threat to the security of the African family in all categories of wage-earners. It is more serious in the case of the uneducated pagan than his counterpart who is a practising Christian or of his educated brother who is earning sufficient to maintain a family adequately. The uneducated pagan woman finds the urban environment a release from the ties of tribal conventions, rules, and obligations. She soon demands the luxuries of expensive food and clothing which she can see her neighbours enjoying and she soon learns that there is a shortage of women and a surplus of men willing to pay for her services.

It is commonplace to find women of this class living as concubines with anyone who attracts them and who is prepared to give them what they want. Many become prostitutes and live with other prostitutes. The husband has recourse to the courts, but urban African courts are ineffectual in this regard because of the mixed tribal backgrounds of the litigants and of the freedom of movement of the parties to the dispute. The woman can simply deny that she is or wants to be the 'wife' of the man charged and that is the end of the matter. The courts remain effective in the tribal areas because public opinion, the chief, headmen, relatives, and the Administration are the agents which enforce the legal sanctions of customary law. The urban culture has not evolved a system of values or social controls at this level.

The illiterate Christian has a better chance of keeping his family intact. He has a new system of values to provide controls and to evaluate behaviour. Particularly if he is a member of the evangelical revival missions which enforce rules by discipline and by African lay-preachers who make it their business to watch over the moral welfare of their flock.

The established churches are also successful by providing a community of interest and fellowship which strengthens and sustains family ties through a group which gives its members a sense of belonging. The group has its values and therefore has effective social controls which help to channel the behaviour of its members.

Most educated Africans are Christians because education has been the prerogative of the Missions. Educated Africans also earn enough to maintain a standard of living commensurate with being a Christian. Africans in this category usually work for the type of employer who provides good housing. Housing is important because a family, adequately housed, is often free from the temptations inherent in the poorer housing provided by Arab and Swahili landlords, where families have little privacy and where the woman is able to make clandestine associations with equanimity.

Highly educated Africans are rarely Christians. They have been educated beyond the old-fashioned concepts of Christianity taught by the missionaries in secondary schools and their reading and experience at higher schools of learning has made them sceptical of the church. They have not replaced either the values of their former culture or those of the Missions and live in a social and moral vacuum.

Families of these persons suffer most because the wife is usually an educated girl, too proud to live with anyone prepared to keep her; is a Christian because she comes from a Mission school and has not had the 'higher' education of her husband; is revolted by the idea of becoming a prostitute and dismayed with the prospect of returning to the tribal area to live with a hoe in one hand and a baby in the other. Marriages of this type frequently break up when the husband returns home with a young concubine or second wife. The pagan wife welcomes a second wife. The educated girl is shocked and humiliated.

It is easier to talk about racial accommodations in Mombasa than about racial tensions. Each 'racial' community has numerous associations all of which are, in practice at least, closed groups.

The Africans have formed over one hundred tribal associations, most of which only function in times of crises. Death is the chief stimulus. The tribal association performs the function of the rural kinship group when a member of the tribe, not necessarily of the association, dies. His body is buried according to the ritual of the tribe. In some cases his body is sent to his home by hired car.

The Luo Welfare Association has a secondary function of preventing Luo women from becoming prostitutes or concubines to men of other tribes. The association uses force to capture, secure, and transport a woman back to her home if she steps out of line. There are no Luo prostitutes in Mombasa.

A class system has not yet emerged in the urban areas of Kenya. Housing is not a status factor as in Western society but the higher paid African is noticeably better dressed. This does not prevent him from associating with his poorly dressed relations or friends.

A measure of achievement is the possession of a car, bicycle, radio, gramophone, and European furniture. An important factor of status is the reputation of being a generous host with good food, drink, and music available for friends. This, of course, comes from indigenous sources and is not exclusive to the towns.

A new measure of status is the company you can keep. The friendship of members of Legislative Council or of current politicians increases your status particularly if they are regularly seen visiting your room or house.

The politician has replaced the teacher, padre, trader, chief, headman, and court elder on the ladder of success and achievement. Being a relative or close friend ensures reflected glory just as being the son of a chief was formerly a status factor.

Within prescribed limits racial tensions are avoided by the tradition of exclusive groups within and between each community. The social structure of Mombasa could be described as a series of parallel vertical groups based on race (or tribe), religion, and occupation. Wealth remains a secondary factor. Groups of voluntary association are secondary to long-established traditional groups.

REFERENCES

Basiles, ed. Schoff, W. H.	1912.	*Periplus of the Erythraean Sea.* London: Longmans Green.
Strong, A. S.	1895.	'History of Kilwa'. *Journal of the Anthropological Institute.*

IV. THE RESTRUCTURING OF SOCIAL RELATIONSHIPS

MICHAEL BANTON

The elaboration of a conceptual framework for studying social change is perhaps the most important—and certainly one of the most difficult—of the tasks confronting contemporary social anthropology. It is not easy to study social change using a functionalist model of society because once some of its component parts have been modified it is no longer the same society. Other approaches starting from variant models of the social system are open to the same objection in differing degrees. The major alternative to this tradition in social theory is that which starts instead from the study of behaviour and explores the operation of institutional and large-scale social influences only in so far as this is necessary to the explanation of problems presented by the behaviour of particular human beings. Progress in this latter approach has been impeded by doubts as to the relative spheres of psychology and sociology which in recent years have been very largely resolved. Without going into all the issues this raises or referring to the considerable literature upon it that has accumulated, it nevertheless seems worth attempting a very rough sketch of a conceptual framework for the study of changes in behavioural patterns and considering in this light certain problems arising from the modification of norms of conduct.

Social anthropologists have chiefly concerned themselves with that aspect of behaviour which can be related to the rights and obligations of parties to structured relationships. The central concept in a structural analysis of this kind is that of the 'person'. By a 'person' jurists mean 'a human being (natural person) or a body corporate (artificial person) having rights and duties recognized by the law'. The sociologist may legitimately extend this usage slightly, for he is concerned with custom as well as law and many norms that cannot be enforced by the courts are nevertheless most effectively upheld by the informal sanctions of public disapproval. In this manner society may be conceptualized as a network of persons. In passing from one situation to another a man becomes a different social person. At one moment he may be landlord, at the next, employer. However, his legal and customary obligations as employer vary from one category of employees to another and different behaviour is expected of him in informal situations from formal ones.

Three particularly important principles by which rights and obligations are allocated to members of societies are descent, social stratification, and contract. All three are probably present to some degree in every society. Tribal societies rely heavily upon descent as a means by which people are linked together in the pursuit of common ends. Social stratification is most important in societies divided into 'estates', whether these be of the variety found in Europe in late medieval and early modern times, or the modern version exemplified in the multi-racial societies of eastern and southern Africa. Estates frequently have their own systems of private law, or the differential position of their members may be recognized in the administration of a law which, formally, makes no distinctions. The courts take cognizance of the fact that a light sentence passed upon someone of high rank may be a far more severe punishment than a heavy sentence upon someone more lowly placed. Personal ties founded upon descent and social stratification rarely conflict with each other because all members of a particular kin-group usually belong to the same estate or stratum. Conflict is however frequent, and indeed inevitable, between these ties and the obligations entered upon by contract, for contractual arrangements are needed only where the status system is inadequate to the demands made upon it. Modern industrial organization requires the flexibility provided by a system of free contract; in societies just embarking upon industrialization people are presented with the choice between loyalty to their traditional values and the opportunity of improving their standard of living at the cost of social readjustment. If they choose the latter, then the principle of contract gains significance not only in commercial transactions, but as a means of allocating rights and obligations throughout the social structure.

The Restructuring of Social Relationships 115

SOURCES OF NEW NORMS

A relationship is structured by the rights and obligations of the parties to it. Social change occurs when, and only when, new norms develop as to these rights and obligations, for until new ideas gain general acceptance and become norms any infraction of the existing code will call forth sanctions and result in a reinforcement of the traditional pattern. No society is ever in perfect equilibrium. Norms of conduct in a particular relationship may remain unchanged over long periods but modifications in other relationships are bound to affect them in some degree. The emergence of new norms may be the outcome of changes in the physical or social environments, or perhaps of tensions within the society. But these norms can never be entirely new. If they are to have meaning, they must have some relation to people's experience of the world. Thus new social institutions can arise only from the re-shuffling of elements already in existence.

In most African urban societies, new expectations and patterns of behaviour are taken over from the European way of life. This process is not one of straightforward imitation. In the first place only certain European practices are emulated while others are ignored. In some regions the copying of European practices is so noticeable that this element of selection is overlooked, but it is always present. In the second place, though Africans may aspire to goals of a European character they may not have the means to achieve them, or they may be denied them by acts of European policy. Thus in certain respects the Central African situation appears to be one in which the acquisition of European skills by Africans is favoured only so long as the estate-like system of racial stratification is not disrupted. However, change may be halted or deflected only at a cost, and the cost may after a while be more than people are willing to bear. The African traditionalist who abjures the white man and his works may not be able to restrain his sons from seeking employment in the mine fields. The benefits to employers of rigid stratification may after a time be outweighed by its disadvantages.

The rate of change is as a rule more rapid in work relationships than in the family. An African immigrant from the rural areas may adjust himself to work in a large industrial plant in a relatively short space of time. He accepts his employers' definition of the norms of the employee–employer relationship. But these norms are not imposed upon him, for he can always withdraw from the relationship if he wishes and it usually happens that employers have to alter their European-type expectations in certain respects to accommodate the customary practices of their workers. Domestic relations—and in particular the husband's and wife's expectations of one another—show much greater resistance to change. For whereas a new role as worker in an industrial concern can be added on to a man's other roles without having many immediate effects upon his relations with his fellows, changes in domestic norms react upon a wide range of relationships. The norms governing relations between members of a community are multifarious and at this stage it would probably be fruitless to try and pinpoint them. But a great deal can be learned from the study of situations (such as those brought before urban courts) in which old and new norms are in conflict. It would also be illuminating to investigate differences in the norms of, say, the marital relationship between country dwellers, unskilled urban labourers, and educated Africans, tracing the effects of changes in style of life.

NEW INSTITUTIONS

Existing research material provides little systematic information upon the working out of social change within particular relationships, but some understanding of the emergence and spread of new norms may be gained from the study of new institutions. Voluntary associations are of particular interest in this respect, for the new norms are frequently rendered explicit in the association's constitution or activities, and are taught to novices as the distinguishing characteristics of the organization.

The casualty rate among urban voluntary associations is high, and even if they survive the first critical years they frequently fail to achieve their ambitious objectives. Nevertheless this trial-and-error social engineering brings into the open forms of change not

The Restructuring of Social Relationships 117

easily detected, and it is of significance in pointing the trend of African social development. The enthusiasm for the founding of such bodies and the writing of constitutions is reminiscent of G. K. Chesterton's observation that 'It is the fashion to talk of institutions as cold and cramping things. The truth is that when people are in exceptionally high spirits, really wild with freedom and invention, they always must, and they always do, create institutions. When men are weary they fall into anarchy; but while they are gay and vigorous they invariably make rules....' In young people's associations in different parts of the world and in different historical periods these rules are often of a negative character, like fines for certain offences, for thus the members' desire to symbolize their unity in distinctive customs is most easily met. But the rules which are written into the constitution are less important than those which successful associations decree by the establishment of conventions.

Young men's associations in many different parts of Africa have shown a consistent pattern of development: at first their formal organization is very simple and the imprint of European institutions is very evident, but quite rapidly the structure differentiates and the associations acquire characteristics of their own. Comparing those on the Copperbelt of Northern Rhodesia with those in Freetown, the apparent imitation of European ways is most noticeable in the Rhodesian *mbeni* of the post-1918 period, which Professor J. Clyde Mitchell describes as 'a sort of pantomime of the social structure of the local European community'. *Kalela*, its successor, broke away from this to become a representation of the way of life of the upper levels of African society.[1] The Freetown dancing societies of the 1930's resembled *Kalela* in many respects though their organization and activities were more differentiated and the European borrowings less important.[2] The new Temne companies of the 1940's marked a further step in the same direction. The élite societies now have a highly developed system of offices so that forty-five to fifty members of a total not exceeding ninety may have some title-bearing office. The wide range from which these are borrowed—compared with the earlier

---
[1] Mitchell, 1956.   [2] Banton, 1957, pp. 164 ff.

adoption of military ranks—gives a good indication of the eclecticism of their founders. The principal title, Sultan, is of Islamic provenance. His female opposite number, Mammy Queen, pays silent homage to Queen Victoria; Pa Kumrabai is a traditional Temne official whose role as the outsider with emergency powers in time of crisis has been adapted to give members an extraordinary court of appeal when in dispute with the Sultan; Judge, Doctor, Manager, Commissioner, Sister, Nurse, Leader, Conductor, Provoe, Reporter, and Bailiff are titles of European derivation but borrowed from different institutions and with an understanding of their incumbents' duties.

The activities of the companies and the style of life of their members show that in some spheres Islamic or tribal values are endorsed in preference to European ones. The dancers are usually from among the younger members; the men wear European-style shoes and trousers, a coloured open-neck shirt and perhaps a trilby. The older and more respected members dance only on special occasions: they wear the slippers, long gowns, and tarbooshes characteristic of Muslims. Tribal norms of obligation to kinsfolk, customary ideas of etiquette, etc., are upheld.[3] Those who seek esteem refrain from alcoholic liquors, but smoking—though light by European standards—is not disapproved of and the younger men show off their cigarettes. Children are given tribal Christian names. Where European practices are adopted, this is frequently for display; their rejection in respect of religion, dress, names, etc., is the more noteworthy in that Creole acceptance of them has been virtually complete. (The Creoles of Sierra Leone are the descendants of Africans liberated from the slave vessels in the last century; having little distinctive culture of their own they readily adopted British values and institutions and helped spread them amongst the tribal peoples.) The success of Islam is particularly interesting in this respect. Apart from the Kru and Bassa headmen (who supported independent Christian Churches) all the fourteen tribal headmen, and all the subordinate officials and important company officers that I met, professed themselves Muslims. The growth of Islam appears to be due in

[3] Cf. Little, 1955, pp. 227-9.

part to its providing a common cultural foundation for an African grouping opposed to the Europeans and the compromising Creoles.

Within the company a different standard of behaviour is required of the member than in most relations between young tribal immigrants. Members have to help one another, especially by moral and pecuniary support upon bereavement. Fighting and quarrelling are forbidden and all disputes must be arbitrated within the company. When attending meetings, members are expected to be smartly dressed. The men are enjoined to show respect to the women members. Great concern is shown for discipline, though company officials sometimes have difficulty in getting their authority acknowledged. Some associations make greater demands upon their members than others and they are respected accordingly. In one case this difference in standards was found within an association. A young Limba leader in creating a society for his fellow-tribesmen divided it into two sections: one was fairly exclusive and designed to appeal to the more self-respecting and ambitious youths, the other a more casual arrangement to provide entertainment on holidays which would draw in the less settled immigrant labourers. Thus at different levels members of these associations take on distinctive rights and obligations; in this sense new statuses or new social persons are created.

The desire of the young Temne to raise tribal standards which found expression in the companies has also been an important political factor. Some four years after the establishment of the first company the post of tribal headman fell vacant. This office had previously been held by illiterate greybeards who were out of touch with the young men. Determined to put an end to the inefficiency and corruption of the old system, the young men nominated the school teacher who had founded the company, and they secured his election. He utilized his position as none of his illiterate predecessors had been able to do, and soon became one of the most important figures in the city. In 1957 he entered the House of Representatives and was immediately appointed Minister of Works and Housing. This exemplifies how the young men's influence has increased and with it the significance of the norms they try to propagate and enforce through the companies. Companies appoint their officers according to their own ideas of suitability in which traditional and modernist values are blended. To some extent they can confer prestige outside their membership, for to be known as an important company official heightens a man's standing in other situations, while older men may solicit the support of these groups for political or personal ends. The plethora of offices and the various requirements of members may therefore be seen as an attempt to translate new norms into structured relationships. This importance is the greater because in the urban situation criteria of rank and norms of conduct are confused.

In several respects the companies take over functions which in tribal society are performed by the lineage. Members help one another, honour each other's dead and provide support in times of difficulty. The company creates new ranks and statuses in lieu of the old ones (deriving from position in descent groups of varying prestige) that are no longer viable. The resemblance is not due to any intrinsic significance in descent organization but to its use in certain kinds of society for allocating rights and obligations. In urban life new institutions have to be created to perform the same functions, though in accordance with different criteria.

SYMBOLS OF STATUS

When a new status is created and a class of persons arise who observe distinctive rights and obligations, some outward sign is often adopted by which they can distinguish themselves. Secret societies have their signs and most associations their badges. Priests, like soldiers, wear a uniform, and missions often require their converts to adopt a different dress, for the individuals' commitment to a new code requires some outward and visible sign. The Freetown companies lack any special means of identifying their members except for the insistence upon cleanliness and smart clothing which is a means of distinguishing social strata in the general tribal population. Social strata are among the most important of the new urban classes of persons, and it is instructive to examine status symbols in this light. When an immigrant adopts the style of clothing distinctive of educated Africans this is construed as a claim on his part to be treated as an educated man: that he is prepared to observe the obligations of members of this class and expects in return their rights. In assuming the symbols which denote this status he is implicitly contracting to perform its duties. Of course, his claim may not succeed and his use of these symbols of higher status be regarded as illegitimate, but the issue may not have to be faced openly because in urban areas symbols of status are always changing. Whenever a new class of persons emerges they try to differentiate themselves from the class from which they came by the adoption of particular symbols; expensive possessions may be particularly effective for this purpose if members of the new class have a higher income, but if other people succeed in buying similar articles then the former class will seek new ways of symbolizing their distinctiveness.

The significance in African culture of items borrowed from the European way of life would appear to be less evident in the Central African situation than it is in the West. Godfrey Wilson maintained that 'Africans cannot but wish to gain the respect . . . of the Europeans, whose general social superiority is always before them'.[4] Clyde Mitchell argues similarly that 'the prestige system in urban areas uses "civilization" or "the European way of life" as a standard or scale'.[5] He does not suggest that the Africans cultivate any distinctive values of their own, as might be anticipated—especially in view of the political tension. In defence of this presentation it might be held that the observance of traditional norms contributes to a man's esteem but is irrelevant to his prestige. He may be esteemed as a very competent boss boy but his position on the scale of prestige is that of his occupation and all boss boys rank alike.[6] Similarly, he may be esteemed for his individual qualities but be allocated a position on the prestige scale according as he approximates to the ideal of a black European. It may be doubted, however, whether the association between prestige and Europeanization is not more apparent than real. To be highly regarded, an African needs to be educated and

[4] Wilson, 1942, Pt. II, p. 15. [5] op. cit., p. 15. [6] Cf. Goffman, 1951, pp. 294–5.

to draw a salary large enough for him to purchase fine clothing and other objects of prestige—as Mitchell says. But this is not because education and fine clothing are European. It is because of the significance Africans have placed upon them. In being transferred from one culture to another the items borrowed undergo a subtle transformation. The same artefact may be a symbol in two cultures, but it cannot symbolize exactly the same things in them both because the two worlds of experience differ.

Two distinctive problems may be confused in discussion of this kind; why some things are borrowed rather than others; and why individuals strive after particular prestige symbols. The second problem is a psychological one and is to be explained in terms of motivations; the 'reference group' concept is only one step on the way. An African may seek a European qualification to demonstrate his abilities to Europeans or to Africans or both; or he may wish to convince his fellows that he is fitted to be their leader because he can fight Europeans with their own weapons. Once a group has adopted new norms the question of where they come from is irrelevant to the explanation of individual attempts to live up to them—just as a London woman's desire to dress according to fashion is not affected by whether the fashions come from Paris or Rome.

Which cultural features are borrowed depends upon the degree and nature of the contact. Initially, it often appears as if the subordinate group seeks to discover the secret of their conquerors' power and copies the artefacts and customs that appear to them most closely associated with this power. Even so, this is not pure imitation; these things are copied because of what they signify in *African* experience. At a much later stage when colonies are seeking independence there is an avoidance of European practices and a revival of traditional lore and customs. In the intermediate stages, two aspects of institutional change deserve attention. In the first place, the acceptance of new values imported by Europeans, especially those relating to material progress, entails the disruption of the old order. People move to the towns, seek education and technical skills, etc. These changes entail the restructuring of one social relationship after another.

If education is to be respected, the schoolmaster must be recognized as possessing special rights and obligations and be accorded prestige. Traditional criteria of authority, rank, and duty must give way to demands deriving from radically new expectations. In the second place, however, when rearranging their system of relations Africans may come back to European culture to borrow certain items as patterns for their new institutions, or as means of differentiation: a large motor-car becomes a better symbol of high status than a bevy of wives. European titles are taken over by the companies where there are no African titles that have the connotations they desire. In these cases cultural borrowing is a consequence, not a cause, of the restructuring of relationships. Frequently, the adoption of European ways appears to be no more than play-acting on the Africans' part or a satire upon European life as they see it. Yet the early stages of the borrowing process are bound to appear like this, for in them the Africans are experimenting with the European customs in question, getting the feel of them, and making them into something of their own. The representations of minor European ceremonials like the conduct of meetings,[7] also serve as a form of socialization by training Africans in skills which may be of use to them in the newly emerging forms of social organization.

These reflections are prompted by the study of voluntary associations, but if they are valid they should be more widely applicable. The restructuring of relations involved in family parasitism and the growing independence of women can be treated as a response to changed material circumstances, but this is only a beginning. The action of young educated men in resisting the importunities of kinsmen, and of women in asserting their independence, cannot be explained as simply responses to their material interests (though Marxists would argue that they are conditioned by their membership in a particular class and that the class so responds). They reject certain of their traditional obligations, thereby losing rights associated with them. They claim certain new rights and have to recognize new obligations in consequence. European activities may entail changes in the

[7] Cf. Valdo Pons's paper in this volume.

African social structure but the mere presence of Europeans or other groups can accelerate change by demonstrating alternative social arrangements. Western expressions of economic individualism and women's rights may be echoed and utilized in establishing new customary relations, but they have no force of their own.

CONCLUSION

This essay has been exploratory and tentative in character. It stems from dissatisfaction with social theories starting from concepts of 'society' and 'group', which, apart from other weaknesses, provide no suitable framework for the detailed study of social change. The possibility has been indicated of an alternative approach starting from the concept of the person, and viewing social relations in terms of a network of rights and obligations. From this standpoint, social change occurs only when new norms arise as to the rights and obligations of a relationship. These norms can never be entirely new as they have to be fashioned out of ideas and practices with which the participants are familiar. While Africans often appear to imitate European ways, their cultural borrowing is in fact selective and the items taken over acquire a different significance in African culture.

Voluntary associations are of interest in showing how in the urban situation new standards of obligation and new relationships are established once satisfactory forms of organization are discovered. In a West African city like Freetown rights and obligations are increasingly allocated upon a contractual basis instead of being ascribed by the traditional kinship structure: a young man may acquire the benefits of company membership by the contract of membership. Anyone who can fulfil the obligations of a higher position in the system of stratification can claim the rights of this status, and in his assuming the symbols which are held to denote the status, he is implicitly contracting to perform its duties.

REFERENCES

Banton, M.	1957.	*West African City: A Study of Tribal Life in Freetown.* London: Oxford University Press for International African Intitute.
Goffman, E.	1951.	'Symbols of Class Status'. *British Journal of Sociology*, Vol. II.
Little, K.	1955.	'Structural Change in the Sierra Leone Protectorate'. *Africa*, Vol. V, No. 3.
Mitchell, J. C.	1956.	*The Kalela Dance.* Rhodes-Livingstone Paper, No. 27.
Wilson, G.	1942.	*An Essay on the Economics of Detribalization in Northern Rhodesia*, Part II. Rhodes-Livingstone Paper, No. 6.

V. SOCIAL STRATIFICATION IN GWELO

W. B. SCHWAB

For nearly a half a century there has been a steady increase in the number of Africans in Central Africa who have been leaving their tribal areas and entering the wage-earning economy of the towns. Some have remained and given their commitment to town life. But the vast majority are transients, living part of the time in a town and part in their rural villages, serving two economic and social systems. Yet despite the continuous ebb and flow of Africans to and from the towns, a uniquely African urban social system is developing. In this paper we confine ourselves to one aspect of this emerging social system and deal with the system by which persons are ranked differentially according to the values attached to their various roles and activities.

This paper is based on a field study in Gwelo,[1] the fourth largest town in Southern Rhodesia. Gwelo was founded in 1896 by Europeans and today has a population of about 7,000 Europeans and 25,000 Africans. Like many other towns in Southern Africa, Gwelo is a commercial and industrial hub for the surrounding farm lands. Most of the African population are segregated residentially and live in specially designated areas peripheral to the town proper.[2] The African population is tribally heterogeneous, and, although the great majority of Africans are of the Shona (60·5%) and Ndebele (13·6%) tribes of Southern Rhodesia, there are segments of the population who have come to work in Gwelo from Portuguese East and West Africa, Northern Rhodesia, South Africa, and especially Nyasaland.[3] The African

---

[1] I am indebted to the Ford Foundation for their financial support of this project. I am also indebted to the Rhodes-Livingstone Institute for their interest and help during my stay in Southern Rhodesia and to the Population Council for their financial aid.

[2] This study was carried out in the municipal location, the largest of the three official African housing areas surrounding Gwelo. For the demographic part of the survey, a 10% random sample of houses was selected and their occupants interviewed. The formal interviews were carried out by an African staff. A sub-sample was chosen from the main sample for more intensive investigation.

[3] Over 50% of the population falls into the working-age group of 20-40. There is a considerable decrease in the older age groups, which results, apart from natural causes,

population is also migratory and unstable. Typically, a man leaves his tribal area to seek work in town. He may or may not bring his family with him. After a varying period in town, he returns to the reserve whether he has accomplished his goals or not. At some later time he may return to the same or a different town. This circulation between town and rural areas may continue for the greater part of a man's life. There is also considerable occupational and residential mobility within a single town.

SOCIAL DIFFERENTIATION AND THE SYSTEM OF VALUES

There are two characteristic themes which pervade all aspects of social life in Gwelo. The first is the cleavage between black and white. Although both black and white are themselves divided by numerous internal cleavages,[4] the most important social fact in Gwelo today is the separation between colour groups. Each forms a stratum in the society clearly separated by customary and statutory laws. Virtually all power in the society is vested in the Europeans, who control the instruments of coercion, whether political, economic, or social. Yet, despite enforced separation and conflicts between the colour groups, black and white are linked by far-reaching and numerous political and economic relationships. As we shall see later, the African system of social stratification in Gwelo derives many of its features from the economic and social bonds between Africans and Europeans as well as from the separation between them.

The transition between the rural economy in the reserves of Southern Rhodesia and the full-scale urban industrialism is sharp. And, in its most general form, the second pervasive characteristic of the African community in Gwelo is the discontinuities in the two social systems. Although the most remote villages in Southern

from the voluntary return of older people to the reserves and the difficulty for older people in securing employment in town. The ratio of men to women shows a preponderance of males over females. There are several reasons for this disproportionate ratio. Many of the men who come to work in town are young and single. In addition, many of the men who are married have left their wives and children on the reserve. There are some detached women in the population, but proportionately they are not significant.

[4] In a series of penetrating books and papers, Gluckman has made clear the meaning and importance of the elaborate divisions and links within and between the colour groups for the social system of South Africa. Gluckman, 1958. See also Mitchell, 1956, and Epstein, 1958, for Northern Rhodesia.

Rhodesia have had some measure of contact with urban industrial patterns, an African farmer is still primarily a subsistence cultivator, conforming to traditional patterns. Familial obligations and particularistic ties are the essential elements in his social world. When a farmer migrates to town, the patterns of town life are imposed upon him and he must live and work in a world which is marked by a complex network of often unfamiliar and conflicting relationships and roles. To a very large extent his position in society and his economic and social relationships are now determined by what he does. In other words, his position in the productive system is now the critical differential rather than kinship, age, and sex, which are commonly used as status differentials in the traditional social structures. Typically, relationships tend to be amorphous, transitory, and impersonal. New sets of values and forms of association develop in response to new alternatives and incentives which have no basis in accustomed ways. Often these are deeply incompatible with and threaten traditional social forms. And, at the same time, no counterparts to the familiar basis of security have as yet developed in the urban industrial patterning of social relations. Thus, when a migrant comes to town he enters a social system which is characterized by conflicts in principles of social organization and the absence of traditional forms of security. And because the entire urban social system in Gwelo is marked by internal inconsistency and disharmony,[5] the system of social stratification is also marked by ambiguity and inconsistency.

A social stratification system is an expression of the differential ranking of functionally significant roles in terms of a common set of values.[6] Or, put another way, it is the result of the interaction of social differentiation and social evaluation. To a greater or lesser extent, all societies have some role differentiation, even if solely on the basis of age and sex. And there is usually some correspondence between the amount of role differentiation and the complexity of the ranking system. Similarly, men in society

---

[5] For an excellent instructive analysis of the inconsistencies and ambiguities in the social system of a Northern Rhodesian town, see Epstein, 1958.

[6] I am indebted to Bernard Barber's analysis of social stratification for many insights and stimulation (Barber, 1957).

inevitably evaluate each other's roles. And while it is likely that in no society do all men invariably hold precisely the same set of values, in any working social system men share, more or less, a common value system. The pertinent questions that must concern us for the developing African urban social stratification system are: (1) what are the functionally significant roles? and (2) is there a shared and common value system by which these roles are evaluated? Clearly, in the African urban social system in Gwelo, which is marked by extreme heterogeneity and fluidity in norms and social behaviour, there is no single system of values by which individuals are ranked higher or lower according to their various roles and activities. Therefore, what we must ask is whether there is one common set of values which predominates, in the urban context, over all other value systems and which then may serve as a source of differential evaluation and thus as a basis for a system of social stratification.

Putting aside the problems of a common value system for a moment, let us first inquire into social differentiation in the Gwelo African community. In any society a person holds numerous roles, any one of which could be used as a basis for evaluation. Here I shall consider that the relevant roles for evaluation in the system of stratification in Gwelo are those that are socially functional within the urban context and require the relatively full-time participation of those who perform them. In Gwelo, this means the roles an individual has within the urban industrial economic system, but might include the witch doctor, who earns his living by providing native cures for various physical or mental ills, as well as the factory labourer.

The most striking feature of the Gwelo social system is the discrimination in roles between Africans and Europeans. By custom and law, occupational categories have been stereotyped and certain categories have been marked off for each group. In a few instances, the categories overlap, but a difference in wages paid to the two groups for the same work is maintained. The professional and managerial roles are virtually debarred to Africans, although there are a small number of African religious leaders who work among the Africans only. There are African teachers teaching at African schools only and African clerks, who are given a narrow range of responsibility and authority. African commercial traders and skilled artisans are allowed to serve the African population on the location only and may not work in Gwelo proper. But the vast majority of Africans in Gwelo fulfil the menial tasks of the society. For the most part an African is confined to unskilled work either as a labourer or as a domestic. Some who are more gifted or educated rise from these ranks to supervisory or semi-skilled positions, but again these are relatively few. Thus, the range in role differentiation among the Africans in Gwelo is exceedingly limited and the higher ranking positions in virtually all functionally significant roles are reserved to the white segment of the population.

The following table gives the occupational distribution of the adult males (over 15 years of age) in the sample.

OCCUPATIONAL COMPOSITION OF ADULT MALES

Occupation	No.	%
Unskilled	245	73·6
Domestic	10	3·0
Skilled	43	12·9
Supervisory	7	2·1
White-collar, professional, and commercial	20	6·0
Student	5	1·5
Unemployed	3	0·9
	333	100·0

Within the changing heterogeneous Gwelo social system there are several other systems of social differentiation which are related, but not identical, to differentiation by the roles held in the industrial economy. The traditional differentiating characteristics of sex, age, kinship relations, and hereditary political position, although modified considerably, still persist in towns as bases for evaluation. Among these, kinship is the most important and provides a significant basis of relationship in the urban areas. People are drawn to certain towns because their kinsmen are there.[7] A man may seek food, shelter, aid in securing

---

[7] Our data show that over 50% of the men came to work in Gwelo because a kinsman was already there.

a job, and other help from his urban kin and he may not be refused. In addition, once he is residing in town, despite differences in neighbourhood, occupation, education, wealth, or even where personal contact is infrequent, many of the traditional rights and duties of kinship are still valid. In all important happenings such as death, sickness, marriage, births, loss of a job, financial embarrassment, or political difficulties, it is to a kinsman, whenever possible, that an African town dweller turns. There are, I think, two main reasons for the persistence and strength of traditional kin ties in town. The first is that the bonds of kinship operate as the primary social and psychological buffers in the system of urban relations in which no new security devices have as yet replaced the traditional ones. Secondly, almost invariably a man in Gwelo looks forward to returning to his kin and reserve permanently. Therefore, the sanctions of kinship still operate in town and a man's refusal to fulfil his obligation to any kin constitutes a transgression against his whole body of kin to whom he hopes to return.

Mitchell[8] has pointed out in a study of tribalism in the Northern Rhodesian Copperbelt, that tribal affiliation is a primary category of social interaction and hence of differentiation in these towns. His comments are equally applicable to Gwelo. In Gwelo, the people are housed without regard to tribal background and a man's neighbours and co-workers may often differ from him in tongue and cultural traditions. In these circumstances, it is not surprising that tribal affiliation is the first and, in some instances, the most important differential between one person and another. Other social variables such as wealth or education provide bases for separating people. But while each of these social variables is an important criterion for evaluating and dividing people in Gwelo, they are not identical to differentiation on the basis of socially functional roles in the urban industrial system, which I have taken to be the primary basis for the system of social stratification. In some cases, the other systems of differentiation are consistent with that of social stratification, but in others they cut across it sharply.

[8] Mitchell, 1956.

McCulloch[9] has asked whether it is correct to assume that all urban Africans are consciously engaged in a struggle for status in terms of an urban prestige system. To put this in more general terms, she posed the problem of a shared and common value system among urban Africans. As we have said earlier, it is unlikely in any society that all men have the same values at all times and in all circumstances. But in any stable society, there is one predominant value system by which the roles of people are evaluated. Does such a system exist in Gwelo?

There are factors in Gwelo which clearly are barriers to the formation of a common value system appropriate to its urban industrial context. The most important is the lack of appreciation of a new status system in terms of the old. Traditional social relationships are made increasingly precarious by urban patterns and, at the same time, no substitute supports and security have emerged in the urban society. For these reasons, an urban African may cling to traditional bases of assurance and resist urban patterns, and, particularly, an urban mode of status fixing.

The movement of people back and forth from reserve to town and between towns also retards the formation and acceptance of common value system appropriate to urban life. The patterns of a residential mobility between town and reserve are individualized and varied. However, only a very few have given complete allegiance to town life and regard town as their home.[10] Even those who have been working for many years in town usually have close links with a reserve and make lengthy visits to it. The high rate of mobility and the discontinuities in residence and occupation result in increased hesitancy and confusion between the two forms of social life and the values they embody.

Furthermore, the African population of Gwelo is tribally heterogeneous. Although many of the tribes have substantially homogeneous cultures, others differ markedly, especially in regard to their political organizations and prestige systems. Therefore, in addition to the disparity between the values of the

[9] McCulloch, 1956.
[10] Usually these have been born or reared in town or have come to a town from a great distance and remained there.

urban and rural life, there is some diversity in attitudes and values brought into town from the tribal areas.

Another barrier to the acceptance of the industrial way of life has its source in the restraints placed on Africans and the workings of the colour bar. The Africans are kept at uniformly low wage standards and have little or no security of tenure. Socially, as well as economically, Africans are subject to regulations and rigid constraints which have no applicability to the white segment of the population. These barriers and restrictions result not only in apathy and frustration, but engender a bitter resentment.

But none of these are insurmountable barriers to the acceptance of an urban value system, nor do they apply with uniform effectiveness to all ranks of the African population. There are varying degrees of commitment to town life and the values for which it stands and the comparative ease or difficulty in giving allegiance to the industrial system is dependent upon a number of social variables. To what extent has the rural way of life been modified by urban contacts? It is my belief that research will show that many of the same inconsistencies and conflicts that are so acute in town are reflected in the reserves. And, as a greater number of men and women come to town, the disparity between the prestige and status systems of town and reserve tends to break down.[11] It also may be assumed that the appeal of new patterns varies according to age, length of urban experience, education, and position in the traditional system. In the tribal community, status is based, in part at least, on age, and it is to be expected that the older men in town will be reluctant to lose their higher tribal status. Similarly, a man holding a high political position in the traditional society may resist a system which subverts his traditional power. On the other side of the picture, young men can achieve some economic independence from their elders in town and may prefer to enter a status system characterized by greater flexibility. For similar reasons, industrial modes may appeal more to members of disaffected groups. Education and length of urban

---

[11] The economic position of a tribe may also play a part in attitude towards town life. However, it is my impression that, for Gwelo at least, the reserves from which most of the population are drawn have substantially the same economic advantages and disadvantages and, therefore, this is not an important factor here.

experience are also important social variables in influencing the acceptance of an urban social structure and a value system appropriate to it. Those who are more educated and those who have had longer urban experiences see the urban social patterns very differently from those who are predominantly rural and uneducated. Through education, Africans assimilate much of western material culture and are better prepared, if only through a working knowledge of English, to make their way in the urban world. And as an African remains in town, by force of circumstances, he becomes increasingly involved in relationships and activities which are outgrowths of the industrial system. Western material culture is rapidly assimilated and, to a lesser extent, there is an absorption of western attitudes and values. As he remains in town, an African townsman becomes a man with divided loyalties and interests. His new interests are expressed in new social groupings and formal associations and the assertion of new goals. At the same time, there are the claims of traditional loyalties which continuously influence behaviour and attitudes. And it is this conflict in principles, which often remains unresolved, which is the characteristic mark of urban social life and hence of urban social stratification.

INDICATORS OF STATUS

In this section we shall be concerned with various accessible behavioural manifestations, which serve as indicators of differential evaluation and hence of status in Gwelo. These include verbal evaluations, patterns of association, and the various social activities and possessions that are held to be symbolic of social status.

VERBAL EVALUATION

What people say about each other is usually a direct expression of their evaluation of one another. One of the most common sociological uses of verbal evaluation, relevant to social stratification, has been the ranking of different occupational roles. The investigations have been based on the assumption that occupational role is one of the simplest and most accessible indicators of stratificational position.

In Gwelo, occupational ranking was measured by the occupational aspirations of two groups.[12] The adults in the survey sample were asked, 'What would you like your children to become?' The second group was composed of schoolchildren in Standards V and VI in the Gwelo Primary School. They were asked, 'When you grow up what would you like to be?' The responses to these questions are given in broad occupational categories in Charts I and II.

CHART I

Schoolchildren's Occupational Aspirations

Category	No.	%
Professional and white-collar	176	65·7
Agricultural	44	16·4
Skilled and supervisory	33	12·3
Commercial	12	4·1
Miscellaneous	3	1·1
Unskilled	0	0·0
	268	99·6

CHART II

Parental Aspirations for Children

Professional and white-collar	162	76·3
Agricultural	0	0·0
Skilled and supervisory	25	11·7
Commercial	12	5·6
Miscellaneous	13	6·1
Unskilled	0	0·0
	212	99·7

There is considerable agreement in the responses of both groups. The most desirable occupations are the professional and white-collar roles. At the bottom is unskilled labour. Between these are the skilled and supervisory roles and the commercial traders. The desire for agricultural pursuits among children will be discussed later.

[12] Strictly speaking, occupation ranking and occupational aspirations are not necessarily concomitants. Aspirations may be affected by many variables not directly related to prestige. Nevertheless, it was felt that in Gwelo, where there is so much fluidity in the social system, prestige and aspirations of and for children were very directly related.

The rank order of the occupations can in part be explained by the differences in wages paid for different types of work. The minimum wages set by law are £4 15s. 6d. a month[13] and it can be assumed that this is the average wage paid to unskilled labour. The white-collar workers and professionals, in general, earn the highest wages and may earn £14 to £16 a month. However, many of the store owners and other commercial traders have considerably higher earnings than those of the professional or white-collar workers.

The social grading of occupations in Gwelo is related also to influence and power. Although most of the power in the community is vested in Europeans, Africans can hold positions through which they can influence the behaviour and thinking of their fellow Africans. For example, through association with and access to Europeans and government, the position of a clerk may carry with it a considerable measure of power and influence. Since it is the white-collar and professional positions which might have influence or power, it appears that prestige and influence are closely co-related.

A third and more general explanation for the ranking of occupations is to link it to the general prestige patterns in which Europeans and the European way of life serve as models against which prestige is measured for all ranks of Africans. Hence the desire for white-collar and professional roles which more closely approximate to the work of Europeans.

There is one difference in the responses of the two groups which needs explanation. Among children there was a comparatively strong desire to follow agricultural pursuits. Among parents there was no desire for children to return to agriculture. The most acceptable explanation for the desires of the children, I think, is that many of them have come to town to live with relatives for the sole purpose of schooling. They are far from home and close kin and their main ties to town are those of school. They have not yet become deeply involved in urban life and still unequivocally regard life on their reserve as their own. Similarly, almost every adult looks upon a reserve area

[13] The minimum wage has recently been raised to £6 15s. 6d. a month.

Social Stratification in Gwelo 137

as his home and expressed a desire to return there eventually and live out his life. Yet at the same time, almost every adult interviewed wanted his child to enter professional, skilled, or commercial occupations, positions for which town life is requisite. Such universally accepted aspirations suggest that there is an appreciation and acceptance of an urban status system by the adults even though there are varying degrees of resistance to it.

PATTERNS OF ASSOCIATION

Men also express their evaluations of themselves and others by their voluntary associations. Social intimacy is often an expression of social equality and the absence or presence of close associations may in some situations provide a fairly reliable guide to a system of social stratification. Although relations between individuals in an urban community tend to be seen as relations between categories, in Gwelo people do have lasting personal relationships based on varying degrees of intimacy. This intimacy may take many forms. Aid in crises and courting and marriage are among the most reliable expressions of social intimacy and indicators of social equality. Other common forms are mutual visiting, eating together, and common participation in leisure activities at sporting clubs or at the beer hall.

But patterns of association in Gwelo are an expression of many social variables and none of these behavioural manifestations alone, except, perhaps, for marriage, can be taken as satisfactory evidence of social intimacy and social equality. In addition voluntary relationships in Gwelo are not an expression of a single set of interests and values, but reflect the co-existence of more than one system of values. Many of the relationships incorporate the allegiances and cleavages of the traditional society. Some genuinely reflect attitudes and values that have been bred in town.

As an illustration of the uncertainties in interpretation of the patterns of association as indicators of social status in Gwelo, we consider here the results of a questionnaire relating to closest friends. The 'closest friend' questionnaire was based on the assumption that a man will tend to associate with those who are his social equals. It was designed to show the similarities or differences in the social characteristics of those considered best friends.

The questionnaire provided us with the following results. Traditional differentials of kin relations and tribal affiliation still persist as important factors in the formation of friendships. Nearly half of those interviewed had formed their friendships outside of an urban community, presumably strongly influenced by traditional sentiments. Many were related through blood or marriage. Most were members of the same tribal group. On the other hand, other factors which have their source in urban life also seem to play a significant part in the formation and maintenance of friendship. The great majority of closest friends live in the same neighbourhood in the location and many have identical church affiliations.

But what of the similarities or differences in occupational categories or education which are primary criteria of evaluation for social stratification? 64% of the people have closest friends in the same occupational category while virtually all closest friends have had the same education. One can argue from this evidence that occupation and education are acknowledged bases for evaluation. However, 73% of the males in Gwelo are in the unskilled labourer occupational category and, therefore, any random selection of a friend by any member of this group would probably fall into the same category.[14] The same sort of interpretation would apply to the lack of differences in education between closest friends. Thus, it is extremely difficult to evaluate the importance of occupation or education as a basis for association and hence social equality in the urban system.

Another difficulty in the interpretation of the results involves a measurement of the degree of intimacy and the durability of friendship. A man may have daily contact and close association with a friend or co-worker. But to whom does he turn in a crisis? What if there are conflicts between familial obligations and

---

[14] Unfortunately, the numbers in our samples in each of the other occupational categories are too small to provide conclusive results.

those of friendship? In one social situation an African may consider a fellow African a close friend, but in another situation he may reject this friend and respond to claims of kin or tribe. This does not deny the existence or importance of patterns of association based on social equality in terms of the urban value patterns, but in different social contexts, other sentiments and values may prevail. For these reasons, this single inquiry into voluntary associations provides us with only limited information about the new forms of association and differentiations in Gwelo.

SYMBOLS

A third, and in some ways, perhaps, the most striking indicator of status in Gwelo are symbolic activities and possessions.[15] Usually, these behaviour patterns and possessions do not occur singly as indicators of higher or lower status, but are manifested in groups or clusters to indicate a way or style of life. In Gwelo, the symbols of status have a common measure; higher status is accorded to those who have possessions or patterns of behaviour that more closely approximate to European standards. The more of these activities and possessions a person has, the higher his prestige. These symbols encompass many diverse matters, but are regulated by the widespread restrictions in the society on both activities and possessions available to Africans.

The most important symbolic indicators of various social roles and positions are occupation, education, dress, furniture, language, etiquette, and leisure activities. The white-collar and professional occupations are valued highly not only because they are often better paid and carry with them some power and influence. They are preferred also because it is these occupations that are similar to those held by Europeans and thus in addition to becoming a criterion of evaluation in a status system, occupation has also become a symbol of it. An educated man is thought to have knowledge of the 'civilized way of life', and relatively high educational

[15] Barber (1957) has pointed out, 'In all societies, certain activities and possessions are taken as the source, consequence, or correlate of functionally significant roles and of the social class positions that are determined thereby. Such activities and possessions are commonly used by the members of the society, therefore, to infer the social class position of a family or an individual.'

qualifications are symbolic of prestige and requisite of high status. The style and quality of clothing for both men and women, but especially for men, are exceedingly important symbolic indicators in Gwelo.[16] Household furnishings, to a lesser but increasing degree, are similar to clothing as available signs of 'civilized' status. Language and etiquette also express differences in status. English is used by those who are able in all social encounters except those with immediate kin, and among those who are aware of them there is a grave observance of correct European manners and customs. Lastly, leisure activities differ to some extent among the various strata. Those who occupy higher social positions tend to avoid beer-hall activities which are the favourite form of recreation for the others. Instead, they occupy their leisure time with private parties and visiting.

Africans of all ranks in Gwelo clearly distinguish certain symbolic differences in the activities and possessions that express higher or lower prestige. Considerable prestige is always attached to educational attainment and the higher ranking occupations. Language and etiquette also carry considerable symbolic significance.[17] But, on the other hand, other symbols, such as dress, occur over a broad range of the social stratificational structure and therefore become only very crude indicators of status. Moreover, there is a large measure of anomalous display of physical possessions by those who, in another social system, would not ordinarily have them. Indeed, the awareness of and aspirations for certain symbols are so marked a part of town patterns that it often appears as if substance and shadow are confused and that symbols are the sole source of stratification and not an indicator of it.

For these reasons, there is only a rough correlation between

[16] In almost all societies, dress is an indication of status. But in Gwelo, and in similar areas, as Wilson and others have pointed out, the social environment has forced an exaggerated display of European clothing as a symbol of prestige. The reasons are clear. Because Africans are denied access to housing and various other symbols which might put in evidence a high social position, and because the uniformly low African wages usually prevent them from obtaining more elaborate or expensive symbols, fine dress has become exaggerated as a symbol of status. See Wilson, 1941; Mitchell, 1956.

[17] For example, when questioned about his visits to neighbours, one labourer replied that he never visited his closest neighbour because the neighbour eats with a fork and knife. The clear implication is that the neighbour ate as a European and he did not and therefore the two were not social equals and could not be friends.

symbols and social position. Certainly, no single symbol invariably indicates higher prestige and position, although the absence of one might be important. But a group of these symbols often does give a good indication of a person's status. Finally, I should like to emphasize again the use of European standards against which prestige is measured.[18] To my knowledge, there is no symbol that is African in origin that confers prestige in Gwelo. This is coupled with an almost indiscriminate acceptance of all accessible European symbols by all groups of Africans. This contrasts sharply with the discrimination employed in the selection and rejection of new elements and the retention of African symbols which is characteristic of some West African societies. An inquiry into the source of these differences could be most instructive.

CONCLUSIONS

It is clearly suggested by the data discussed in this paper that a system of stratification based on Western industrial values is emerging in the Gwelo African location. Earlier we indicated the underlying importance of a common value system in the formation of a system of social stratification. The central importance of urban occupations as a primary category of evaluation, the almost universal striving for European symbols and the beginnings of urban forms of personal association suggest that there is a shared and common value system appropriate to the urban industrial context.

Although there are certain differences among African territories, the basic characteristics of the prestige and social stratification emerging in Gwelo have been noted throughout most of urban Africa. It is perhaps to be concluded that whenever Africans enter a wage-earning industrialized economy, a generalized status system closely related to that in the West usually results. In other words, there are general forms of social differentiation inherent in the western industrial system which occur wherever these economic patterns prevail.

[18] This point has been made again and again by observers of urban African communities. See Mitchell, 1956.

There is no doubt, however, that the acceptance of the urban value system varies according to several social variables including age, length of urban experience, education, and position in the traditional system, although we were unable to discuss fully in this paper the varying influences of these variables. Traditional patterns and values still persist strongly and an African in town is divided in his allegiances. The awareness of one's position in the status hierarchy and the consciousness of tribal and kin affiliation may provoke conflict in an individual. The obligations and loyalties of an individual as a member of a tribe or as a kinsman may in certain circumstances be in opposition to those demanded by his position in the status continuum. Here the conflict is not between groups or representatives of groups or even between individuals, but is centred on a single individual who must resolve in his person the desires and obligations associated with his many roles.

There has been some discussion of the formation of social classes in urban Africa, but in my view it is premature to speak now of a full-fledged class system among Africans in Southern Rhodesia. Although the system of social stratification in Gwelo provides, in its way, a rudimentary set of rules and procedures regulating social relations and there is an awareness of status, the structure of the stratification system is extremely amorphous. The units of division are not clearly defined. This is, in part, a consequence of the various often conflicting sets of interests and values which actuate a Gwelo African and make uncertain his allegiances and his position in the urban status system. It is also a consequence of the social and economic barriers largely imposed by Europeans. Apart from a numerically insignificant group of men who are educated, relatively wealthy, and who have important occupational roles, the actual social distinctions and differences in prestige between any two persons are very slight indeed. Thus, although there is an acknowledged prestige scale, for the vast majority there is little opportunity to secure the higher positions and the respect that they command.

Another difficulty associated with the concept of social classes in Gwelo is that, in general, it is a family rather than an individual which is the basic unit in a social class system. By referring to a family as the basic unit, qualities of persistence and continuity are given to the concept of social class. In Gwelo, a large percentage of married males have left their families behind on the reserves. Even when families accompany or join the husband or father in town, they rarely remain there for the full length of his stay. For this reason, it is usually the male, as the worker, who has a position in the urban system of stratification and his status is usually not conferred or transmitted to his wife or children. When, or if, the African urban population becomes more stable and the family, rather than the individual, becomes the basic urban social unit it may be more meaningful to speak of social class.

Finally, it has been suggested that a social class must be seen as a category of persons who form the basis for corporate political groups.[19] In Gwelo, there is very little evidence pointing to internal political divisions among Africans. To be sure, the political appetites of educated Africans have been awakened. But because the Africans are inexperienced and unorganized and because there are virtually no avenues open for African political expression, there is little or no actual organized political behaviour. Moreover, the political activity that does occur is primarily an expression of the acute antagonism and the predominant cleavages between black and white, rather than an expression of the internal cleavages in the African population.

REFERENCES

Barber, Bernard	1957.	*Social Stratification.* New York: Harcourt, Brace.
Cox, Oliver Cromwell	1948.	*Caste, Class, and Race.* New York: Doubleday.
Epstein, A. L.	1958.	*Politics in an Urban African Community.* Manchester University Press for the Rhodes-Livingstone Institute.
Gluckman, Max	1955.	*Custom and Conflict in Africa.* Oxford: Blackwell.
	1958.	*Analysis of a Social Situation in Modern Zululand.* Rhodes-Livingstone Paper No. 28.
Hellmann, Ellen	1948.	*Rooiyard.* London: Oxford University Press.

---

[19] See Cox, 1945; Mitchell, 1956.

McCulloch, Merran	1956.	*A Social Survey of the African Population of Livingstone.* Rhodes-Livingstone Paper, No. 26.
Mitchell, J. Clyde	1956.	*The Kalela Dance.* Rhodes-Livingstone Paper, No. 27.
Moore, Wilbert E.	1951.	*Industrialization and Labor.* New York: Cornell University Press.
Wilson, Godfrey	1941-2.	*An Essay on the Economics of Detribalization in Northern Rhodesia.* Parts I and II. Rhodes-Livingstone Paper, Nos. 5 and 6.

VI. EDUCATED AFRICANS: SOME CONCEPTUAL AND TERMINOLOGICAL PROBLEMS

J. E. GOLDTHORPE

This paper is prompted by the perhaps somewhat naïve question: what, from the point of view of sociological analysis, *are* educated Africans? We often speak of the educated African élite; is this a proper usage of the term *élite*? Is there an educated African *class*? Are educated Africans a *group*? or a *category*? These might seem relatively trivial questions, but a clarification of concepts may sometimes be valuable.

'EDUCATED AFRICANS'

By educated we mean, of course, Western-educated, and we use the term in neither ignorance nor disparagement of traditional African modes of education. More precisely, we mean by educated those Africans whose education, in the Western sense, carries them far beyond the average level. Where we draw the line is of course arbitrary, and may depend on circumstances. Obviously we would always include African doctors, graduates, qualified professional men. But in the circumstances of Buganda in the 1920's, or of Karamoja now, a secondary-educated clerk is of the educated élite also; as the general level of popular education rises we may have to raise the line we draw.

The term African might seem relatively unambiguous, and in practice little difficulty does arise, though like all racial concepts it tends to be slightly fuzzy at the edges. In a racially segmented society such as that of many African territories, the educated élite of the African sector may be thought of as a sufficient research field in itself, and the inclusion of non-Africans might make the problem bigger than is conveniently manageable. But the question is more than one of mere convenience. To speak of the African sector in a racially segmented society may correspond well enough with realities to be meaningful as a first approximation at least; but it becomes increasingly difficult to delineate, as educated men of different racial statuses enter more and more into social relations with one another independently of race.

CATEGORY, ÉLITE, GROUP, CLASS?

Category seems an unexceptionable but unhelpful term. If cyclists, women aged 25, and educated Africans are alike categories this does not take us very far. Will *élite* do for what we are talking about? It is perhaps the term in commonest usage in this context; 'African élites' was the title of a special issue of the *International Social Science Bulletin*,[1] and the term has been similarly used by other writers including the present.[2] The *locus classicus* on élite as a sociological category is of course Pareto.[3] It is used also by Raymond Aron;[4] and by Lasswell and others;[5] it is defined in English and French by authoritative committees of the British Sociological Association and the Fondation Nationale des Sciences Politiques;[6] and it is carefully analysed by the late Professor Nadel, with particular reference to African élites, in the *International Social Science Bulletin* already referred to.

A careful reading of these sources seems to make it clear that in its general sociological usage the term élite is not quite right for what we have in mind; there is a considerable power component in the term which is not quite, or not necessarily, justified when we speak of the educated African élite. It is obvious enough that the term is literally applicable in fully self-governing African territories like Liberia, Ethiopia, and Ghana. Elsewhere, however, as in Nigeria or Uganda, to insist on using some other term until Independence Day and then suddenly to start talking about the élite would appear a highly arbitrary procedure. Yet if we can talk about the African élite in Uganda it seems unreasonable not to do so in Kenya or Nyasaland.

To get over this difficulty was perhaps one of Nadel's aims in

---

[1] Vol. VIII, No. 3, 1956. [2] Goldthorpe, 1955. [3] Pareto, 1935, para. 2025.
[4] Aron, 1950. [5] Lasswell *et al.*, 1952.
[6] *International Social Science Bulletin*, Vol. VII, 1955, pp. 474–6.

Educated Africans: Conceptual and Terminological Problems 147

his extremely careful analysis of 'The Concept of Social Elites'.[7] He concludes that an élite is a plurality of people with main characteristics—a position of pre-eminence over all others; some degree of corporate group character and exclusiveness ('there must be barriers to admission'); awareness of their pre-eminent position as the consequence of some attribute which they share by right; the recognition of their general superiority by the society at large; and imitability—'the élite, by its very manner of acting and thinking, sets the standards for the whole society, its influence or power being that of a model accepted and considered worth following'.

Applying these criteria to Ghana, Professor Busia writes:

> It is suggested that there are three classes of élites in Gold Coast society; the traditional 'royal' families, the European or alien rulers, and the educated Africans, or those who have been most successful in learning the skills and mode of life introduced by the European.

He goes on:

> With the adoption of British parliamentary institutions and elective local councils, the new élite have become a ruling class; for though there is universal adult suffrage, only those who are literate qualify for election to the Legislative Assembly. The new élite are thus able to monopolize political power.... It is permissible in the Gold Coast situation to regard all who are literate as an élite because their patterns of aspiration are 'Western': that is, European orientated.[8]

Do educated Africans form a *group*? This term is not particularly well defined; yet it seems probable that most sociologists would agree that to qualify as a group an assemblage or collection of people must have three things—communication, interaction, and awareness. The educated Africans with whom the writer is most familiar—former students of Makerere College—are not a group in this full sense; they do not all regularly communicate with one another, and the old student body as a whole does not possess a recognizable structure. I think, however, that many if not most of them are aware of being educated Africans, and to that extent

[7] *International Social Science Bulletin*, Vol. VIII, pp. 413–24.   [8] ibid., pp. 426–9.

of belonging to something—a category or assemblage of people —a little apart in some ways from the non-educated. Rumney and Maier, in elucidating first principles, describe groups as 'collections of individuals in regular contact or communication, each possessing a certain structure'. But, they add,

> not all collections of individuals are groups; they may lack a recognizable structure, in which case they may be conveniently designated as quasi-groups. If, however, these individuals have certain interests in common they may in time form groups. Thus a social class without being a group itself usually generates groups, such as political parties.[9]

Educated Africans can, I think, well be regarded as a quasi-group or incipient group in that sense, readily lending itself to the formation of true groups on a basis either of tribe or locality.

The word *class* has already crept in to the discussion, and this too is not a well-defined term. Attempting, however, an elucidation if not a definition, it seems that when we speak of social class in Western societies we mean a system of inequality; or rather, several systems of inequality, which can be distinguished in principle, but which partially coincide, overlap or diverge, in ways which afford great complexity to actual systems. The more important inequalities may be tabulated:

(a) Wealth; or, more precisely, (i) income and
(ii) capital
(b) Occupational status
(c) Education
(d) Culture
(e) Ascribed status due to birth

Social class has two further important characteristics, which are variable within limits:

1. Social mobility is possible, but limited. That it is possible marks off social class systems from systems such as caste or institutional inequalities based on race; yet mobility is not perfect, and in practice people are more likely to have a social class stand-

[9] Rumney and Maier, 1953.

Educated Africans: Conceptual and Terminological Problems 149

ing somewhat like that of their parents than they are to have one widely different.[10] This is in turn related to the fact that:

2. The family is the unit of social class. Though the attributes of social class position such as wealth and occupational status belong largely to men, and almost exclusively to adults, yet it makes sense to speak of 'wives of the professional class', or 'working-class children'. And on the whole a group of brothers and sisters generally have similar social class status, as a consequence of the imperfect social mobility already noted.

Finally, social class manifests itself in three main ways:

(a) Differential behaviour, including deferential behaviour.

(b) Residential segregation, the fact that people of similar social class mix and entertain more freely and frequently than do people of different class, and an appreciable degree of social class endogamy.

(c) Generally accepted beliefs that social class exists, and a general readiness to place one's self and other people in social class categories.[11]

Broadly speaking, the social class system in all its aspects does not yet seem to exist in territories like these. The more important inequalities and segregations follow the lines of race rather than class. Awareness of social class distinctions in the population as a whole is incomplete, and distinctions are more readily attributed to race than to class, as is interestingly shown by the term 'black European' to describe Africans of the highest social rank and greatest degree of Western acculturation. But at the same time some of the elements of the social class system are undoubtedly beginning to emerge.[12]

For example, it makes very good sense to speak as Fallers does of 'social class in modern Buganda';[13] and he shows how many of the attributes of a social class system have come into being in

---

[10] In a highly sophisticated treatment of the subject by D. V. Glass and his colleagues it was discovered, for example, that in Britain unskilled workers' sons are 2·6 times as likely to become unskilled workers as are the population at large, while in the case of professional and administrative men the 'index of association' is as high as 13. See Glass (ed.), 1954, p. 18.

[11] This has been demonstrated in very many surveys; see, for example, Hall and Caradog Jones, 1950, pp. 31–55; Bott, 1954, pp. 259–85.

[12] For a fuller treatment see Goldthorpe, 1956, Also 1958, Ch. IX.

[13] Fallers, 1957.

Buganda. Inequalities of income and capital seem clearly to be greater than in traditional conditions now that money serves as a store of value and power, and land can be individually owned. Specialized occupations, particularly those carrying high social class evaluation, are differently evaluated and carry different social prestige. There are the widest possible inequalities in education. And Fallers is surely arguing against his own data when he suggests that 'the new élite do not seem to have acquired a class culture any more than did their predecessors in the nineteenth century'. The Buganda equivalents of the English public schools—King's College, Budo and St. Mary's, Kisubi, to which he refers—ensure that to some extent they do. The new élite share a knowledge of English and indeed often tend to speak among themselves a curious mixture of English and Luganda which must be almost incomprehensible to a peasant. Material possessions, as Fallers says—'fine houses, large cars and fine clothes'—involve possession also of immaterial aspects of culture, the knowledge of how to use them—how to drive a car, for instance. Moreover, a protracted visit to England has become the hall-mark of élite membership among the Ganda; and this results in a noticeable accentuation of Westernization and helps to lend the culture of the Ganda upper class a definite flavour of its own, markedly different from that of peasant Ganda society. And though hardly half the Ganda are Christian by even the widest definition, the great majority of the upper class are Protestant or, to a less extent, Catholic adherents, and conspicuous attendance at the fashionable church parade on Sunday morning at the cathedrals remains an almost indispensable badge of upper-class status. Surely these add up to a highly distinctive class culture?

Where it seems more likely that social class in Buganda—and very possibly elsewhere in Africa—falls short of the Western model is in the relations between class and kinship. Fallers reports a tendency to intermarry, but it seems probable that social class endogamy in this case is very incomplete, if only because women's education still lags. Thus the present writer found in his follow-up of former Makerere students that out of

Educated Africans: Conceptual and Terminological Problems

33 Ganda members of the sample year, the wives of 15 knew little or no English. (12 knew some, and information was not obtained about 6.) In another study, of students entering Makerere in 1954, out of 18 Ganda freshmen—drawn largely from the élite or upper-class families described by Fallers—13 had fathers literate in English but only 3 had mothers who knew English. Information about the occupational status of siblings is unfortunately scanty; Fallers draws attention to the positive correlations, for instance, the very strong tendency for present-day chiefs to be the grandsons of the men who got the lions' shares of land under the 1900 Agreement; but he does not indicate how many of their brothers and sisters are in humbler circumstances today. Quite possibly the proportion is not high, yet the writer's impression is that Ganda would see nothing strange in a doctor having a brother working as a clerk or a sister married to a carpenter. Certainly one of the chief personal problems of educated Africans, including Ganda, is the avalanche of poor relations who descend on them as soon as they get their first salaried job. Though Buganda may be exceptional, evidence is not lacking of similar situations elsewhere. Leith-Ross writes, for example, of the Nigerian élite:

> The family is not the unit of parents and children but the extended family which looks for financial help or moral support to whatever member has made good. The Minister has a 'sister' selling cassava in the market; the successful doctor has a 'brother' working as a Public Works Department labourer.
>
> The family bond linking rich and poor, literate, influential and insignificant, militates against any idea of a strictly isolated 'class'. It also prevents the group, though increasingly Westernized, from being cut off from its origins.[14]

It would not be difficult to multiply examples.

Whether this difference from Western societies makes it difficult to apply the term 'social class', or whether we can still do so with the reservation that social class and kinship are differently related in Africa, seems largely to be a verbal question. If we agree that something with some resemblance to social class is coming into being in Africa, especially in parts most affected

[14] INCIDI, 1956, pp. 181-2.

by contact with the wider world, we must now ask how the educated élite fit into it.

In what may be rather loosely termed the colonial situation, with the first establishment of administration and business there comes a demand for the services of clerks and other junior officials and managerial staff which it is uneconomic to meet by bringing in expatriates. Meanwhile the activities of Christian missions have come to include the establishment of schools and the provision of education; and we have the establishment of a pattern in which mission schools are seen as the avenue to the white-collar jobs of 'fonctionnaires' and professional men.

It is of these circumstances that observers use such phrases as 'the magic of literacy'. Paper qualifications become an end in themselves. Mission-educated clerks, sous-officiers, fonctionnaires, *et al.*, embrace a Western way of life—or as near to one as their resources allow. This has been documented, for example, by Busia in Ghana,[15] by le Tourneau in French North Africa,[16] and by Pierre Razafy-Andriamihaingo in Madagascar,[17] while Little's description of young educated Mende men is something of a classic.[18]

The wholehearted adoption of Western ways seems to follow from two factors. First, the close association of education with missionary influence, so that Western education seems inseparable from Christianity (this, obviously, would not apply in North Africa and other Muslim lands, however) and from Western influence generally. At the same time, the nature of white-collar employment very generally causes white-collar workers to be associated with, and to associate themselves with, their employers, whether 'management', Government, or the Church. Thus to some extent Europeans become a 'reference group', as is more fully discussed below.

In the early stages, therefore, educated Africans set the pace for the emerging middle class and make up the greater part of it. But there are additional contributions of at least two other sorts. Economic development creates an indigenous business class of

---

[15] *International Social Science Bulletin*, Vol. VIII, 1956, p. 429.
[16] INCIDI, 1956, p. 109.   [17] ibid., p. 250.   [18] Little, 1951, pp. 255–6.

Educated Africans: Conceptual and Terminological Problems 153

traders, shopkeepers, larger-scale peasant farmers growing cash crops and beginning to employ labour, transport owners, and even—though usually less importantly—small-scale industrialists. Thus Razafy-Andriamihaingo writes of a rural middle class of progressive farmers, and of traders, shopkeepers, and small industrialists as contributing to the middle class in Madagascar,[19] while Assane Seck notes a similar development in French West Africa.[20]

At first, the business class are quite separate from the educated élite; very many of them are illiterate and quite usually many are not Christian. In Buganda, for example, Islam is widespread among the small business–large farmer class in marked contrast to Christianity among the élite. In Kikuyu, the writer has been told of wealthy lorry-owners going about with hundreds of pounds in notes in the pockets of tattered raincoats, outwardly indistinguishable from peasants, while wealthy Kikuyu traders are said to be openly polygamous in contrast to the respectability of Christian schoolteachers. Though Western consumer goods such as car, radio, and comfortable furniture may be bought and enjoyed, the style of life could rather be described as modified-traditional than Western; and this is intelligible, for the business interest of the class lies partly in their not being too remote from their customers.

This separation can last only for a time, however. Members of the élite become farmers and businessmen part-time and in retirement. Thus Balandier suggests that in Brazzaville the nucleus of a true bourgeoisie is to be found among some chiefs and members of parliament who have gone into trading or transport businesses. 'C'est à un tel niveau que s'effectue la rencontre entre les élites éduquées et les élites économiques, entre le pouvoir et l'avoir.'[21] And even more importantly, the children of both classes go to the same schools; while education overseas is an aspiration of both also, as is reported by Leith-Ross of Western Nigeria;[22] while Assane Seck, too, sees the fusion of the two classes in somewhat similar terms.

[19] INCIDI, 1956, pp. 246–9.   [20] ibid., p. 161.   [21] Balandier, 1955, p. 161.
[22] INCIDI, 1956, p. 178.

As an intermediate category, we have the traditional or modern African ruling class. Though in some areas traditional political status may continue to be recognized, especially for instance where there are hereditary chiefs, there seems everywhere to be some infiltration into positions of authority of men of the new educated élite. This is documented, for example, in a recent review of the careers of former students of Makerere College.[23] Sometimes there may have been a deliberate policy on the part of Government and missions of concentrating education to some extent on the traditional ruling class if there was one; the secondary school at Old Moshi in Tanganyika was, it is said, set up specifically for the sons of chiefs, while the education of the new Protestant oligarchy of Buganda after 1900 was almost certainly one of the motives for the foundation of King's College, Budo. The selection of future rulers for education, however, has probably been outweighed in most places by the selection for positions of authority of men already educated. Putting it at its lowest, a European administration will tend for obvious reasons to prefer chiefs who can read and write; even more will prefer chiefs with some knowledge and experience in one of the technical branches of modern African administration such as agricultural or veterinary services or education.

The style of life of men in this position is often a real compromise. They have more inducement than the business class to Westernize, partly in order to attain and maintain a standard that will impress Europeans with their status. The more they succeed in that direction, however, the more they become cut off from African society, which, especially when the office they occupy is elective, may make it difficult to maintain their position and perform their functions. Thus ceremonial occasions like the anniversary of a prince's accession come to wear a double aspect, a polite garden party or select dinner largely for European guests with drumming, dancing, beer, and traditional rites somewhat separate in time and space.

We may suggest, then, that in African territories under European administration the educated African élite, itself largely

[23] Goldthorpe and Macpherson, 1958.

the product of mission schools, constitutes at first the main part of the emergent middle class, and sets the pace for that class; that it infiltrates also into the positions of political authority in African society, whether they be traditional or modern; that it is later joined with a business class of very different social and cultural origins; and that the two, or three, elements finally may be expected to fuse. Following Baltzell's useful distinction, we may say that it is in these stages an élite of individuals rather than a class of families, owing to the toughness of the wide African kinship ties and to the lag in women's education behind that of men which forces many educated men to marry beneath them (purely, that is, in terms of years of schooling).

CULTURAL ASPECTS AND THE REFERENCE GROUP IDEA

The problem of a class culture, raised by Fallers, has been dealt with in very general terms in a neglected contribution by J. Obrebski, 'The Sociology of Rising Nations'.[24] Over a large part of the world, he points out, typical of rising nations is a 'basic cultural dichotomy, the split of the society into two different social and cultural universes: the literate "national" civilization limited to a small layer of the society, and the folk-culture, embracing the originally non-literate masses'.

> Owing to the fundamental differences in culture, the whole social structure takes the shape of a two-class system, particularly in societies where the national culture group is of foreign origin, as, for instance, in the colonies.
> Operating within this culture-and-class dichotomy the institutions of the national culture group produce two-fold effects: they detach, physically and spiritually, the members of the folk-society from their own group and they reject them from the full participation in the national culture groups.

Race discrimination, or 'cultural ethnocentrism', may therefore work in Africa in much the same way as, for instance, the resistance of an established upper class to the intrusions of *nouveaux riches* in more homogeneous societies; while the breaking down of regional or tribal cultures by the metropolitan 'national

[24] *International Social Science Bulletin*, Vol. III, 1951, pp. 237–43.

culture' can equally be paralleled, outside Africa, in Western societies themselves. In these circumstances, the more the established élite resist the newcomers, the more the latter strive to make themselves acceptable by adopting their values and way of life.

It is at this point that reference group theory seems clearly to have something to say on our topic.[25] Merton and Kitt have coined the useful phrase 'anticipatory socialization', and point out that men who undergo it are neither always readily received by the group to which they aspire nor approved by their own group, by whom indeed they are often regarded as renegades or traitors.

This obviously is relevant to African élites, and it is noticeable that in times of stress such as Mau Mau in Kenya or the 1949 riots in Buganda the group most consistently under attack have been the most Westernized Africans, for whom a fury has been reserved distinctly reminiscent of that against Quislings in German-occupied Europe.

They also say something of direct relevance on marginal men; when the social climber is excluded in principle from the group to which he aspires, 'anticipatory socialization becomes dysfunctional for the individual who becomes the victim of aspirations he cannot achieve and hopes he cannot satisfy'. The life-history of Jomo Kenyatta would make a fascinating case-study from exactly that point of view, and it is not difficult to understand how an educated man in a society where his hopes are raised to the maximum extent by his education, and then disappointed to the maximum extent by the self-protecting colour bar thrown round itself by the dominant group, may react into chauvinism—'Facing Mount Kenya'.

Like all good ideas, however, reference group theory is not without its dangers, and in attempting to make it explain too much there is likely to be an emphasis on trivialities while essentials may be overlooked. It is obvious enough that in many parts of Africa, Europeans as the most powerful group afford

[25] 'Contributions to the Theory of Reference Group Behaviour', Merton and Lazarsfeld (eds.), 1950.

the model for reference group behaviour by aspiring Africans; yet two important qualifications need to be made.

First, when educated Africans buy Western consumer goods or adopt European ways, their behaviour is not necessarily determined solely by a desire to emulate the reference group. Thus when Mitchell found Africans using 'sewing machines, bicycles, shot-guns, etc.',[26] it was hardly necessary to invoke reference group theory; such articles have an obvious utility in enabling existing wants to be met with less effort and greater technical effectiveness. Similarly, the adoption of rice, butter, and tinned foods may be a rational adjustment to life in town, while new tastes like those for European beer and cowboy music may arise in response to a situation affording a far greater range of choice than traditional African culture did. Indeed, when we eliminate behaviour for which other explanations are possible we may be left with relative trivialities, such as pith helmets and nameboards—and this is, perhaps, a criticism of reference group theory itself. This is not to deny that such reference group behaviour occurs—(very obviously it does)—but to suggest that the patterns of life of educated Africans need to be seen also in relation to other factors in their total situation.

Secondly, the extent to which Europeans form a dominant and exclusive group varies, of course, in different parts of Africa. The situation in Central Africa is near to one extreme of European dominance and exclusiveness, and it would appear to be no accident that Mitchell and other workers have found their behaviour demanding little other than the reference group explanation. In West Africa at the other extreme even the wearing of Western dress has ceased to be a mark of high social status, while here in East Africa the situation is intermediate.

REFERENCES

Aron, R. 1950. 'Social Structure and the Ruling Class'. *British Journal of Sociology*, Vol. I, pp. 1–16, 126–43.

Balandier, G. 1955. *Sociologie des Brazzavilles Noires*. Paris: Armand Colin.

---

[26] INCIDI, 1956, pp. 222–32.

Bott, Elizabeth	1954.	'Class as Reference Group'. *Human Relations*, Vol. VII, pp. 259-85.
Fallers, L. A.	1957.	'Social Class in Modern Buganda'. (Mimeographed.) (Paper read at a Conference of the East African Institute of Social Research in June 1957.)
Glass, D. V. (ed.)	1954.	*Social Mobility in Britain*.
Goldthorpe, J. E.	1955.	'An African Elite'. *British Journal of Sociology*, Vol. VI, pp. 31-47.
	1956.	'Social Class and Education in East Africa'. *Transactions of the Third World Congress of Sociology*, Amsterdam, Vol. V, pp. 115-22.
	1958.	*Outlines of East African Society*. Kampala: Makerere College, Dept. of Sociology.
Goldthorpe, J. E., and Macpherson, M.	1958.	'Makerere College and its Old Students'. *Zaïre*, Vol. XII, pp. 349-63.
Hall., J., and Caradog Jones, D.	1950.	'The Social Grading of Occupations'. *British Journal of Sociology*, Vol. I, pp. 31-55.
INCIDI	1956.	*Record of the 29th Session*. 'Development of a middle class in tropical and sub-tropical countries'.
Lasswell, H. D., Lerner, D., and Rothwell, C. E.	1952.	*The Comparative Study of Elites*. Stanford: University Press.
Little, K. L.	1951.	*The Mende of Sierra Leone*. London: Routledge and Kegan Paul.
Merton, R. K., and M. Lazarsfeld, P. (eds.)	1950.	*Continuities in Social Research: Studies in the Scope and Method of 'The American Soldier'*.
Pareto, V.	1935.	*The Mind and Society* (Tr. Bongiorno and Livingstone). London: Cape.
Rumney, J., and Maier, J.	1953.	*Sociology: The Science of Society* (2nd ed.). New York: Schuman.

VII. AN EXPENDITURE STUDY OF THE CONGOLESE *ÉVOLUÉS* OF LEOPOLDVILLE, BELGIAN CONGO[1]

L. BAECK

PRELIMINARY REMARKS

Our factual knowledge of consumption patterns in underdeveloped countries in general may still be in an embryonic state.[2] Statistical material on the spending habits of Africans only recently emerging from a barter economy at a subsistence level is scarcer still.[3] Moreover, a great many of the available studies have been inspired by such practical considerations as the just wage, the vital minimum, sanitary and hygienic conditions, etc. As a rule they have dealt with elements of society which have benefited least—the sub-proletariat of the African *bidon-villes*.

Recent studies have thrown more light upon the socio-economic problem connected with the rapid transition of more or less backward agricultural societies into industrialized ones. The characteristic pattern of this process of change may be described as one of growing differentiation of society into its sub-systems.[4] Moreover, it is recognized that the realignment of different sub-systems may result in tension. This is because some elements are exposed to, and do respond more readily to, outside stimuli and pressure than others. The very pattern of the transformation process depends also on the different adaptive capacities of the sub-systems.

In the economic sphere, for example, modern division of labour and a money economy were forced upon the African if he did not adopt them voluntarily. By contrast, kinship structure, land tenure, and political organization are not impinged upon as long

---

[1] This paper is based on the partial results of field-work carried out in the urban centre of Leopoldville (Belgian Congo) during the year 1956 under the auspices of l'Institut pour la Recherche Scientifique en Afrique Centrale (IRSAC).
[2] Hoyt, 1956, pp. 12–22.
[3] Mersadier, 1957; Accra: 1956b; 1956a.
[4] Parsons and Smelser, 1957, Chap. II; Southall, 1957.

as they do not get in the way of Western codes of administration and economic development.[5] The unbalance resulting from the unequal differentiation of traditional sub-systems is more or less proportional with the speed as well as with the bearing of the impact of modern Western society on indigenous societies.

The prodigious economic development of the Congo during the last two decades has made an abrupt change in the material and social structures of indigenous society.[6] Many thousands of Africans migrated to the newly created industrial and commercial centres. Completely rural only thirty years ago, with an average population density of about 6 people per square kilometer, the Congo nowadays shelters 8% of its total African population in localities of more than 10,000 inhabitants. The growth rate of urban agglomerations is, even by modern standards, enormous.[7] The city of Leopoldville, for example, with its 46,880 inhabitants, in 1940 mushroomed into a sprawling city of 348,763 Africans and 18,056 Europeans.

The study of consumption patterns of the newly urbanized Africans of the Congo, moreover, is of particular interest in that they are astride two civilizations. The problem involved, then, is to find out how the urban African distributes his newly acquired purchasing power and to assess the social factors—traditional and modern—that influence him in the way he spends his income.

The present analysis concentrates on the distribution of the expenditure of relatively well-to-do Africans, referred to in the Congo as the *évolués*.[8] The *évolué* is confronted today by the tremendous range of goods and services which modern society can offer him and he makes his choice from them according to several criteria of varying complexities. Our hypothesis will be

---

[5] Greaves, 1935.
[6] About 38% of the available manpower of the Congo is employed as salaried workers. In the province of Leopoldville this proportion amounts to 50%.
[7] Supplementary material on the general social consequences of this rapid development of the Belgian Congo are to be found in: Grévisse, 1951; Pons, Clément, Xydias, 1956, pp. 255–524; Minon, 1957, pp. 5–51; Baeck, 1956 and 1957a.
[8] The group of *évolués* studied here form a sharp contrast as far as their income is concerned with the rest of the population. We observed that the yearly *per capita* income of people living outside the money economy amounts to approximately 29 dollars, while the yearly *per capita* income of people inside the money economy amounts to 76 dollars. The group of *évolués* studied here, however, have a *monthly income* (salary plus family allowances) of between 70 and 150 dollars per household.

An Expenditure Study of Congolese 'Évolués'

that there are two fundamental tendencies in play which govern the consumption patterns of the Congolese.

The first is signified by the fact that the consumption patterns of Europeans tend to capture the imagination of the Africans. There, in general, the Africans have found a reference of consumption among the different possibilities in order to share their purchasing power among the array of goods and services which the modern material world can offer them. However, the *évolué* of the Congolese towns has just emerged geographically—but not socially—from his traditional social structure. He is still tied to it by certain links which find their overt expression in his budget. Concerning food, the inhabitant of Leopoldville continues to show his preference for certain traditional meals where native products, such as vegetables and oils, predominate. Also, in managing his resources in general—the flow of money, credit, and commodities—the *évolué* remains tied to a certain extent to his system of traditional values, while on the other hand he adopts specific new Western techniques. We shall indicate below the importance of certain kinship obligations in the balance sheet of this new class of well-to-do Africans. The abrupt increase in buying power has pre-empted the old preoccupation with subsistence and thus leaves more free play for considerations of choice between goods and services. We shall say, then, that for these Africans most overt expressions like mutual aid, gifts, etc. derive from a traditional value system *which is being inflated by modern times and circumstances.*

The selection they arrive at and which is translated into their expenditure on goods and services may throw some light upon the complicated problem of social change in general and change in consumer behaviour in particular. Furthermore, the selection they make, finding overt expression in their expenditure, may be indicative of the more general problem of choice-factors in a development process.

METHODOLOGY

The choice of the households was made from the pay-roll list of Government clerks on a stratified sampling basis.[9] In order to be included in the sample, the household had to have an overall income of 3,500 francs (i.e. 70 dollars, 50 francs being equal to 1 dollar) a month. The composition of the family was also taken into consideration in order that the sampling correspond as much as possible with the composition of the *évolué* population in town. Table I shows the composition of the sample according to income and family composition.

TABLE I

Composition of the sampling according to income and family status

Overall income (in dollars)	Number of children								Total
	0	1	2	3	4	5	6	7	
70·00– 79·99	1								1
80·00– 89·99	4	2							6
90·00– 99·99		8	2						10
100·00–109·99		1	1	5					7
110·00–119·99			3	1	3				7
120·00–129·99					5	1	1		7
130·00–139·99						1	2		3
140·00–149·99						1	2	2	5
Total	5	11	6	6	8	3	5	2	46

The method of daily visits and interviews in the households proved to be the best one for collecting material since most of the African housewives are illiterate and unable to keep a record book themselves. It was decided that a very intensive study of short duration would be most fruitful. The period of one month seemed adequate.

During the daily visits, which were made before the midday

---

[9] From the statistical point of view we tried to respect as much as possible the method of random choice inside the various strata. Unfortunately, we were not able completely to apply this technique because of the refusal of certain households. This refusal appeared generally at the moment when the housewife learned of the daily visits. The original choice included 52 households, of which we were not able to complete our study in six.

An Expenditure Study of Congolese 'Évolués'

meal, the food bought for the day's meals was weighed on a scale. The husband was contacted regularly since he does a good deal of the shopping. In addition, at the end of the inquiry, we took a complete inventory of the goods available in the households. This inventory, which one might call a cumulative statement of durable expenditure, permits us to estimate easily the order of preference for any particular kind of item and saved us the expense of a more lengthy study.

THE RESULTS

I. THE FLOW OF MONEY AND EXPENDITURE

A. *The Data*. In the collection of the basic material we have tried to classify income and outlay in the most detailed manner possible. The elements of the overall income, deriving from earnings—above and beyond the salary and family allowances—were separated by its earner, head of the family or family member. This breakdown of income according to the earner proves to be useful in societies where the wife used to be an important economic agent. From our statistics we concluded that the wife of the *évolué* is not an important money earner. This is in marked contrast to the wives of the urban proletariat who are mostly engaged in petty trade. The income, in cash, of the husband constitutes the most important element of the overall income.

Another useful distinction is one between cash income and income in kind, especially in a society which gives and receives gifts to such an extent. Furthermore, we have to introduce the rubric 'transactions'. It comprises any exchange, in cash or kind, which alters the status of credit, debt or the reimbursement of a debt of the household. These transactions may include the following: the deposit or withdrawal of an amount at the Savings Bank, the contract or repayment of a charge-account (*bon pour*), sums received through *ikelemba*[10] or loans made to a stranger. We shall see that these transactions are quite important in the budget of the *évolué* and that without taking them into consideration his budget would be unintelligible.

[10] For a definition of *ikelemba*, see text p. 168.

However, in such conditions can we use the term 'budget' at all? Would it not be more exact to say simply 'balance sheet'? As one author remarks, a budget implies making provision, whether premeditated or unconscious, methodical or approximate.[11] It conveys the idea of equilibrium or a tendency towards equilibrium: whereas a balance sheet is only an *a posteriori* observation. A budget is set up for a determined period of time, while a balance sheet may be drawn up at any time, when its usefulness becomes obvious.

During the course of the month, the receipts of the total 46 households amounted to 5,289 dollars and 6 cents while the expenditure came to 5,305 dollars and 40 cents. This shows that the total of 46 households registered a deficit of expenditure over receipts during the month of 0·3%.

Furthermore, we observe that 94·8% of the overall receipts derive from wages, 4·1% from supplementary earnings, and 6·7% from dependants' contributions.

The observation alone of this balance sheet of receipts and expenditure would leave us with the impression of a rather neat balance. But in fact it gives us only a very incomplete idea of the attitude of the households in handling their affairs. We noted already that to have a more complete idea, one must also follow the fluctuation of their cash balances, their debts, and their credit situations. Moreover, the households did not begin their month with a clean slate. There were pre-existing debts and credits and during the course of the month they modified the situation.

The total of the transactions that result in either an inflow of money or an inflow in kind amounted for the 46 households to 461 dollars 10 cents, of which the detail is as follows: receipts in *ikelemba* 25·2%; withdrawals from the Savings Bank 0·4%; creation of new charge-account liabilities 74·4%. The outflow represents 515 dollars 64 cents and breaks down into: loans to strangers 11·6%; deposits to the Savings Bank 10·7%; repayment of charge-account liabilities 77·7%.

What can be learnt from the above-mentioned balance sheet of receipts, expenditures and monetary flows combined?

[11] Mersadier, op. cit.; Cochrane and Bell, 1956,

(a) If the balance sheet shows a deficit: the household has used some of its cash in hand; or else contracted a formal liability such as the charge-account or a less formal liability with a traditional flavour such as *ikelemba*. In either case the result is the same: a decrease in the cash in hand or an increase in debts.

(b) If the balance sheet shows a surplus: the household has either increased its cash balance or its credit situation by a formal action—granting charge-account credit—or less formal action such as *ikelemba*. Here, as in the preceding case, the net effect is the same.

Up to this point we have not yet taken into consideration such transactions as gifts and credit grants, which are not properly classifiable under the more formal headings above. The fact of having obtained an advance from a relative whom one is housing or of having granted a loan to a family member in whose village one spends one's yearly leaves or who has safeguarded the traditional interests of the *évolué* in his native village, do not create contractual obligations, similar to the charge-accounts, for example. They are to be considered rather as quasi-debts and quasi-credits. What was the numerical importance of these more hybrid quasi-transactions? As far as gifts from and to relatives are concerned the following data were obtained: the total of 46 households gave to the value of 145 dollars 5 cents during the month and received to the value of 74 dollars 10 cents.

The importance of hospitality to kinsfolk proves to be more tangible still for the new townsmen. Each day we noted the number of people participating in the meals, who did not belong to the nuclear family. This kinship hospitality extends, in our sample, to brothers of the clan or tribe, sometimes friends from back home or from the city who are in difficulty or temporary need. The greatest number, though, are visitors from the bush—adults and children—who remain for some time in town in order to share the spoils of their more fortunate brethren.

We computed one person remaining in the household for the two meals—midday and night—for the whole month as a complete consumer unit. From these daily results we calculated for each household individually the burden attributable to dependants. Certain households supported the burden of a supplementary consumer unit, and sometimes more, even for the entire month. Our results bear out that:

(a) The average of dependent adults which is added daily to the adult family amounts to 0·39 units, which is equivalent to 16·3% of the total adults under consideration in the sample.

(b) The average of minor dependants—that is, those who are added daily to the number of children in the nuclear family—average 2·87 units—amounts to 0·37 units, which means 11·4% of the total minors in the sample.

What are the implications to be drawn from the foregoing results for the behaviour of the emerging well-to-do classes in their new urban environment? Under the following heading we will put forward some tentative interpretations.

B. *The Implications.* In the society in which the *évolués* were reared money and money transactions played only a negligible role. Furthermore, as far as the statistics on the national income of the Congo show, their material situation is one of privilege, not only *vis-à-vis* the subsistence sector but even if we take the majority of the salaried workers into account. That this rapid ascent to upper-class status alters their behaviour in the sheer material domain goes without saying. New wants develop by contact and social and economic reference, and new ways of living are acquired. However, before tackling this problem we will concern ourselves with how receipts and expenditure are canalized between production and consumption units among the family and kinship groups. In other words, it is an inquiry into what may be called the substructural elements of income and expenditure.

First of all we will stress the ambiguous nature of the distribution of the spoils inside the nuclear family. Indeed, this bears the mark of traditional as well as modern valuations and role structures. We observed above that the spouse of the *évolué* contributes little or nothing to the family income. Unlike her rural sisters or her proletarian counterpart of the urban centres she has ceased to be an economic agent in the household. For the rural African housewives indeed, opportunities for work are mainly limited to tilling the soil while the women of the urban centres may make a living out of petty trade. On the one hand there seems to be a tendency among *évolués* to consider that menial tasks, especially the overt ones such as petty trading, are beneath the dignity of their wives in the newly acquired social standing of the household. On the other hand, there is some bitter feeling that since she has ceased to be an economic agent, as she was in the traditional rural milieu, a wife has become a liability instead of an asset.

The role differentiation in the production process, where the husband becomes the sole breadwinner for his family, affects the traditional pattern of the allocation of resources inside the restricted family unit. How does the housewife fare in an economy where men are the sole breadwinners? As far as we could observe in our sample the old principle of the separation of goods still obtains, with the result that the husband considers his salary as his own and not that of his family. This means first of all that the husband in the *évolué* households holds the purse and secondly that he keeps the strings tight for expenditure that concerns his wife and children. The family allowances, however, are considered to be the normal source of income for the wife and children. They are thought of as a kind of compensation for the new leisurely status of the housewife. Of the salary proper, however, the husband surrenders only a minor part for family expenditure. Outside the general food items he himself buys clothes for his wife and children and perhaps kitchen equipment, etc. However, the proportion spent on clothes, etc. is largely in his favour, as we shall see later on.

Another significant aspect borne out by our statistical material is the importance of debtor and credit flows in the balance sheets of the *évolué* households as well as the particular blend of new and traditional formulae in meeting the debtor and credit situations. Various authors have drawn attention to the carelessness with which Africans handle their budgets, and this irrespective of the fact that they get high or low wages. This, however, is not the point we want to make. We are concerned more with the ways and means by which they meet their debtor situation—or credit situation—and to find out how they make their choice between traditional and new ways of settling it. For this we will not take into consideration the withdrawals from and deposits to the Savings Bank, but rather the *ikelemba* and the charge-account flows.

Ikelemba constitutes a traditional type of credit which has undergone some modifications in the urban money economy as far as its form is concerned. In the rural environment it consisted of a pooling of labour or goods to build a hut or clear a plot in the forest for cultivation. The sanctions involved in such a pooling of resources are by the origin of the procedure traditional ones which limit their applicability to partners of the same kin or clan. This limited applicability of the rules of the game is one of the reasons why more formal and contractual forms replace the older ones in meeting debtor or credit situations with strangers. *Ikelemba* is nowadays a procedure by which one receives the salary of two or more partners in order to live for some time ostentatiously or to meet a sudden and great expense. Our figures indicate the relative importance of the new charge-account techniques or loans as against less formal and traditionally established credit pooling under *ikelemba*. The social dimension of these customary credit techniques is the clan or the extended kin. The town with its heterogeneous population places a check on the existing credit institution or forces it to adapt itself in its form as well as in its sanctions to the prevailing modern conditions. Moreover, even among members of the same kin the applicability of a traditional credit formula is limited. This is because traditional sanctions are less feasible in urban surroundings. In town, in fact, contact between kinsfolk becomes less direct and intimate than in village or tribal surroundings.

Nevertheless, as we have pointed out in another context, customary credit institutions show more adaptive capacity to new conditions and sanctions in the case of credit for *productive* uses than in the case of credit for consumption uses.[12] In other words,

[12] Baeck, 1957b.

ikelemba is practised more easily among businessmen, for the buying of a truck for example, because in this case a tangible counterpart can always be seized. Finally we observed that *ikelemba* proves to be less popular among the *évolués* than among the proletarian urban masses, who, by their near subsistence salary level, hold more together and resort more often to traditional means of coping with a situation of deficit.

A third point clearly brought to the fore by our statistical material is the importance of kinship obligations for the recently urbanized *évolués*. One part of these manifestations derives from real kinship obligations and is therefore to be considered not as gratuitous gifts or fortuitous hospitality, but rather as a solid social investment based on a certain reciprocity. The urban dweller pays, as in earlier days, his tribute to his social superior in the customary society, as well as for those to whom he is a traditional custodian. Furthermore, the settler in town is not yet totally convinced about the solvency of our Western society from the social point of view and this explains that his effort to stay in contact with people back home goes beyond paying mere lip-service to some customary institutions.

Especially nowadays when there is a growing concern in the rural milieus about the fast-increasing importance in public affairs and the economic success of the educated salaried *évolués* the latter have to give their rural or proletarian clanspeople gifts and prodigal hospitality lest they be ostracized and disenfranchised of traditional rights back home.

On the other hand, the *évolué* is in a certain sense the prisoner of the value system typical of the *homines novi*. In order to prove to his clan the importance of his success in town—and he wants to prove it—he must demonstrate it by tangible goods and services which he obtains for them. We have here a certain extravagant consumption which makes, in reality, for a vicious circle of inflation in the kinship obligations.

Finally it would be an error to think of the kinship obligations as following essentially a one-way movement: from the town to the rural areas. As our statistical evidence indicates, the movement from country to town was, as far as gifts were concerned, equal to a sum of 74 dollars 10 cents. All these factors combined ensure that the nuclear family is still solidly embedded—socially, psychologically, and economically—in the broader kinship network. Loss of function may lead to disintegration and, in the economic sense, the broader kinship ties may have become a nuisance rather than an asset for the bulk of salaried people in the towns.[13] But if some specific function may be lost by the extended kinship structure, other imperative forces—like social security, prestige, etc.—make for a new integration on a level that incorporates modern as well as traditional values and motivations.

II. THE FLOW OF GOODS AND SERVICES

Up to this point we have shown where the receipts came from and where they go, and this from a bookkeeper's standpoint. The flows of cash and credit ultimately find their expression in goods and services, of which we will analyse the relative importance here below.

We have already remarked that the households disposed of 5,305 dollars and 40 cents on goods and services which have been divided into three functional items; food, drink, miscellaneous. On the average the households spent 2,484 dollars 96 cents or 64·8% for food, 327 dollars or 6·2% for drinks, and 2,493 dollars 42 cents or 46·9% for miscellaneous. The two large items, food and miscellaneous, merit by their importance a more detailed analysis.

A. *Analysis of the Food Items.* The first question we may ask, since we are interested in the change in consumption patterns, is what was the pre-European food consumption in the broad regions of the Congo? It would be difficult to answer this question precisely since few or no nutritional studies are available for this immense region. Nevertheless a general description of alimentary preparations and the basis of nutrition may be given here as a point of departure. In the basic nutrition one may distinguish between the grains, leguminous, and tuber foods. For each of these, subdivisions appear according to whether the initial product

---

[13] See Merton, 1949, pp. 21–81, and Levy, 1952, pp. 55 et seq., for loss of function.

is used in raw form, fresh or dried, or whether it is reduced to flour by pounding or milling, which is more frequently the case. The quality of this flour, whether preferred coarse or finely pulverized, will lead towards carefully defined preparations. In the last analyses enters the composition of the product which accompanies the basic nutrition or is incorporated into it; sauce or milk or any other, but above all the 'sauce' which lends a complementary element to each dish, or at least strives to.

For the majority of the population even now, meat or fish rarely provides the principal dish. These are expensive and the preservation of meat and fish is difficult. The typical Congolese food, then, is a dish with a vegetable base accompanied by a meat or fish sauce. Although this pattern may still be valid for the majority of the population, some signs in certain circles and especially in the urban environment show that the traditional nutrition base is more and more complemented by European food items and preparations. In this particular domain of material living, European food patterns constitute a new test of change.

In Table II we have computed in detail the food pattern of our households in order to indicate the specific food items and their relative importance in the culinary composition of our well-to-do urban Congolese.

It should be noted that the weights mentioned in Table II are gross weights. Account should be taken of the fact that a good number of those items are perishable products—like meat, fish, vegetables—which are sometimes exposed for hours in a tropical market. Thus the above-mentioned quantities include a rather high proportion of wastage which the households could not use.

For the other, non-perishable products—such as rice, roots and tubers, sugar—the indicated quantities do not always equal the quantities consumed during the month. In fact, for certain households we were not able to make an account of their stock of these products at the beginning and the end of the month. However, the possible errors may not be considerable if one takes into consideration the buying methods of the African households. Food is bought every day at one of the numerous local markets by the housewife. She receives in the morning the necessary sum to buy

TABLE II
Breakdown of the Heading—Nutrition

	Item	Total monthly quantity in kg.	Average price per kg. in francs (1 dollar = 50 frs.)	Average monthly quantity per household in kg.	In % of total value
I.	*Roots, tubers, and mealy fruits*				3·36
	Manioc	445,000	6·04	9,670	2·16
	Sweet potatoes	70,000	4·50	1,520	0·25
	Potatoes	99,000	7·62	2,150	0·61
	Yams				0·22
	Dry manioc in stalks				0·12
II.	*Animal products*				49·01
	1. *Meats*				20·97
	Fresh pork and beef	374,000	50·60	8,130	15·22
	Goat meat	9,300	46·23	0,200	0·36
	Antelope meat	2,150	79·07	0,470	0·13
	Poultry				3·31
	Smoked meat	12,350	65·55	0,270	0·65
	Dried meat				0·19
	Preserved meat				0·78
	Sausage, etc.				0·33
	2. *Fish*				22·83
	Fresh fish	248,420	34·36	5,400	6·86
	Dried smoked fish	111,145	76·70	2,410	6·87
	Salted fish	130,955	37·52	2,840	3·95
	Canned sardine, salmon, etc.				1·83
	Dried fish				3·32
	3. *Milk and cheese*				4·95
	Powdered and condensed milk				4·69
	Cheese				0·26
	4. *Eggs*				0·16
	Caterpillars				0·10
III.	*Cereals, cereal flour and derived products*				12·64
	Rice, polished	644,100	8·97	14,000	4·65
	Bread				6·76
	Bread rolls				0·78
	Corn	8,200	16·58	0,170	0·15
	Corn meal	40,950	7·89	0,890	0·25
	Corn silk				0·05
IV.	*Other vegetable flour and derived products*				8·55
	Manioc flour	1,113,400	6·22	24,200	5·57
	Chikwangue				2·29
	Fritters				0·32
	Corn and manioc cakes				0·28
	Manioc dough				0·09

Item	Total monthly quantity in kg.	Average price per kg. in francs (1 dollar = 50 frs.)	Average monthly quantity per household in kg.	In % of total value
V. *Ripe leguminous seeds*				2·18
Dried green beans	230,500	10·81	5,010	2·00
Peas				0·18
VI. *Oil-seeds*				0·52
Palm and coconuts				0·52
VII. *Edible nuts and grains*				0·61
Peanuts	47,900	11·41	1,040	0·45
Shelled peanuts				0·13
Grilled shelled peanuts				0·03
VIII. *Fats and oils*				5·59
Butter	15,400	8·72		1·08
Margarine				0·13
Palm oil				3·72
Peanut oil				0·34
Cotton-seed oil				0·28
Olive oil				0·04
IX. *Vegetables*				4·25
Manioc leaves	493,900	3·04	10,730	1·21
Native vegetables	185,000	8·04	4,020	1·19
Onions	95,160	15·50	2,060	1·19
Fresh tomatoes	39,300	15·90	0,850	0·50
Squash				0·11
Egg-plant				0·03
X. *Fruits*				3·77
Bananas	658,000	4·33	14,300	2·29
Other fruits				2·48
XI. *Miscellaneous*				9·52
Sugar	247,200	12·55	5,370	2·49
Pili-pili	59,590	22·60	1,290	1·08
Tomato paste				1·43
Fortifiers (ovomaltine, etc.)				2·74
Tea				0·75
Delicacies				0·49
Coffee				0·19
Salt	54,240	5·17	1,180	0·22
Sugar cane	19,200	5·36	0,430	0·08
Mushrooms				0·03
Misc. (vinegar, pepper, etc.)				0·02
Total				100·00

the meal items for the day. Even tea and sugar are bought in infinitesimal quantities for daily consumption. At Leopoldville, in the market as in the shops, numerous commodities such as rice, sugar, sweet potatoes, manioc, etc. are sold 'by the pile'. Likewise, for liquids such as palm oil, peanut oil, the measurement is in small cans—tomato juice cans, for example—rather than by calibrated measures. This is one of the reasons why the prices of certain basic articles reveal a considerable dispersion around the mean. The explanation why even well-to-do Africans do not buy in bigger quantities the non-perishable articles such as sugar, manioc, tea, etc. is to be sought in tradition. Furthermore, the fear that a stock for several days in consumption articles will draw too many kinsfolk to the house to profit from the wealth of their fortunate brethren, is very strong.

Whereas the traditional native diet consisted of roots, tubers, mealy fruits, vegetable flour, fats, oils, and vegetables, the present pattern of expenditure for diet in *évolué* households shows a different tendency. What is most striking in reading Table II above is the importance of a few animal products. Meat and fish account respectively for 20·97% and 22·83% of the total food expenditure. If we compute, as in the list below, the relative value on the different meat and fish categories, we observe that fresh meat clearly dominates the other categories, while for fish the items are more evenly distributed.

Meats	*100%*
Fresh butcher's meat	72·6
Goat meat	1·6
Antelope meat	0·7
Poultry	15·8
Smoked meat	3·1
Dried meat	0·9
Preserved meat	3·8
Sausage, etc.	1·5

For fish the figures are:

Fish	*100%*
Fresh fish	30;1
Smoked dried fish	30·0
Salted fish	17·4
Dried fish	14·5
Canned fish	8·0

The preference for fresh meat—mostly pork and beef—over items such as antelope, poultry, dried meat and smoked meat, marks a clear tendency to an urban pattern of consumption, where modern distribution facilities are more available. It is also interesting to note that canned fish proves to be more popular than preserved meat. This preference is largely due to the fact that canned fish, unlike preserved meat, is generally canned in sauces.

As far as the general orientation of nutrition towards an urban occidental pattern is concerned—and so depends more on imported goods—the results are clear. Milk, powdered or condensed, accounts for 4·7% of the total food expenditure. The results for the other articles are, respectively: 7·5% for bread and rolls; 1·2% for butter and margarine; 2·5% for sugar; 2·7% for fortifiers such as ovomaltine; 2·6% for canned meat and fish. Thus the total of these products—for which there was no traditional or rural precedent—equals 23·2% of the total food expenditure. Together with the important expenditure on meat and fish which, in the rural areas, are consumed on a more modest scale, we observe a clear tendency to new items—such as bread, butter, powdered milk, etc., as well as a stressing of older ones (meat and fish) under the new urban conditions.

This does not mean that the Congolese *évolués* have completely lost the food preference of their ancestors. A glance at the figures for the quantitative importance of certain native products—manioc, oils, legumes, etc.—indicates that the traditional basic nutrition is always present.

B. *Analysis of the Miscellaneous Heading*. The notation of the expenditure under the heading *miscellaneous* was made, as we have mentioned, in two ways. First, by daily investigation of furnishings, clothing, etc., as they appeared during the course of the month. Since this is a question mainly of durable goods purchased over a long period, such an investigation would not yield complete results. Moreover the frequency of a purchase is not the only difficulty. There is what one might call the differential degree of depreciation between more or less durable goods, such as between furniture and clothing. The purchase of furniture will leave, in general, evidence for about ten years, whereas clothing is used up more quickly. In fact, the inventory indicates the crystallization of certain expenditure which would escape us even in an inquiry covering a whole year.

To begin with we have centralized, in Table III, the monthly flow of expenditure for goods and services which were classified under the heading *miscellaneous*.

TABLE III

Breakdown of the Heading Miscellaneous [1]

Item	Monthly total for all households, dollars	Percentage
Housekeeping	271·36	10·9
Personnel	62·70	2·5
Furniture	168·74	6·7
Small appliances, utensils	149·16	5·9
Water	34·68	1·4
Charcoal and fuel-wood	46·16	1·8
House construction and improvement	105·90	4·2
Books, schooling, etc.	48·00	1·9
Participation in celebrations	25·32	1·0
Leisure	104·04	4·2
Jewellery	25·28	1·0
Travel	95·64	3·2
Pharmaceutical products	94·97	3·8
Clothing	655·20	26·3
Rent[2]	130·70	5·6
Fonds d'Avance[2]	250·70	10·0
Other	216·58	8·6
Total	2,493·34	100·0

[1] The classification of certain articles in the respective headings sometimes presents difficulties of a practical nature. For this reason there is listed below the contents of the various headings which might leave room for different interpretations.

Housekeeping: kerosene, matches, soap, brushes, baby-bottles, candles, wax, brooms, pans, glasses, buckets, scissors, dishes, etc.
Furniture: tables, chairs, curios, beds, cradles, rugs, pictures, ?-boxes.
Personnel: houseboys and laundry-boys.
House construction and improvement: sheet-metal, barbed wire, boards, cement, bricks, paint, etc.
Small appliances and utensils: kerosene lamps, cameras, sewing machines, irons, etc.
Travel: Out-of-town bus tickets, taxis, train tickets, etc.
Pleasure: lottery tickets, football, cigarettes, records, newspapers, movies, etc.

[2] Rent was paid by 18 households, while 13 households paid into the Fonds d'Avance.

An Expenditure Study of Congolese 'Évolués'

It should be noted that the individual variation among households about these figures is considerable, and that these results only accentuate a certain tendency. Nevertheless, some articles are bought with the same frequency by each family—kerosene, candles, glasses, etc. Other equally homogeneous headings are: charcoal, fire-wood, water, and rent.

With reference to the other expenditure the results of the inventory alone are indicative of their structure over a long period. Table IV represents an *overall* inventory, set up on the basis of the individual inventories. Its tendency is towards an average.

TABLE IV

Overall Inventory [1]

Item	Average per household in dollars	As % of total
Furniture and appliances	537·20	38·9
Bedding	50·40	3·6
Household utensils	52·60	3·8
Furnishings	46·60	3·4
Plates and dishes	41·80	3·0
Linen	8·20	0·6
Travel objects	20·80	1·5
Men's clothing	352·80	25·5
Women's clothing	111·40	8·1
Children's clothing	61·80	4·4
Other	96·40	6·9
Total	1,380·00	100·0

Furniture: armchairs, cupboards, tables, refrigerators, radios, phonographs, sewing machines, desks, bookcases.
Bedding: mattresses, sheets, blankets, pillow-slips, etc.
Linen: tablecloths, towels, etc.
Furnishings: lamps, cushions, lamp-standards, mats, etc.
Travel objects: trunks, suitcases, etc.
Other: alarm clocks, eyeglasses, hatchets, shovels, toilet articles.

As for the technique of calculating the value of the different articles, we evaluated them at their purchase price. When the wife or husband did not know the price, the estimate was made by using the current price for a new article. This should be taken into account in reading this table.

What can these combined results of daily and inventory inquiries tell us about the structure of expenditure towards various goods and services?

The first observation is certainly that the Congolese *évolué* spends a large part of his resources on furniture, furnishings, and clothing. Furniture constitutes 6·7% of the total monthly miscellaneous expenditure and 42·7% of the total inventory. Clothing expenditure is also a fundamental item in the budget of the Congolese *évolués*, all the more so as new purchases are made much more frequently than for furniture. Clothing constitutes 26·3% of the monthly total. Clothing for men, women, and children accounts for 38% of the total inventory. It is striking to note that the husband corners the lion's share of the clothing budget for the family. At the present time the Congolese *évolué* still lives, from the budgetary point of view, by the principle of separation of goods. Moreover, the man occupies, as traditionally, the primordial place here.

Finally, their preference tends above all towards tangible and visible goods that place them before the eyes of their less fortunate brethren.

It is not fitting to close without mentioning that a part of the resources of some of them is devoted to what one might call an investment. In fact, two households in our inquiry are in the process of constructing houses with their own resources. Also, thirteen households have concluded contracts with the Fonds d'Avance for the acquisition of their houses and pay in a monthly average sum of 19 dollars and 28 cents.

III. CONCLUSIONS

Theoretical research has recently laid more stress upon the 'group reference functions' underlying consumption behaviour as against the bias towards utility functions expressed by earlier writings.[14] It clearly moves towards an integration of consumer behaviour in the general framework of social behaviour and towards incorporation of this behaviour in a structured role

[14] Duesenberry, 1949, pp. 25–30.

expectation system in particular.[15] The urban African milieu may be called a social milieu where pluralistic role structures are abruptly juxtaposed. However, the theoretical framework seems actually too embryonic and the empirical data too scarce to draw —even tentatively—lasting conclusions on the consumption functions and consumer behaviour in the case of fast transition and change in the structured role expectations system.

Nevertheless it may be of interest to indicate some of the factors that possibly underlie and influence our particular group in their choice within the specific context of rapid economic and social development. One of the consequences of economic development is that it generally brings together, especially in the case of 'implanted development', two different plateaus of consumption. The attraction exercised by an implanted consumption pattern coming from a more developed economy affects the traditional consumption behaviour in the sense that it provides a reference schema to all income strata and this in relation to the immediate upper income level. This change in consumption patterns must be seen in the background of the overall social and economic change in these milieus. Modernistic elements of social and economic stratification are superimposed on the native pattern of status and performance. Performance in the new urban conditions finds its overt expression in the income group to which one belongs. The mixture of income-group-relativism on western lines and traditional status requirements and standards results in the inflation already mentioned. In an underdeveloped economy such as that of the Belgian Congo, the resulting demonstration effect proves to be even more substantial, owing to the great inequality between income groups, enhanced by such factors as the socially and politically dominant position of the upper income groups, the Europeans. In other words, consumer behaviour in order to be socially intelligible cannot ignore the transitional social system to which it is referred.

The reference group for the *évolué* of the Belgian Congo proves to be his traditional social system from which he recently emerged and to which he continues to pay allegiance, as well as the

---

[15] Parsons and Smelser, op. cit., pp. 230–2.

European one with its corresponding consumption pattern from a more mature economy. One aspect of importance in the decision-making in this frame of reference is the choice between consumption and saving. Another concerns the way purchasing power is oriented towards the various possible goods and services —what may be called the consumption pattern by reference to transitional societal roles.

As far as the first point is concerned, our analysis clearly points out the preference of the *évolués* for goods and services over savings and liquid assets. In fact, a minimum amount of liquid assets is amassed in such modern and formal ways as deposits into the Savings Bank. Furthermore, it proves that savings at random are less attractive than investment-savings for definite projects like routine payments to the Fonds d'Avance, sums employed in the improvement of the house, or in minor construction. It follows then that the propensity to consume, marginal and absolute, is extremely high. But in appreciating this we make an exception of the customary channels of investment and saving which get their full significance in traditional total structure. The numerous expenditures made in favour of dependants, gifts to clan brethren and kin are solid social investments. Part of these expenses, it should be added, have their origin in the fact that the individual wants to display his prosperity conspicuously to his kin in the rural areas.

To prove that he is prosperous he, for preference, models his choice of goods and services on the consumption pattern of the Europeans. That the selection made from among the range of goods and services is not devoid of a certain bias to conspicuousness follows from the clothing example. However, with the scant statistical and socio-economic evidence at our disposal it is difficult to draw more than broad conclusions. Consumption behaviour like all human behaviour will be, to a certain extent— and this applies equally to the Africans in a fast-changing world— irrational, chaotic, and hence imponderable.

REFERENCES

Accra: Government Statistician	1956a.	*Secondi Takoradi Survey of Population and Household Budgets, 1955.* Statistical and Economic Papers, No. 4.
	1956b.	*Kumasi Survey of Population and Household Budgets, 1955.* Statistical and Economic Papers, No. 5.
Baeck, L.	1956.	'Léopoldville, Phénomène Urbain africain'. *Zaïre*, No. 6.
	1957a.	*Étude Socio-économique du Centre Extra-coutumier d'Usumbura.* Bruxelles: Académie royale des sciences coloniales.
	1957b.	'Une Société Rurale en Transition: étude sociologique de la région de Thysville'. *Zaïre*, No. 2, pp. 115–86.
Cochrane, W. W., and Bell, C. S.	1956.	*The Economics of Consumption.* New York: McGraw-Hill.
Duesenberry, J.	1949.	*Income, Saving and the Theory of Consumer Behavior.* Cambridge (Mass.): Harvard University Press.
Greaves, I. C.	1935.	*Modern Production among Backward Peoples.* London: Allen & Unwin.
Grévisse, F.	1951.	*Le Centre Extra-coutumier d'Elisabethville.* Bruxelles: Académie royale des sciences coloniales.
Hoyt, Elizabeth E.	1956.	'The Impact of a Money Economy on Consumption Patterns'. *Annals of the American Academy of Political and Social Science*, Vol. 305, May.
Levy, M. J., Jr.	1952.	*The Structure of Society.* Princeton: University Press.
Mersadier, Y.	1957.	'Budgets Familiaux Africains'. Dakar: Centre IFAN.
Merton, R. K.	1949.	*Social Theory and Social Structure.* Glencoe (Ill.): Free Press.
Minon, P.	1957.	'Quelques Aspects de l'Evolution Récente du Centre Extra-coutumier d'Elisabethville'. *Bulletin du CEPSI*, No. 36.
Parsons, T., and Smelser, Neil	1956.	*Economy and Society.* London: Routledge & Kegan Paul.
Pons, V. G., Clément, P., and Xydias, N.	1956.	'Effets Sociaux de l'Urbanisation à Stanleyville'. In Forde, D. (ed.), *Aspects sociaux de l'industrialisation et urbanisation en Afrique au Sud du Sahara.* Paris: UNESCO.
Southall, A. W.	1957.	*The Theory of Urban Sociology.* East African Institute of Social Research. (Mimeographed.)

VIII. MIEUX-ÊTRE ET PROMOTION SOCIALE CHEZ LES SALARIÉS AFRICAINS DE BRAZZAVILLE

R. DEVAUGES

(Extrait d'une étude effectuée pour le compte du Haut-Commissariat de la République en Afrique Equatoriale Française, Service de la Coordination des Problèmes de l'Equipement de Base.)

APERÇU MÉTHODOLOGIQUE

Les résultats exploités ici sont extraits d'une étude sociologique destinée à préparer le plan d'urbanisme de Poto-Poto, la principale cité africaine de Brazzaville. Un des objectifs proposés à cette enquête était de pouvoir préciser à l'Administration, à propos des faits étudiés:

— quels groupes ils concernaient,
— de combien de personnes ces groupes se composaient,
— où résidaient à Poto-Poto les membres de ces groupes.

Il s'agit certes là d'un schéma idéal qui n'a pu être réalisé qu'avec une précision variable. Mais la nécessité de s'y conformer a commandé l'orientation du travail qui a comporté deux phases principales:

— dans une première partie, on s'est efforcé de découvrir et d'exploiter des documents déjà existants, tenus à jour par l'administration pour des raisons diverses, et permettant de déterminer certaines catégories de la population présentant un intérêt pur l'enquête: commerçants patentés, salariés imposables, possesseurs de véhicules automobiles, de maisons 'en dur', etc. L'exploitation statistique et cartographique de ces documents, qu'il fallait interpréter et souvent compléter, a permis, d'une part de définir des groupes sociaux d'après certains signes extérieurs de niveau de vie, d'autre part, de situer les membres de ces groupes à l'intérieur de Poto-Poto, au moyen d'une

Mieux-Être et Promotion sociale chez les Salariés africains 183

série de cartes de répartition. Ces cartes ne seront pas utilisées dans la présente étude.

— la seconde phase du travail consistait en une enquête par sondage, destinée à inventorier le contenu et à apprécier le degré de signification des catégories ci-dessus définies. Ce sondage portait sur une population stratifiée suivant les critères retenus dans la partie précédente et, en particulier, la catégorie socio-professionnelle. La ventilation des réponses a été faite, non pas *a priori*, mais au moment du dépouillement, compte-tenu de la nature même de ces réponses. On s'est efforcé de corriger par cette méthode très souple ce que la première partie de l'enquête risquait d'avoir de trop artificiel. Moyennant des ajustements de détail, il a alors été possible de faire apparaître, au moyen du sondage, des courants et des tendances significatifs dans les catégories sociales, préalablement définies par leur aspect externe.

Après une brève présentation de Brazzavaille, nous reprendrons dans le présent travail la démarche même de l'enquête. Pour cela, nous commencerons par définir, dans leur volume et dans leurs revenus, les principaux groupes de la population salariée.

Utilisant ensuite les résultats du sondage, nous comparerons ceux de ces groupes entre lesquels sont apparues des oppositions et des relations significatives. Nous examinerons successivement certains aspects des modes d'alimentation, de la façon de se loger et de s'habiller, ainsi que l'acquisition de certains objets de luxe.

Dans une dernière partie, enfin, nous essaierons de dégager une hiérarchie des appréciations relativement aux différents aspects étudiés de la vie domestique, ainsi que les relations que cette hiérarchie laisse apparaître d'un groupe à l'autre.

LE MILIEU ÉTUDIÉ

Brazzaville comptait, au recensement de 1955, une population africaine de 87,279 habitants.[1] Capitale fédérale de l'Afrique

[1] On possède pour Brazzaville deux recensements établis de façon satisfaisante par le Bureau de Statistiques du Haut-Commissariat. Cf. Soret, 1954, *Recensement et Démographie des Principales Agglomérations d'A.E.F.* Brazzaville, 1955—1956.

Equatoriale Française, Brazzaville est essentiellement une ville administrative et commerciale, située à la limite des rapides du Congo, au point de rupture de charge entre le fleuve et le chemin de fer conduisant au port de Pointe-Noire.

Après une période de prospérité quelque peu artificielle au cours des années 47–50, où la ville a connu une expansion démographique rapide, une crise économique grave est apparue, qui, quoique stabilisée, continue encore à faire sentir ses effets. Cette crise s'est traduite pour les Africains par un chômage étendu qui touche aujourd'hui à peu près le tiers de la population active.[2]

Le cité africaine de Poto-Poto, qui est la plus importante de Brazzaville, comportait, au recensement de 1955, une soixantaine de mille habitants, représentant toutes les races du moyen-Congo, ainsi que d'importantes minorités venues d'A.O.F. ou des Territoires voisins. Dans ce 'melting pot', les caractéristiques culturelles des différents groupes—à commencer par les plus voyantes—tendent progressivement à s'effacer, en même temps qu'une 'conscience de Brazzavillois', née de conditions de vie et de préoccupations communes, fait peu à peu son apparition.[3]

LES GROUPES DE NIVEAU DE VIE

Née des activités européennes, la cité de Poto-Poto est essentiellement composée de salariés. A côté, cependant, et pour satisfaire aux besoins de cette population, se sont installés des commerçants et quelques artisans. La proximité du Congo et l'existance de quelques terres de culture aux abords immédiats de la ville, ont permis également l'installation de pêcheurs et d'agriculteurs professionnels.

Le sondage utilisé ici n'ayant porté—pour les nécessités de l'enquête—que sur les salariés, nous ne considérerons donc que cette catégorie, que nous définirons dans son volume et dans ses revenus.

Nous dénombrerons ici les salariés, non pas à partir des professions déclarées, qui comportent aussi des chômeurs, mais à

[2] Cf. Devauges, 1958, Chap. II.
[3] Cf. Devauges, *Les Conditions sociologiques d'une politique d'urbanisme à Brazzaville.* (Rapport à l'Orstom à paraître.)

partir de déclarations des employeurs qui indiquent seulement les emplois réellement existants. Il faut toutefois signaler, dans ces déclarations, une certaine tendance à diminuer à la fois le nombre des emplois et les qualifications. En outre, un certain nombre de petits employeurs—africains particulièrement—n'ont pas répondu au questionnaire. Les chiffres exploités ici constituent donc *un minimum*. Ces réserves faites, les diverses catégories de salariés, d'après la qualification et le mode d'activité, se répartissent de la façon suivante:

	pour l'ensemble de Brazzaville	dont à peu près les 2/3 à Poto-Poto[1] soit
Manœuvres	3,896	2,600
Gens de Maison[2]	3,000	2,000
Ouvriers[3]	5,367	3,580
Cadres	122	80
	15,224	10,150

[1] En supposant la proportion des emplois occupés égale à celle des professions déclarées, pour lesquelles, seules, nous possédons des chiffres détaillés pour l'une et l'autre cité.
[2] Chiffre estimatif.
[3] Y compris les ouvriers et employés du CFCO, chiffre pour 1957 communiqué par la gare de Brazzaville.

La répartition des niveaux de revenu parmi les salariés peut s'établir avec une approximation satisfaisante à partir de documents officiels. Voici, d'après ces documents, la répartition des tranches de salaires annuels:

— salaires jusqu'à 60.000 francs	6,741[1]
— salaires de 60 à 100.000 francs	1,911
— salaires de 100 à 150.000 francs	813
— salaires de 150 à 250.000 francs	600[2]
— salaires de plus de 250.000 francs	75[2]
	10,140

[1] Chiffre obtenu par soustraction des suivants du total des emplois déclarés.
[2] Estimation à partir des chiffres fournis par les Services du Personnel des principales Administrations.

Les 7/10 environ de l'effectif se composaient donc, en 1957, de salaires ne dépassant pas 5.000 francs par mois. Seule, une toute petite minorité dépassait 8.000 francs par mois.

En fait, si le salaire est une indication importante, il ne suffit pas à caractériser un niveau de vie. Il faudrait faire apparaître la position du salarié: chef de famille ou simple commensal n'apportant à la famille qu'une partie de son salaire. Il faudrait également faire intervenir dans un ménage donné, l'apport éventuel des femmes, soit par la culture, soit par le commerce ainsi que le nombre de personnes à charge, chômeurs en particulier. Ceux-ci, en effet, tendent à se fixer chez les parents ayant les moyens les plus étendus et contribuent par là à une égalisation sensible des niveaux de consommation.

Au point de vue des types de professions correspondant aux salaires définis ci-dessus, la première catégorie comporte exclusivement des manœuvres, la seconde, des manœuvres spécialisés et des ouvriers spécialisés. La troisième tranche correspond aux salaires des ouvriers qualifiés. Les ouvriers hautement qualifiés, très rares, les employés et les cadres locaux, composent la quatrième. Enfin, il faut établir une cinquième catégorie avec quelques dizaines de Cadres Supérieurs ayant des traitements se situant autour de 500.000 francs par an.

En fait, cette coincidence entre le salaire et le type d'activité—les manuels se trouvant parmi les salaires inférieurs à 150.000 francs et les employés parmi les salaires plus élevés—ne correspond que très grossièrement à la réalité. Il existe une 'frange' très importante entre 60 et 150.000 francs, où l'on trouve à la fois les manuels les mieux payés et les employés à plus faible salaire. Il reste toutefois que, en moyenne, la répartition des salaires est sensiblement décalée d'un groupe à l'autre. Les deux catégories: revenus inférieurs et revenus supérieurs, conservées dans les tableaux qui vont suivre et qui ont été établies empiriquement, entrent assez bien dans ces cadres rectifiés. La première correspond à un groupe comportant exclusivement des manuels, tous illettrés ou, au mieux, sous-scolarisés. La moyenne des salaires devrait s'y situer entre 60 et 100.000 francs. La seconde, avec quelques capitas ou des manuels ayant achevé leurs études primaires, comporte surtout des employés. Le salaire moyen devrait se situer pour celle-ci au-delà de 150.000 francs. Malgré le chevauchement partiel des deux catégories ainsi définies, l'analyse des sondages dans les parties qui vont suivre va nous montrer que, dans chacune d'elles, comportements et aspirations tendent à se cristalliser autour de modèles relativement homogènes et présentant de l'une à l'autre des écarts intéressants.

NIVEAU DE VIE ET MODE D'ALIMENTATION

Bien que l'alimentation demeure chez les Africains de Brazzaville un des secteurs où la coutume a le mieux conservé ses droits, certaines denrées d'origine européenne font progressivement leur apparition. Comme ce phénomène est lié à la fois à une conception du bien-manger et à l'étendue des moyens économiques, son étude devrait faire apparaître des différences caractéristiques entre les catégories socio-professionnelles. Nous examinerons ici la composition générale des menus, puis la consommation du pain, qui constitue un aliment privilégié et, enfin, les désirs exprimés en matière d'alimentation.

A. *Les aliments de base*

Le critère adapté pour la classification des aliments de base a été le prix de revient. Etant donné d'une part, la présentation différente des produits et les modes archaïques de vente de certains d'entre eux,[4] d'autre part, leur inégale valeur nutritive, il n'était pas possible de comparer simplement les prix d'achat. On a donc classé ces denrées d'après le coût approximatif des plats qu'elles servaient à préparer. Cette notion est peut-être inexacte, objectivement parlant, mais elle correspond à l'idée que se font de leurs dépenses alimentaires les habitants de Poto-Poto. Dans cette perspective, on peut classifier ces aliments de base de la façon suivante:

— Poisson salé, séché ou fumé[5]
— Poisson frais
— Viande de brousse ou de boucherie
— Conserves (sardines, maquereaux, corned-beef)

[4] Le poisson salé est vendu en morceaux de 20, 50 ou 100 Fr., les poissons frais à raison de 4 ou 5 de grosseur déterminée pour 100 Fr., la viande de boucherie au poids, les conserves à la boite. En économie coutumière, il semble que l'unité la plus fréquente soit non pas le poids, mais la somme d'argent: 10 Fr., 20 Fr., 50 Fr., etc. C'est la marque d'une économie pauvre.

[5] Les poissons séchés et fumés de préparation locale coûtent plus cher que le poisson frais. Mais ils servent à la confection de plats bon marché accompagnés de légumes locaux, de la même façon que le poisson salé (qui est d'ailleurs de préparation européenne).

Ce classement selon le prix de revient se trouve aussi coincider avec le passage des denrées coutumières aux produits européens. Le tableau ci-dessous étudie les modes de nutrition d'après la fréquence hebdomadaire de ces différents types d'aliments: on a regroupé dans la catégorie des aliments chers le poisson frais, la viande et les conserves. Les aliments 'bon marché' comportent uniquement les poissons conservés.

TABLEAU I

Type d'alimentation dominant

	Dominance des aliments 'chers'	Egalité approximative	Dominance des aliments 'bon marché'	Réponses inexploitables	Ensemble
Revenus inférieurs (66 rép.)	36	25	36	3	100
(dont Ouvriers) (34 rép.)	(36)	(29)	(29)	6	(100)
Revenus supérieurs (64 rép.)	56	19	22	2	100
(dont Employés) (36 rép.)	(50)	(11)	(33)	2	(100)

Dans le groupe à niveaux de vie inférieurs, les deux types d'alimentation arrivent à égalité. Parmi le groupe à plus hauts revenus ou à niveau d'instruction plus élevé, les aliments 'chers' dominent nettement, traduisant à la fois un budget alimentaire plus élevé et un mode de vie plus européanisé.

B. *La consommation du pain*

Le pain est considéré à Poto-Poto comme un aliment de prestige par opposition au manioc qui constitue la base de l'alimentation coutumière, du moins pour les Moyens-Congolais. Comme le poisson, le pain se vend non pas au poids mais à l'unité monétaire, sous forme de petits pains de 5, 10, 15, ou 20 francs.

Le pain n'accompagne qu'exceptionnellement les repas de midi ou du soir, sauf pour des repas de gala à l'Européenne. Chez les Employés, il est consommé parfois à midi, accompagné ou non d'arachides grillées ou d'une boîte de sardines. Mais, le plus fréquemment, le pain est réservé au petit déjeuner du matin, accompagné de thé ou de café. De petits Cafés sont spécialisés à Poto-Poto dans la distribution de ce seul repas du matin.[6] Prendre le petit déjeuner dans ces Cafés est un luxe réservé aux hommes; la famille n'en bénéficie pas. Dans d'autres cas, surtout chez les plus pauvres, le pain est réservé au petit déjeuner des enfants. Dans le tableau II, la consommation de pain a été etudiée selon sa fréquence relative.

Comme dans le tableau précédent, la consommation de pain augmente de façon sensible avec le niveau de vie. Mais, dans le détail, d'autres éléments de différenciation apparaissent, qui montrent que la consommation de pain est un critère plus sensible que celui des aliments de base. On remarque en particulier le renversement des proportions entre les 'tous les jours' et les 'jamais' lorsqu'on compare les Ouvriers aux Employés. La consommation quotidienne ou presque quotidienne du pain tend à apparaître, dans ce tableau, comme un trait distinctif des Employés. Elle est beaucoup plus rare chez les Ouvriers malgré des conditions de salaire souvent voisines.

TABLEAU II

Consommation de pain

	Tous les jours	Périodiquement dans le mois	Ocasionnellement	Jamais	Ensemble
Revenus inférieurs (66 rép.)	24	27	3	46	100
(dont Ouvriers) (34 rép.)	(23)	(18)	—	(59)	(100)
Revenus supérieurs (64 rép.)	34	34	3	29	100
(dont Employés) (36 rép.)	(44)	(28)	(6)	(22)	(100)

C. *Les désirs en matière d'alimentation*

Après les principaux types d'aliments effectivement consommés, il était intéressant d'interroger les gens sur ce qu'ils auraient aimé ajouter à leur nourriture s'ils avaient eu davantage de moyens

[6] On compte 43 Cafés déclarés à Poto-Poto en 1958.

à y consacrer. Les réponses ont été en général multiples. On les a regroupées en trois catégories qui ont paru correspondre à des types de besoins différents.

La première catégorie comporte exclusivement, à l'exception du poisson salé, des produits d'origine locale existant dans la tradition africaine. Le désir de consommer davantage de ces denrées devrait exprimer une insuffisance réelle de nourriture et, en tous cas, l'absence actuelle de désir d'evolution sur le plan alimentaire.

On a regroupé dans la seconde catégorie tous les aliments d'origine européenne cités avec une fréquence suffisante dans les réponses précédentes pour être considérés comme faisant partie de l'alimentation normale. La viande joue ici un rôle prépondérant. C'est d'ailleurs l'aliment le plus souvent cité avec les conserves et le poisson frais. On peut estimer que les réponses rentrant dans cette catégorie, qui est la plus fréquemment citée, expriment le désir d'une amélioration à la fois qualitative et quantitative de l'alimentation.

Dans la troisième catégorie, enfin, on a réuni tous les produits, également d'origine européenne, qui n'avaient jamais été cités dans les questions relatives à l'alimentation réelle. Il s'agit de produits peu habituels ou chers, paraissant exprimer une volonté d'evolution, de promotion sociale, beaucoup plus que le besoin fondamental de manger davantage. Il convient de constater que cette catégorie est plus souvent citée que la première qui exprimait pourtant, en principe, une sous-nutrition réelle. Dans les deux groupes de niveau de vie définis (tableau III), ces trois catégories se classent dans le même ordre, mais avec des proportions différentes.

Pour les aliments coutumiers, les moins souvent désignés, les chiffres sont trop faibles pour tenir compte de leur écart. Par contre, la comparaison des deux catégories suivantes fait apparaître des différences significatives. Dans le groupe à faibles revenus, les produits rares ou chers sont cités dans une proportion trois fois moindre que les denrées européennes courantes. Dans le second groupe, au contraire, les deux catégories arrivent sensiblement à égalité. En outre, les produits rares ou chers y sont cités dans une proportion double de celle trouvée pour le groupe I. Il apparaît

TABLEAU III
Les desirs matière d'alimentation

	Nourriture coutumière	Denrées Europ. relativement courantes	Produits rares ou chers	Ensemble
Revenus inférieurs (66 rép.)	20	60	20	100
(dont Ouvriers) (34 rép.)	(20)	(60)	(20)	(100)
Revenus supérieurs (64 rép.)	15	44	41	100
(dont Employés) (36 rép.)	(15)	(44)	(42)	(101)

ainsi que dans les deux groupes le désir d'améliorer la quantité est, dans la plupart des cas, associé à celui de modifier la qualité (par augmentation de la consommation d'aliments européens). Mais le désir de consommer des produits rares ou chers, pratiquement indépendant de celui de manger davantage, est beaucoup plus marqué dans le groupe à niveau de vie supérieur. On émet l'hypothèse qu'il traduit avant tout un désir de promotion sociale

LES TYPES D'ÉQUIPEMENT DOMESTIQUE

Plus que l'alimentation peut-être, l'équipement domestique, dans la mesure ou il fait intervenir des installations plus coûteuses, a des chances d'être représentatif des différentes catégories sociales. Nous en étudierons ici deux aspects qui ont paru à la fois significatifs et faciles à hiérarchiser: l'existance et l'organisation dans la maison de pièces 'd'apparat', c'est-à-dire non réservées aux usages domestiques quotidiens, et la possession d'appareils de radio ou de phonographes. Nous y ajouterons la répartition des moyens de transport individuels.

A. *Les pièces 'd'apparat'*

La persistance en ville des structures familiales traditionnelles, qui impose aux citadins d'héberger libéralement aussi bien les aînés que les jeunes frères et les neveux, fait que la maison considérée comme idéale à Poto-Poto comporte 5 ou 6 pièces. En fait, les maisons de cette importance ne sont l'apanage que d'une partie assez restreinte de la population. Cependant, même dans les plus petites, il est fréquent qu'une pièce soit réservée plus ou moins exclusivement à des usages qui ne sont plus précisément domestiques: salle à manger, pièce 'pour recevoir les amis' baptisée pompeusement 'salon', parfois vide, parfois possèdant un mobilier spécialisé pour ces différents usages. Le tableau suivant donne une idée de la fréquence avec laquelle on rencontre ce genre de pièces à usage non domestique dans un échantillon pris au hasard de la population:

	%
— Groupe à revenus inférieurs (66 réponses)	67
— (dont Ouvriers: 34 réponses)	71
— Groupe à revenus supérieurs (64 réponses)	81
— (dont Employés 36 réponses)	83

Si le second groupe présente dans ce domaine une certaine supériorité sur le premier il est frappant que, même parmi les niveaux de vie les plus médiocres, l'existence de pièces d'apparat demeure remarquablement répandu.

Dans de nombreux cas, cette pièce d'apparat est une pièce vide ou presque et où, simplement, on ne mange pas; d'autre fois au contraire elle possède un mobilier spécialisé plus ou moins complet. L'analyse des réponses fait apparaître des étapes que l'on peut considérer comme constituant une hiérarchie dans cette installation:

— Pièce vide ou pas de mobilier spécial
— Chaises et table, ou fauteuils
— Chaises et table, et fauteuils, ou l'un des deux avec un buffet
— Mobilier complet, éléments de décoration (fleurs, etc. . . .)

Ces types d'installation intérieure se répartissent suivant les groupes de façon significative (tableau IV). On rencontre une absence complète d'ameublement spécial dans le quart environ du premier groupe, contre 10% seulement du second.

L'ameublement minimum (chaises et table ou fauteuils) apparaît comme la catégorie dominante dans les deux groupes. Cette étape paraît constituer un seuil inférieur de l'équipement, en

TABLEAU IV
Le mode d'installation des pièces 'd'apparat'

	Pas d'installation spéciale	Chaises et table ou fauteuils	Les deux ou l'une et buffet en plus	Mobilier complet avec décoration	Ensemble
Revenus inférieurs (66 rép.)	24	34	30	12	100
(dont Ouvriers) (34 rép.)	(29)	(29)	(29)	(13)	(100)
Revenus supérieurs (64 rép.)	12	41	19	28	100
(dont Employés) (36 rép.)	(11)	(39)	(22)	(28)	(100)

particulier dans le second groupe. L'installation plus complète, avec souvent un buffet en plus du mobilier déjà cité (le buffet est une pièce relativement importante coûtant de 3 à 5,000 frs. chez un menuisier africain) représente le seuil supérieur de l'équipement dans le groupe I: il n'y est qu'exceptionnellement dépassé. Pour le groupe II au contraire, c'est au niveau de la catégorie supérieure (mobilier complet, avec, souvent, des éléments de décorations), rencontrée dans plus du quart de l'échantillon, qu'il faut situer le seuil supérieur d'équipement. Une inégale répartition des types d'équipement avec un décalage vers les types 'supérieurs' des seuils minima et maxima parait ainsi distinguer les deux groupes.

B. *Phonographes et appareils de radio*

Ils constituent l'équipement de luxe par excellence dont la possession est la marque à Poto-Poto d'une aisance certaine. On a ventilé séparément l'appareil hors d'usage, que l'on n'a pas les moyens de faire réparer, le phonographe qui était un instrument très apprécié naguère chez les citadins mais qui est en train de se démoder et enfin le poste de TSF, qui est le plus coûteux à acquérir et nécessite en outre la possession d'une installation électrique ou l'achat périodique de piles d'un prix relativement élevé.

De tous les dépouillements effectués jusqu'à maintenant, c'est ici que les différences entre les deux groupes de niveau de vie sont les plus nettes (tableau V). Les 3/4 du groupe à revenus inférieurs ne possèdent ni radio ni phono alors que cette proportion tombe aux 2/5 pour le groupe II et au tiers seulement chez les Employés. La moitié de ce dernier groupe déclare posséder un appareil de radio contre 1/5 à peine des Ouvriers. Ce tableau fait ressortir également la suprématie du poste de radio sur le phonographe, ce qui constitue un phénomène relativement récent dû surtout au développement du réseau électrique et au perfectionnement des appareils à piles.

TABLEAU V

Phonographes et appareils de radio

	Rien	Appareil hors d'usage	Phono	Radio	Ensemble
Revenus inférieurs (66 rép.)	76	3	6	15	100
(dont Ouvriers) (34 rép.)	(76)	—	(6)	(18)	(100)
Revenus supérieurs (64 rép.)	41	6	6	47	100
(dont Employés) (36 rép.)	(33)	(6)	(11)	(50)	(100)

TABLEAU VI

Moyens individuels de transport

	Rien	Bicyclette	Bicyclette à moteur	Ensemble
Revenus inférieurs (66 rép.)	36	61	3	100
(dont Ouvriers) (34 rép.)	(29)	(65)	(6)	(100)
Revenus supérieurs (64 rép.)	19	53	28	100
(dont Employés) (36 rép.)	(17)	(55)	(28)	(100)

C. Les moyens de transport individuels

Bien qu'ils n'appartiennent pas à proprement parler à l'équipement domestique, nous étudierons ici la repartition des moyens de transport individuels qui, plus encore que les appareils de radio, représentent une dépense importante et supposent sur le plan professionnel un niveau déjà élevé et une stabilité suffisante.[7] La, bicyclette mise à part, qui demeure avant tout un engin utilitaire, ces équipements représentent, autant et peut-être plus que des commodités, des éléments de prestige social particulièrement appréciés.

L'échantillon étudié ici ne possède que des bicyclettes ordinaires et des bicyclettes à moteur. Cependant, malgré la modestie de ces équipements, des différences sensibles apparaissent d'un groupe à l'autre. Précisons que la réponse de l'interviewé a été faite non pas pour lui seul mais pour la famille au sens étroit. Les très rares cas où celle-ci possédait deux moyens de transport n'ont été comptés que pour un (tableau VI), le plus important.

Les 3/5 du groupe à revenus inférieurs possèdent des bicyclettes, mais les bicyclettes à moteur y sont à peu près inexistantes. Celles que l'on y trouve appartiennent uniquement à des Ouvriers, qui révèlent ainsi une position légèrement supérieure à l'ensemble de leur groupe. Dans le groupe à revenus supérieurs par contre, si la proportion de bicyclettes diminue par rapport au groupe précédent, plus du 1/4 de l'échantillon possède des bicyclettes à moteur. En outre le nombre de ceux ne possèdant aucun moyen individuel de transport a diminué de plus de moitié comparativement au premier groupe. Il y a là une différence significative à rapprocher de celles rencontrées à propos du mobilier 'd'apparat' et des postes de radio.

LES VARIATIONS DANS L'HABILLEMENT

L'habillement est un signe extérieur auquel les habitants de Poto-Poto sont en général extrêmement sensibles. Les coutumes

---

[7] La plupart des bicyclettes et des scooters sont acquis aujourd'hui par le moyen d'un système de crédit. Celui-ci n'est consenti, la plupart du temps, qu'aux fonctionnaires ou aux salariés présentant des garanties suffisantes.

traditionnelles ont dans ce domaine entièrement disparu à l'exception de celle de marcher nus-pieds. La tenue habituelle des hommes va du short avec une chemisette jusqu'au complet veston avec cravate, rare il est vrai, et réservé en principe aux tenues de sortie ou de cérémonie.

Nous n'étudierons ici que l'habillement masculin des jours de semaine qui est apparu le plus significatif des différences socio-économiques. Afin d'alléger le tableau, on n'y a introduit que ce qui constituait une amélioration par rapport à la tenue minimum: short, chemise ou chemisette et pieds-nus. On a distingué le port des sandales de celui des chaussures, ces dernières représentant une dépense sensiblement plus élevée. On a considéré le pantalon comme plus 'habillé' que le short, ce qui n'est d'ailleurs pas forcément exact, les travailleurs manuels, maçons, etc., portant fréquemment des pantalons, même s'ils sont en guenilles. On a regroupé enfin, parmi les marques d'un soin vestimentaire et d'une aisance plus grande, le port du blouson ou du veston et celui de la cravate. Enfin, on a ventilé à part les possesseurs d'un bracelet-montre: il s'agit là un engin de luxe à rapprocher (bien qu'à un degré moindre en raison de son prix plus modéré) de l'appareil de radio et de la bicyclette à moteur parmi les marques extérieures d'aisance matérielle (tableau VII).

Les 2/5 seulement des revenus inférieurs portent des sandales

TABLEAU VII

La tenue vestimentaire des hommes en semaine

	Sandales	Chaussures	Pantalon	Veston Blouson Cravate	Montre bracelets
Revenus inférieurs (66 rép.)	42	21	39	3	—
(dont Ouvriers) (34 rép.)	(41)	(24)	(41)	—	—
Revenus supérieurs (64 rép.)	22	66	81	16	25
(dont Employés) (36 rép.)	(17)	(72)	(94)	(17)	(33)

Pour 100 réponses dans chaque catégorie

et 1/5 des chaussures, ce qui signifie que les 2/5 restants marchent normalement nus-pieds. Les proportions se renversent avec le groupe II. Les 2/3 déclarent porter normalement des chaussures et 1/5 seulement des sandales. En fait une certaine ambiguité de la question apparaît ici puisqu'il semble ressortir de ces réponses qu'une petite partie du groupe II marche nus-pieds. Cela semble indiquer en fait que certains interviewés ont décrit leur tenue vestimentaire au travail, d'autres à la maison. Cette différence ne joue d'ailleurs un rôle que dans le groupe II; il n'y a pratiquement pas à en tenir compte dans le groupe I. En dépit de cette imprécision, la transformation de l'habillement d'un groupe à l'autre apparaît avec netteté. Plus qu'au niveau réel de revenus, celle-ci est sans doute partiellement imputable à des obligations (on ne peut pas aller au Bureau nus-pieds). Mais elle indique aussi une conception différente du vêtement 'décent' lorsqu'elle fait apparaître, par exemple, une prédominance du port des chaussures sur celui des sandales. Il en est de même du choix du pantalon à la place du short: le pantalon est cité dans une proportion plus de deux fois supérieure dans le groupe II comparé au groupe I. Il faut noter que tous les 'Cadres' interviewés ont répondu porter à la fois pantalon et chaussures.

On a rapproché, comme constituant des suppléments vestimentaires rares, le port du blouson ou du veston et celui de la cravate. Deux interviewés seulement dans le groupe I ont déclaré mettre normalement un blouson en plus de leur chemise. Dans le groupe II ces suppléments apparaissent beaucoup plus fréquemment bien qu'ils demeurent toujours relativement rares. On n'a rencontré en particulier que quatre interviewés (deux Employés et deux Cadres) ayant déclaré porter la cravate de façon quotidienne. Notons que cet usage n'apparaît chez les Européens qu'au niveau des cadres supérieurs.

Enfin la montre-bracelet, objet de luxe et de prestige, ne fait son apparition que dans le groupe II: elle apparaît dans 1/4 de l'échantillon. C'est dans le sous-groupe des Employés qu'on la rencontre avec la plus grande fréquence: 1/3 des cas. Elle apparaît ainsi comme un trait distinctif de cette categorie.

LA HIÉRARCHIE DES DÉSIRS EN MATIÈRE D'ÉQUIPEMENT

Une question ouverte terminait la série consacrée à la consommation et à l'équipement. Elle était formulée selon un mode classique dans les enquêtes d'opinion: 'Qu'achèteriez-vous en premier lieu si vous aviez davantage d'argent?' Comme on avait préalablement passé en revue les différentes catégories de besoins, on s'est volontairement abstenu de préciser davantage, dans l'espoir de faire apparaître une hiérarchie spontanée des besoins.

On a rangé dans les 'objets de luxe', des objets complexes et coûteux pour lesquels on a estimé que l'élément de prestige social l'emportait nettement sur l'aspect utilitaire: bracelets-montres, radios, frigidaires, bicyclettes, vélomoteurs, etc. Quand plusieurs objets d'une catégorie ont été désignés plusieurs fois au cours d'une énumération (bracelet-montre et vélomoteur dans les objets de luxe par exemple), on n'a compté la catégorie qu'une seule fois. De nombreux cas d'énumération de meubles ou de vêtements formant en réalité un ensemble ont conduit à adopter ce protocole simplifié qui évitait au maximum les distinctions arbitraires. Du fait qu'on a tenu compte des réponses multiples sans avoir fixé à l'avance de liste pouvant servir de référence, les chiffres obtenus sont affectés d'une grande variabilité (Tableau VIII).

Pour les rendre plus facilement comparables on a figuré entre tirets dans chaque case leur classement pour chaque groupe de revenus, les proportions les plus fortes étant citées les premières. Dans les deux groupes, les vêtements arrivent largement en tête et sont cités par plus de la moitié des interviewés. Toutefois une différence très significative apparaît ici entre Ouvriers et Employés : la proportion presque double de réponses trouvées chez les seconds montre que l'élément de prestige attaché au vêtement est beaucoup plus important pour eux, même s'il domine également chez les Ouvriers.

On trouve une opposition du même genre entre les groupes I et II à propos des objets de luxe. Ceux-ci arrivent au deuxième rang des désignations dans le groupe II (où ils sont cités presque dans la moitié des cas) alors qu'ils sont mentionnés par moins d'un tiers du groupe I où ils arrivent au troisième rang.

Avec le Mobilier, on entre davantage dans le domaine utilitaire.

TABLEAU VIII
Les désirs en matière d'équipement

	Alimentation	Vêtements	Mobilier	Objets de luxe	Maison, Commerce	Economies
Revenus inférieurs	18	55	39	30	21	6
(66 rép.)	–5–	–1–	–2–	–3–	–4–	–6–
(dont Ouvriers	(12)	(35)	(24)	(29)	(35)	(12)
(34 rép.)	–5–	–1–	–4–	–3–	–1–	–5–
Revenus supérieurs	6	59	37	47	19	22
(64 rép.)	–6–	–1–	–3–	–2–	–5–	–4–
(dont Employés)	(11)	(61)	(39)	(39)	(6)	(22)
(36 rép.)	–5–	–1–	–2–	–2–	–6–	–4–

Bien qu'elles aient un rang d'écart d'un groupe a l'autre, les désignations relatives à ce type d'équipement restent dans des proportions voisines et dépassent le tiers des échantillons. Le désir d'acquérir une clôture, de construire une maison ou d'ouvrir un commerce, qui représente à la fois une dépense assez importante et un effort de fixation et d'organisation domestique, offre un classement très inégal. S'il obtient un rang médiocre dans les groupes I et II, il arrive en tête à égalité avec les préoccupations vestimentaires, chez les Ouvriers. Chez les Employés, par contre, ces préoccupations-par un phénomène d'opposition remarquable —n'arrivent qu'au dernier rang.

La perspective de faire des économies n'obtient qu'un rang très reculé pour toutes les catégories sans distinction. Observons toutefois qu'elle est un peu plus fréquente dans le groupe à revenus supérieurs (environ 1/5ème de l'échantillon).

Enfin, il parait extrêmement significatif que le désir de consacrer un supplément d'argent à l'alimentation arrive pour toutes les catégories dans les derniers rangs, avec des proportions de choix qui n'atteignent jamais le 1/5ème des échantillons. Il y a là un phénomène délicat à interpréter, surtout que, dans une question non exploitée ici, on a décelé l'expression absolument généralisée d'un désir de manger davantage. On émet l'hypothèse que, sauf les cas extrêmes,[8] le régime alimentaire paraît insuffisant

---

[8] Le fait de rester un jour ou deux sans manger au cours de la semaine parait fréquent dans certaines couches de la population et, en particulier, chez les chômeurs. Cf. Devauges 1958.

mais normal et qu'on préfère réserver une rentrée supplémentaire d'argent à des achats d'équipement plutôt que de l'investir sans résultats apparents dans des dépenses alimentaires quotidiennes.

Les résultats obtenus ici permettent au total de classer par ordre d'importance relative les aspects de la vie domestique analysés dans les questions précédentes. Ils donnent une idée de la façon dont se modifierait la consommation au sens le plus général du mot dans la perspective d'un relèvement du niveau de vie. Pour toutes les catégories sociales, les achats vestimentaires arriveraient sans doute en premier lieu suivis de ceux d'objets de luxe divers (montres, cyclomoteurs, appareils de radio etc.) et de mobilier. Des dépenses d'un caractère plus utilitaire (terrain, maison installation d'un commerce) apparaîtraient sans doute chez les Ouvriers. Mais—toujours d'après les résultats obtenus ici—il ne semble pas que la consommation de produits alimentaires (et en particulier des denrées européennes que nous avons vu faire leur apparition dans les menus) s'accroîtrait, du moins au début, de façon importante.

CONCLUSION

Cette brève analyse des principaux aspects de la vie quotidienne montre que des processus de différenciation d'un type nouveau ont fait leur apparition au sein des populations africaines de Brazzaville. Un désir général de transformation apparaît, dont on peut mesurer le degré de pénétration, variable selon les groupes humains ou selon les aspects de la vie domestique considérés.

La comparaison, dans chaque domaine étudié, des situations de fait et des aspirations, montre une continuité des unes aux autres, non seulement à l'intérieur d'un même groupe de niveau de vie, mais encore d'un groupe à l'autre. Elle fait ressortir en particulier que le passage des types coutumiers aux types plus européanisés est considéré comme une promotion sociale progressivement réalisée en fonction des moyens économiques. Les inégalités d'avancement des groupes, classés selon le niveau de revenus et les types de profession, font apparaître un 'retard' dans cette évolution des moins favorisés. Il apparaît hors de doute sur ce point que le chômage, en limitant les moyens matériels des populations, a contribué à retarder le processus 'd'européanisation' qui était la conséquence de cette évolution.

Le vêtement apparaît comme le domaine où la transformation est le plus achevée. C'est également celui où le désir d'améliorer son équipement est le plus fréquemment exprimé. Après l'habillement, c'est l'équipement domestique au sens large qui arrive en tête des préoccupations: les désirs exprimés concernent des acquisitions à caractère plus utilitaire (mais non pas moins coûteux) chez les groupes à plus faibles revenus et davantage des objets luxueux ou témoignant d'un désir de prestige social dans les groupes à revenus plus élevés. Une différenciation profonde à propos de la conception même de l'évolution, commence à se dessiner dans ces domaines entre Ouvriers et Employés. L'alimentation par contre, même si des denrées d'origine européenne y ont fait leur apparition, apparaît comme le secteur où la tradition s'est le mieux maintenue et où les désirs de changement sont les plus faibles.

REFERENCES

Devauges, R. 1958. *Le Chômage à Brazzaville en 1957.* Étude sociologique. Rapport à l'Orstom.
Les Conditions sociologiques d'une politique d'urbanisme à Brazzaville. Rapport à l'Orstom à paraître.
Recensement et Démographie des Principales Agglomérations d'A.E.F. Brazzaville, 1955–1956.
Soret, M. 1954. *Démographie et Problèmes Urbains en A.E.F.* Mémoires de l'Institut d'Études centrafricaines, Brazzaville.

SUMMARY

Improvement of living standards and social status among African wage-earners in Brazzaville

This paper describes part of a sociological study carried out in Brazzaville at the instance of the Government of French Equatorial Africa as a preliminary stage in the planned urban development of Poto-Poto, the chief African quarter of the city. One of the purposes of the study was to provide the Administration with accurate information concerning the living standards, social status, and ambitions for betterment of certain groups among African wage-earners, together with particulars of the sizes of these groups and their location in the area studied. These purposes determined to some extent the scope and direction of the investigation. A preliminary study of government records and other documents made it possible to classify the population into occupational categories and social groups in accordance with certain external criteria relating to income levels and standards of living. A subsequent survey, carried out by sampling, provided supplementary information concerning the content and the significance of the categories thus established. The analysis of the findings of the survey was made as the answers received were classified, and not according to a prearranged system; thus it was possible to correct the somewhat artificial classification arrived at by the preliminary study.

Brazzaville, the Federal capital of French Equatorial Africa, after a period of considerable prosperity and rapid expansion, suffered a severe economic crisis the effects of which are still patent. In particular there is widespread unemployment affecting perhaps one-third of the African population. Poto-Poto, the largest African quarter in the city, has a population of roughly 60,000, including members of all the Middle Congo tribes as well as some from French West Africa. The diverse cultural characteristics of these peoples are gradually being submerged in a common local consciousness resulting from living conditions and common interests. Apart from a small number of fishermen and cultivators, the majority of the inhabitants of Poto-Poto are wage-earners; the survey was concerned only with these, and among them, only with those actually in employment. These were classified in five categories according to the scale of earnings, from which it appeared that only about three-tenths of the labour force earned more than 5,000 francs per month; moreover, in relation to standards of living, the domestic circumstances of the wage-earner—e.g. number of dependants, wife's contribution to expenses, etc.—had to be taken into account. Classification by earnings corresponded roughly to classification by qualifications—

Mieux-Être et Promotion sociale chez les Salariés africains 203

i.e. general labourers, specialized artisans and craftsmen, qualified technicians, clerical and managerial staff, and a very small group of higher grade managerial staff whose annual earnings might amount to 500,000 francs. This correspondence was not of course exact; among manual workers, for example, some were earning more than the lower grades of clerks. In practice it was found that a classification into two groups characterized by lower and higher levels of earned income provided a useful and reliable basis for the investigation. The first group consisted only of manual workers, mainly illiterate or of very low educational standard, earning an average monthly wage of from 60,000 to 100,000 francs. The second was composed mainly of clerical workers whose average monthly wage exceeded 150,000 francs. The sample survey showed that in each of these groups, behaviour and ambitions tended to conform to a specific pattern.

Standards of living in each of these groups were estimated in relation to the following criteria:

- *a.* Nature of feeding habits: use of traditional or European, cheap or more expensive, foodstuffs; consumption of bread; preferences as regards improvements in diet.
- *b.* Types of household equipment, including furniture, decoration, luxury articles such as radios, gramophones, etc.
- *c.* Possession of means of transport such as bicycles, motorbicycles.
- *d.* Difference in dress: wearing of sandals or shoes; shorts or trousers; coats, waistcoats, ties; wrist-watches.
- *e.* Desires and ambitions as regards improved household equipment, luxuries, ownership of businesses, savings.

The information received on these points from roughly 66 individuals in each group was set out in the form of tables, and an analysis of these results reveals the emergence, within the African population of Brazzaville, of a new type of social differentiation; a general desire for change is manifest, though its intensity varies in different groups. The gradual adoption of European habits and standards, as this becomes economically possible, is regarded as social advancement. The process of Europeanization is noticeably less advanced among the lower income groups and is probably attributable to the effects of unemployment. The transformation is most clearly seen in the matter of clothing—traditional costume has entirely disappeared among wage-earners—and ambitions and preferences are most frequently expressed in terms of dress. Next in order comes household equipment, and here there is noticeable difference in outlook between manual and clerical workers. In the matter of food, on the other hand, even where European foodstuffs are used, traditional habits remain strongly rooted and the desire for change is small.

IX. TWO SMALL GROUPS IN AVENUE 21: SOME ASPECTS OF THE SYSTEM OF SOCIAL RELATIONS IN A REMOTE CORNER OF STANLEYVILLE, BELGIAN CONGO

V. G. PONS

Avenue 21 is the name I have given to a group of 23 dwelling compounds which face each other across one end of a single street in the *centre extra-coutumier* of Stanleyville. In 1952–3 I conducted a small-scale 'family-and-community' study amongst the inhabitants of these compounds.[1] Early in the course of my field inquiries I was struck by what seemed to me to be the overriding influence of tribal and kinship affiliations on the pattern of neighbourhood relations. As my field work progressed, however, it became apparent that the inhabitants were also continually distinguishing and grouping themselves according to norms and values with a clear 'urban' reference, and I realized that if I was to gain any understanding of neighbourhood relations in the avenue it would be necessary for me to start by observing relations between particular people in particular situations.

In the present paper I report on two small leisure-time groups which I was able to observe for several months. I shall first describe a few aspects of the overall social situation in the avenue, and then focus on the two groups which I shall refer to as the 'club' and Christine's 'guests'.

AVENUE 21 AND ITS PEOPLE

To describe the nature of Avenue 21, we must briefly recall two main features of Stanleyville at the time of this study. First, the

[1] At the time of this study I was a member of a team of three social scientists appointed by the International African Institute (under the terms of a contract with UNESCO) to conduct a wide programme of investigations in Stanleyville. My colleagues were Mademoiselle N. Xydias and Monsieur Pierre Clément. The study of Avenue 21 was my individual responsibility but I frequently discussed observations made there with my two colleagues and I gratefully acknowledge the stimulation received from them.

town was in a state of rapid expansion and far-reaching change. In pre-war days it had been a quiet and slow-moving centre of administration, transport, and commerce, but by 1952–3 it had developed into a minor boom-town with an appreciable measure of industrialization taking place against a general background of vigorous economic growth in the colony as a whole.[2]

Secondly, the *centre extra-coutumier* of the town already had a comparatively well-differentiated ecological structure and each of the three large African 'townships' or 'suburbs' lying around the 'European town' contained distinctly different kinds of neighbourhoods. In general, the more 'civilized' neighbourhoods lay close to the European town and there was a steady transition to less 'civilized' neighbourhoods as one moved out towards the peripheral areas.[3]

Avenue 21 lay in a far corner of the *centre extra-coutumier* in one of its poorest and least 'civilized' neighbourhoods. The area had first been settled in 1930 and had thus been in existence for a little over 20 years. In general appearance, however, it remained more 'village-like' than 'town-like'; nearly all the dwellings were native-type huts built by the inhabitants themselves, and in most cases the dwelling compounds were still partly covered with trees and bush.

A census of Avenue 21 late in 1952 revealed a *de facto* population of 128 men, women, and children, but there was a high rate of movement in and out of the avenue and the population fluctuated from week to week and even from day to day. In an effort to gain a working impression of this movement, I tried, with the assistance of several informants, to keep a daily register of the population from 1 August 1952 to 31 March 1953. Excluding 'visitors', whom I defined as persons who came to the avenue without their goods and chattels, I recorded 164 'permanent inhabitants' of whom only 82 (exactly 50%) were living there throughout the eight-month period.

I also tried to record and classify the places of origin and the destinations of persons coming to and departing from the avenue. This task proved more difficult than the first, but my attempts to

[2] Pons, 1956a.   [3] Pons, 1956b.

carry it out did lead me to the conclusion that the bulk of the movement was between the avenue and other parts of the town and not between town and country.

The *de facto* population of 128 persons recorded during the course of my census made up 43 separate households. These were distributed over the 23 dwelling compounds as follows: nine compounds had a single household each, nine had two households each, four had three, and one had four.

To distinguish between the households of title-holders ('owners') of compounds and those accommodated on a compound 'owned' by someone else, I use the terms 'principal household' and 'subsidiary household'. From the above figures it follows that there were 23 principal households and 20 subsidiary households. Of the heads of the 20 subsidiary households, only two were occupying their own houses which one and the same title-holder had given them permission to build on his compound. The remaining 18 subsidiary households were accommodated in houses or rooms owned by title-holders, 12 as rent-paying tenants and six free of charge. Of the six free tenants, four were related by kinship to the title-holders of their respective compounds; the remaining two and all 12 rent-paying tenants were not related to their landlords, though in two cases landlord and tenant were members of the same tribe.

The substantial proportion of subsidiary households encountered in the avenue points to an important change in the neighbourhood. Up to a few years earlier, the sharing of compounds by two or more households, especially on a rent-paying basis, had been largely confined to areas of the *centre extra-coutumier* near the 'European town'. Very recently, however, the continued rapid growth of the town's population had led to the practices of letting and renting accommodation to spread progressively from the central to the peripheral areas.

In the absence of data for earlier years it is impossible to arrive at a precise assessment of recent changes in the composition of the population, but an indication of the main trends can be inferred from knowledge of the characteristics of heads of principal and subsidiary households. The heads of principal households were mostly middle-aged and elderly people who had lived in Stanleyville for many years and most of them were engaged in occupations with relatively high prestige such as carpenter, shopkeeper, tailor, and mason. In sharp contrast, the heads of subsidiary households were mainly young adults who were comparative newcomers to the town and were in most cases ordinary manual labourers.

The two categories of householders also differed appreciably in tribal composition, the heads of principal households making up an appreciably more homogeneous group than the heads of subsidiary households.

These differences between heads of principal and subsidiary households suggest that the current trend of change was in the direction of a population more varied and more heterogeneous than it had formerly been.

KNOWING ONE'S NEIGHBOURS

There were two factors in the avenue situation which might have led us to expect comparatively little anonymity despite the high rate of mobility and the increasingly heterogeneous character of the population. First, title-holders and members of their families were on the whole persons who had lived not only in the town but in Avenue 21 itself for many years. The actual figures for the 23 title-holders were as follows: five had lived in the avenue continuously since it was first settled in 1930, six had been there between 11 and 20 years, seven for 6 to 10 years and only five for less than 6 years.

Secondly, conditions in the avenue were such that it is difficult to imagine how anyone could have lived there, even if only for a few weeks, without learning to identify many of his neighbours. In a general description of daily life in Stanleyville, Clément has drawn attention to this. He explains that there was, 'at the neighbourhood level, an exchange of paid services involving almost every one in a network of relationships', while the lay-out of compounds and houses was such 'that people see what their neighbours are doing, . . . talk to each other from compound to compound, ... and are of necessity in unbroken contact'. Under such conditions, Clément points out, every newcomer is inevitably 'spotted, observed, catalogued, and located with reference to his tribe, the village he came from, the relatives who are putting him up, his trade, etc.'[4]

Being able to 'place' a neighbour, however, does not necessarily involve knowing him as an individual personality. In an attempt to gauge the extent to which 'old' residents knew their neighbours in this latter sense, I ask four of them, all men, to describe every other man living in the avenue.

My working procedure was as follows. I drew up a list of all men who were either living in the avenue or who had left it within the past few weeks. There were 50 names in all. I then interviewed the four men individually asking them to tell me 'what sort of person' each of the 50 subjects was.

Below are some specimen answers, freely translated from French and Kingwana:

> (1) He is a good man. He gives sound advice to anyone in trouble. The people listen to him, and if there is a quarrel, people call him ... He treats all young people like his children.
> (2) He is just a drunkard ... he does not treat his 'brothers' well ... he will eat with you, yet when he has food he eats by himself.
> (3) He is from 'my country', but I do not know him. All I see is that he still follows 'uncivilized' ways.
> (4) That is Jean's 'brother' ... I do not know his 'character' or his 'ways'.

Answers (1) and (2) are given as examples of descriptions based on personal knowledge of an individual, whereas (3) and (4) represent the kind of answers which revealed little or no personal knowledge of the subjects being described.

Omitting all descriptions of the latter kind, I found that the four interviewees between them gave me 126 descriptions out of a possible total of 200. Their individual scores—out of 50—were 36, 33, 30, and 27, and the distribution of subjects according to the number of interviewees by whom they were known as individual personalities was as follows: 16 were 'known' by all four interviewees, 12 by three, 9 by two, 8 by one, and only 5 by none.

[4] Clément, 1956, p. 375.

Although such figures necessarily constitute an arbitrary and inadequate measure, they do, I believe, help to describe an important aspect of the social situation in Avenue 21. Complete anonymity was almost impossible, but there was a very wide range in the extent to which people really knew each other.

THE 'CLUB'

The 'club' was in essence a small group of friends. Its members were six adult men who lived close to each other and who had constituted themselves into a kind of mock-formal association. They referred to their group as *l'association*, and they gave each other titles such as *président, gouverneur, commissaire de district, comptable*, and *avocat*. The activities of the 'club' were mainly celebrations as, for example, on Christmas Day. At such meetings, one man would act as 'chairman' another as 'secretary', and so on. The roles assumed by various members at any one meeting did not necessarily correspond to the formal titles they held, nor would one man necessarily keep the same role throughout a meeting.

During meetings, which consisted mainly of drinking and joking, the group would fine members for 'offences' such as arriving late or for 'allowing' a wife to call her husband away. After a fine had been imposed, the 'offender' would invariably 'lodge an appeal'. Similarly, there was much mock formality in the calling of meetings, and on one occasion during the period of my field-work a 'secretary' sent a written notice announcing a forthcoming meeting to each member despite the fact that all were neighbours who inevitably saw each other daily.

Although the 'club' had only six members, attendances at two prearranged meetings which I attended were 9 and 13. On the first of these occasions, the number was made up by three kinsmen of the man in whose house the meeting was held; two were living on his compound at the time and the other happened to be visiting him from another part of the town. At the second meeting, which was on Christmas Day, three men had brought their wives, and there were four additional men, all kinsmen of one or other member of the group.

A few general characteristics of the six regular members of the club are shown in Table I. Members A, B, and C constituted an inner clique which had been primarily responsible for establishing the 'club'. A, in whose house the 'club' used to meet, lived opposite B, and C lived on a compound next to B's. These three men were often to be found sitting together in the evenings, chatting outside A's house, and it was on one such occasion that the formation of the 'club' was first proposed. The three acted on the proposal the same evening, A going to call E who lived on the compound next to his, and E in turn calling in F who lived on the same compound as himself. B went to call D who lived a few compounds away.

D and B had for long been close associates, both as kinsmen and near-neighbours, and B used to call at D's house almost every evening on his way home from work. D later became 'president' of the 'club' and this fact is significant for, unlike the titles carried by other members, that of 'president' was only conferred after some little deliberation. I give a brief account of the incident.

At the first prearranged meeting, which took place on a public holiday a few days after the formation of the 'club', the members began to choose office-bearers—to distribute titles, one might say. After some discussion, they decided to invite X, who was not present, to be 'president'. X was an elderly and much respected man, who had come to Avenue 21 when it was first settled in 1930. One member was sent, there and then, to invite X, who, however, was not at home at the time. On hearing this the meeting unanimously chose D as their 'president'. D was thus a second choice, but from the particular circumstances of his election it is evident that he was genuinely held in high regard by the other members.

As shown in Table I, D was the youngest member of the group, but he had grown up in the avenue and was better educated than anyone else there.

B's status within the group and in the avenue was intermediate to that of D on the one hand and of A, C, E, and F on the other. Like D, B was known as an exemplary man—one who did not roam about the town, who was quiet with his wife, who always

Special Studies

TABLE I

Members of the 'Club'

	Tribe	App. age, yrs.	Marital status	Schooling, yrs.	Occupation	Yrs. in Stanley-ville	Yrs. in Ave. 21
A	Mukumu	50	Married	Nil	Mason	7	7
B	Mubali	30	,,	3	,,	6	4
C	Mubali	30	,,	3	Labourer's foreman	7	5
D	Mubali	26	,,	10	Carpenter	Since birth	21
E	Murumbi	40	Div.	Nil	Mason	21	21
F	Mukusu	30	,,	,,	Carpenter	Since birth	18

welcomed his 'brothers', and was polite to everyone. Although B was a member of the 'club's' inner clique consisting of himself, A and C, the link between him and D was a much stronger one than that between himself and either A or C. Somewhat similarly,

Diagram depicting the relative status of members and the principal lines of association between them

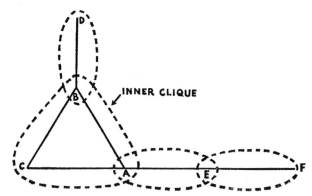

E and F were much closer to each other than either of them was to A; E and F had lived on the same compound for many years, the 'owner', E, having even given F permission to build a house there.

From the foregoing account, it is clear that the 'club' was established on the basis of a set of pre-existing relations and that these had in some cases developed over a period of many years. When I left Stanleyville, the 'club' had been in existence for a few months only, and it is quite possible that it failed to endure in this particular form. Our interest, however, is in the nature of the social relations which existed between the members of the 'club' irrespective of whether it continued to exist as a mock-formal association for any length of time.

CHRISTINE'S 'GUESTS'

Christine's 'guests' constituted a group which, unlike the 'club', had no semblance of formal organization. Christine was a woman of about 45 years of age. She was a petty shopkeeper and a landlady with a small fluctuating number of tenants and lodgers. Also, like a number of other women in the avenue, she occasionally sold beer illicitly at a slightly higher retail price than she had paid for it. The group I have in mind consisted of those of Christine's clients, tenants, and lodgers who were often to be found lingering, chatting, drinking, and, sometimes, playing a gramophone and dancing, in her house in the evenings.

Christine had never been married by tribal custom, but had for some years before coming to Stanleyville been the concubine of three successive Europeans. After her arrival in Stanleyville, some ten years ago, she had entered into one 'temporary marriage' after another in the *centre extra-coutumier*, and had finally settled in Avenue 21 about five years before I met her. She was now living singly, depending on her 'guests' and customers for her livelihood. Some of her neighbours said that she was mad, and she had the general reputation of being quarrelsome and unreliable.

On many week-day evenings, the main room in Christine's house was empty, and on others one would find only one or two people chatting to Christine as she waited for customers who might buy two or three cigarettes or a box of matches or half a bottle of paraffin. But on pay-days and usually on Saturdays and Sundays, the evening scene changed appreciably. I describe it as I saw it one Sunday evening between seven and eight o'clock.

Christine was sitting in the corner, next to the table on which she kept her small stock of goods for sale. There were ten people in the room; all but two were inhabitants of Avenue 21, eight were men and two women. (For details of the eight who lived in the avenue, see Table II.) Two of the men were drinking bottled beer at a table in another corner. One or two others had bottles in their hands and they would occasionally pass these to a friend. The gramophone was playing continuously, and a few of those present danced on and off. Of the two girls, one was standing at the door watching, the other danced, occasionally with a partner but usually by herself. Similarly, the men who danced did so either

TABLE II

Some of Christine's 'Guests'

Guest	Tribe	App. age, yrs.	Marital status	Schooling, yrs.	Occupation	Yrs. in Stanleyville
Man	Muleka	30	Single	3	Labourer	Under 1
"	"	20	"	3	"	"
"	Mubali	25	Married	5	Mason	3
"	Mogandu	25	Single	2	Chauffeur	3
"	Muleka	22	Married	6	Labourer	Under 1
"	Mubali	25	Divorced	3	Houseboy	5
Woman	Lokele	15	Single	Nil	—	1
"	Mubali	20	"	Nil	—	2

with each other or on their own. During the hour that I was there, several passers-by stopped at the door for a short while, and a few came in to buy something. For example, a woman from the next compound bought one franc's worth of paraffin which she poured straight into her lamp. She then lingered on, talking to Christine for about five minutes.

Of the ten 'guests' who were present throughout the hour, three were Christine's tenants, one was a man who normally lived in another part of the town but was staying on Christine's compound for a few days, two were from a compound next to Christine's, two from further down the road, and two from a nearby avenue.

A few of Christine's 'guests', and especially those who were also her tenants, were fairly regular clients, but even her tenants were usually short-term clients for the population living on Christine's compound was itself of a very transient nature.

From Table II it can be seen that there were some important differences between the composition of Christine's 'guests' and the 'club'. Like the 'club' members, Christine's 'guests' were drawn from several different tribes, but most of them were younger and they consisted mainly of comparatively recent immigrants.

Amongst Christine's 'guests' I occasionally encountered one or two pairs of friends or kinsmen, people who knew each other well, but normally the company assembled in her house consisted of persons amongst whom there was no chain or network of pre-existing relations. On the contrary, persons making use of the establishment were often complete strangers to each other, or had been so until very recently; they were not friends seeking each other out, but people thrown together as new arrivals in a neighbourhood where most of their social relations were of a fleeting and superficial nature.

THE SIGNIFICANCE OF THE TWO GROUPS

The 'club' and Christine's 'guests' had some general features in common: each was a leisure-time group operating at the level of the immediate locality and each was essentially an 'urban' group in the sense that it met only needs and interests arising directly out of the 'urban' experiences and circumstances of its participants. When I first began to take notice of the two groups, these common features were uppermost in my mind, and my main interest in each was as an example of social life unaffected by 'tribalism'. As I came to see the two groups in their total setting, however, I began to realize that there were fundamentally important differences between them. Each drew its participants from fairly distinct sections of the avenue's population; the one had a stable membership, the other had a membership which was continually changing; the one was built on a set of close pre-existing relationships between persons who knew each other as individual personalities and thus had comparatively secure expectations of each other's behaviour, the other clearly operated on 'type' rather than on personal expectations. In short, the quality and character of social relations within the two groups were completely different.

In depicting the contrast between the 'club' and Christine's 'guests' I have, of course, neglected innumerable important and interesting aspects of social relations in Avenue 21. This was inevitable. It was also quite deliberate in so far as the purpose of this paper was to attempt to demonstrate the need for intensive small-group studies to shed light on the system of social relations in African towns. In Mitchell's *The Kalela Dance*[5] and Epstein's *Politics in an Urban African Community*[6] we have recently received two valuable contributions to the analysis of the modern urban African social system. The conceptual approach used by Mitchell and Epstein is a highly suggestive one, but it needs to be tested and developed at different 'levels' of the social structure, and not least in face-to-face groups. The present paper, based on field materials gathered several years before the publication of Mitchell's and Epstein's contributions, clearly does not constitute such a 'test', but it is hoped that it may help to encourage rigorous small-group studies with this specific objective.

REFERENCES

Clément, P. C.	1956.	'Social Patterns of Urban Life', in *Social Implications of Industrialization and Urbanization in Africa South of the Sahara*, pp. 229-73. UNESCO Tension and Technology, Series, ed. D. Forde.
Epstein, A. L.	1958.	*Politics in an Urban African Community*. Manchester University Press for the Rhodes-Livingstone Institute.
Mitchell, J. C.	1956.	*The Kalela Dance*. Rhodes-Livingstone Paper, No. 27.
Pons, V. G.	1956a.	'The Growth of Stanleyville and the Composition of its African Population', in *Social Implications of Industrialization . . .*, pp. 229-73.
	1956b.	'The Changing Significance of Ethnic Affiliation and of Westernization in the African Settlement Patterns in Stanleyville (Belgian Congo)', in *Social Implications of Industrialization . . .*, pp. 638-69.

[5] Mitchell, 1956.   [6] Epstein, 1958.

X. KINSHIP, FRIENDSHIP, AND THE NETWORK OF RELATIONS IN KISENYI, KAMPALA

A. W. SOUTHALL

I. INTRODUCTION

Kisenyi is a suburb of Kampala in which intensive investigations were made mainly between 1953 and 1955 as part of a wider study of Kampala. Some of the results have already been published elsewhere.[1] It lies half-way between the main commercial centre of Kampala Municipality and the headquarters of the Kabaka's Government in Mengo two miles away. It is the densest African settlement in the urban area, but is not exclusively African. The sample area consisted of eighty acres occupied at an average density of 35·9. In a country where urban life and commerce are of very recent growth, it hums with petty trade. Its population contains a core of highly urbanized Africans, mostly but by no means exclusively Ganda, who have been in the area for at least several years and in many cases have land, property, or business interests. These seem to form the more stable points round which flows a host of Africans of many tribes whose residence there is much more ephemeral. Kisenyi also attracts crowds of visitors from other parts of the town and the neighbouring countryside to its beer bars, its prostitutes, its butchers, and its petty trade. The area lies within Mengo parish, itself part of the *Kibuga* or Capital of Buganda. The formal structure has already been described[2] and the present purpose is to give some of the results of investigations intended to throw light on the nature of informal relationships among the residents of Kisenyi.

II. THE NETWORK OF SOCIAL RELATIONS IN KISENYI

A sample of 145 household heads was drawn from the questionnaires of a previous 100% sample in this area. It was based on

[1] See Southall and Gutkind, 1957. [2] ibid., Chaps. I and X.

10% of the Ganda and 5% of the other tribes. The questions asked, and to some extent the quantity and quality of the answers, were not such as to justify extensive statistical treatment or tests of significance. But they form quite an adequate basis for representative description in a field where our ignorance is still so particularly profound.

The householders were asked to say who their best friends were. Most gave only one. Comparatively few gave kin as friends; from a sixth to a quarter in most tribes, including the Ganda, though over a third of the Luo cited kinsfolk, a fact highly consonant with Luo kinship structure. Another quarter of most tribes gave common tribe or country of origin as the basis of their friendship, but less than a tenth of the Ganda cited this and none of the Rwanda.

The factor of mutual assistance and also of gratuitous help from older to newer residents was stressed in another quarter of cases, especially by the Haya and Ganda. The giving of food, or of initial accommodation, lending of money, giving of medicine or of treatment when sick, being in general a kind person especially to foreigners, help in getting a job, loaning a bicycle, and protecting property were all mentioned.

Another fifth of all tribes gave different aspects of local association as the basis of friendship, mentioning the actual sharing of a room or the simple fact of being neighbours, visiting each other and meeting to talk or drink together.

It is interesting to distinguish between the actual fact of the friend cited being a fellow-tribesman and whether this or some other reason was given to account for the friendship. In the Ganda category all the friends except two, one a Luo and one a Soga, were Ganda. This is not particularly surprising in the case of the local tribe. But it was only a minority of cases in which the tribal bond appeared as the recognized reason for friendship. Very few Ganda cited actual kin and in over half the cases the friend's occupation was that of beerseller.

Two Luo cited Ganda, but all the rest had friends of their own tribe. Over half the Rwanda and nearly half the Haya and Toro had friends of other tribes. The five Nubis in the sample all gave

Kinship, Friendship, and Relations in Kisenyi, Kampala 219

Nubi friends and it may be noted that they are a very solidary category bound by common occupation, common religion, and in almost all families some common experience of military service. Among the smaller tribal categories in the sample there were eight cases of friendship between fellow-tribesmen and fourteen of cross-tribal friendship.

If we are to rationalize these data with hypotheses which are in line with the facts, although they cannot be proved, we may make the following suggestions: friendship is usually made with persons of the same tribe, but the number of cross-tribal friendships is considerable and certainly significant. Furthermore, the factor of opportunity has to be borne in mind. Thus it is easier, or more likely by chance, that a Ganda will make a Ganda friend because the Ganda are numerous. Similarly, it is more difficult for members of tribes with a very small representation to find fellow-tribesmen as friends and they are that much more likely to strike up an acquaintance with those they encounter frequently at home, in leisure hours or at work. It is interesting that three short-term residents of minority tribes cited relatives or neighbours in their tribal homes as their only friends and another said that his children living with him were his only friends in town.

Members of the sample were also asked whether they had any close kin in town and what they were doing. Obviously differing tribal conceptions of kinship are involved here. Nearly all the Ganda had relatives in town. They were of very diverse kinds, from brothers and sisters to wife's father or father's sister's son. Less than one in ten of these relatives in town were cited as friends. Nearly all the Luo had kin in town and though nearly half of them cited kin as friends, it is noticeable that most of these were affinal rather than agnatic, though very many Luo had brothers or half-brothers in town. Luo probably felt that relations with affines are not by definition good in town, therefore when they are they are more like relations of friendship, whereas the agnatic bond is more ineluctable and taken for granted even in town. Very few Toro had kin in town, but the tribal bond was important. Nearly all Haya had kin in town but did not cite them as friends. Half the Rwanda and the minority tribes had kin in town but only a few cited them as friends.

In the conditions of Kisenyi, kinsfolk remain very important, but the corporate significance which kinship has in most of the tribes from which Kisenyi people come cannot be reproduced. Town life enforces what might be called in a sense bilateral kinship behaviour: the strength of the fundamental ties is still generally assumed, but rather on a reciprocal basis which precludes long-term parasitism. Other kinsfolk, both consanguineal and affinal, present options which may or may not be taken up for friendship or assistance on a situational basis. Casual friendships may be between kin because they are liable to meet and become acquainted, rather than because non-kin are unacceptable. In other words, such friendship roles are more achieved than ascribed. There is clear empirical recognition of neighbourhood, common interest, joint residence, profession or occupation, in various combinations, as valid foundations for friendship and reciprocal obligation.

As has been done in the case of urban sociology in the United States, we have to distinguish between the supposedly impersonal and anomic elements in town life and what may be attempts to surmount them. It is unquestionable that the solidary roles and corporate groups of rural tribal society cannot be reproduced in town. Africans coming to town must either enter a new social structure ready made and foreign to them, or create a new structure for themselves. Of course, both processes occur. For the Ganda the case is somewhat different, in that their traditional capital provided an embryonic introduction to town life from which there has been a continuous development to the present Kibuga and its increasing involvement with Kampala as a whole. For the Ganda, therefore, the shock of change was cushioned, and through them indirectly rendered gentler for other tribes also. In many respects the present Kibuga is completely transformed, while Kampala is an entirely new phenomenon without precedent in the traditional structure. Therefore all new arrivals, even Ganda, have to make radical adjustments to town life. But the fact that for Ganda at any rate the Kibuga represents

Kinship, Friendship, and Relations in Kisenyi, Kampala 221

their traditional Kibuga, the forerunner of Kampala, provides a thread of continuity which undoubtedly aids in the adjustment.

Members of the Kisenyi sample were asked what they considered to be the source of order in their community. This is a sophisticated question and the results are only taken as a qualitative indication of the outlook and awareness of these people. There was a high rate of failure in response, 46 giving no answer or saying that they did not know. However, some declarations of ignorance were in themselves positively illuminating, as in the case of the woman who said that she was a peasant and therefore could not be a chief, a woman so that she had never asked her father, and how then could she know. Several women showed similar reactions.

The majority view was given in 42 answers all of which attributed order to the chiefs. Most referred in particular to the local headmen and parish chief of Kisenyi, but some also mentioned the sub-county chief. Four attributed order to the Kabaka, two to the landowners, another two to the *Lukiko* and one to the Katikiro. One said it was due to the house-owners who provided accommodation for them. By contrast, 18 attributed it to the Government, or the Governor, or to Europeans. All these implied that the source of order was quite foreign to themselves and only passively accepted by them, whereas those who referred to chiefs, Kabaka, landowners, or *Lukiko*, probably saw order as belonging to a social system recognized and respected by them, though not their personal concern.

Eight answers gave the police as the source of order, several adding that this was because they arrested thieves and drunkards. One attributed it to the fear of prison, another to the courts, and another to people's sense of guilt. A Nubi attributed it to the King's African Rifles. Three said that there was order if taxes were paid.

Eighteen other answers revealed interesting opinions, attributing order more directly to the positive attitudes of ordinary persons. These answers ranged over: love of country or of neighbours, education, the influence of parents, good manners, religion, people themselves making friends, and freedom from discrimination between tribes. One stressed that chiefs should be immune to bribery, two said that if there was plenty of money no one would steal, and one said that if every man worked and every woman was married there would be no trouble.

A somewhat different insight was gained by asking who was considered most popular and who most important in the community. Out of 165 persons mentioned as of importance, the largest category was that of the chiefs, who were cited 63 times. The next largest category was of local residents prominent as shopkeepers, traders, and craftsmen, who were cited 42 times. Large landowners of the area, including several members of the royal family, were mentioned 32 times. Several of these are not resident in the area. Women were cited 28 times and most of these were beersellers. Persons of tribes other than the Ganda were cited 29 times and these included many citations by Ganda as well as non-Ganda.

There was little overlap between those cited as important and those cited as popular. Nearly all respondents gave different people as popular and important. But some of the female beersellers, the male headmen, and the main landowners were cited as both important and popular, though by different people. Males were mentioned 87 times for popularity and females 63 times, including 51 different men and 24 different women. Non-Ganda were cited 46 times, 26 different persons being mentioned. The Haya headman was cited four times by Haya and once by a Rwanda; a Ganda shopkeeper was mentioned twice by Ganda, once by Haya, and once by Luo; a Teso laundryman twice by Teso, once by Lango, and once by Ganda; a Teso eating-house keeper four times by Teso and once by Acholi.

Outstanding in popularity were the Ganda women beersellers. Some of them combined other roles such as dancer, house-owner, food-seller, matmaker, or member of the royal family. They were mentioned by members of all tribes and seem to occupy key positions as focal points in the network of social relations.

III. WOMEN IN THE SOCIAL STRUCTURE

The emergence of women as heads of independent households is an objective indication of radical change from the traditional organization of society. In these tribes women were usually legal minors, necessarily under the guardianship of either a husband or a male kinsman. This is largely true in most rural areas today, though the state of affairs which has arisen in towns is also spreading into the countryside around them, especially in the case of the Ganda round Kampala.

In Kisenyi 23% of all households were headed by women. Two-thirds of these were accounted for by single women, just as in the case of male households many consist of single men. But in the other third a variety of situations were found. Several women might be living together, or a woman might be supporting her own children, or even a brother of almost her own age. Often these women were also house-owners. In the other Kampala suburb of Mulago it was found that 34% of house-owners were women. Besides this there were many women of very indeterminate status. Some were working in eating-houses or shops and counted as members of their employer's household. Some were living with male relatives but obviously leading quite independent lives. A number gave shadow husbands who were never tracked down. This was probably because they were afraid of being rounded up as prostitutes, a fate which indeed befell independent women in this area from time to time, if they could not prove that they were in an officially recognized type of employment, or otherwise bring pressure to bear on the local authorities.

Ganda women accounted for 69% of the female household heads, Haya for 11%, Toro 5%, and Rwanda 3%. From another point of view, 43% of all Ganda households had female heads, 35% of Haya, 13% of Toro, and 15% of Rwanda. The rest were Soga, Swahili, Half-caste, Teso, and five other tribes.

The women household heads have a longer average period of residence in Kisenyi than adult males as a whole.

Figures from Jinja show a longer average residence for women

PERIOD OF RESIDENCE IN KISENYI

	Up to 1 yr.	1–4 yrs.	4–10 yrs.	Over 10 yrs.	Total
Women household heads	31%	29%	18%	22%	100
Adult men	28%	43%	14%	15%	100

than for men and both in Jinja[3] and in Dar es Salaam[4] a higher proportion of female than of male residents were born in town.

A hypothesis which would repay careful testing is that while towns attract fewer women than men, they attract women for a longer time. The nature of the urban attraction for the two sexes is in some respects radically different. While for men it provides the opportunity to supplement, perhaps quite frequently, the amenities of rural life, for women it provides a total and permanent escape from rural and tribal society. The oscillation between town and country, with its overtones of oscillation between traditional and secular contexts, is much less characteristic of women than of men. This is particularly the case with independent women. Women who simply accompany their husbands to and fro, play a largely passive role in this process, but the women who come to town as a more permanent escape make a crucial contribution to the evolving pattern of urban social structure. Not only do they escape from tribal sanctions, kinship obligations and male dominance, but in many cases from marriage itself.

IV. DEFINITION OF THE STRUCTURE

The corporate structures of the wider economic and political system provide an outer framework within which the people of Kisenyi live. Those who make their living in Kisenyi, or who sleep, eat, or spend their leisure there, discover and create their own field of social relations to a large extent. It is therefore new, variable, and uncertain. Corporate groups and well-defined roles contribute little to it. The use of strings of qualitative phrases or adjectives to describe these situations as amorphous, hetero-

[3] Sofer, 1955, pp, 18–19.   [4] Leslie, 1957.

geneous, fluctuating, or unstructured, does little to reveal their inner meaning. Strictly speaking, they could only be accurately defined by innumerable statistical statements of the frequency and interrelation of an infinitude of transient behaviour patterns. These are unmanageable for both writer and reader as even some of the primitive data adduced in this paper must indicate. The alternative is to try to pick out recurring features and to discern trends, providing evidence which may seem plausible but cannot amount to proof.

We may recapitulate the situation in respect of the main aspects of social life. The containing corporate political structure lies largely outside Kisenyi. It appears foreign to most of the inhabitants or to many more as belonging to the dominant local tribe. Only a very few saw it as concerned with the personal relations of themselves and their neighbours, over which they had some control. The political structure enters Kisenyi in the form of the parish chief and his headmen. Their power is limited, but their influence is very great, because they really belong to the area and are involved in its life and its problems. They are pivots or focal points of dense networks of relationships. They see their political responsibilities in terms of preservation of harmony, the smoothing of the rough edges in social life, as well as against the background necessity of securing their own livelihood. They humanize the power structure. If they themselves transgress or twist the law to their personal advantage and are open to persuasion, this is really the obverse to their ability to sympathize with the day-to-day problems of others as well as their own. Some people prefer a person who, in every sense, speaks their own language, who has time to spare for them and makes them feel better and have more sense of belonging, even if he cannot solve their problems and in fact profits from them. This seems better than an outsider who might dispense impersonal and inflexible justice, without any human involvement. Personal contact is very highly valued. The African population has never recovered from the loss of personal contact with British officials which has resulted from improved communications and increasing paper work. They used to see and know the District

Commissioner, as a person, in the bush on safari and round the camp fire. Now they rarely see him except as a figurehead at a mass ceremony or impersonally at a formal meeting. This is frequently lamented.

The majority of Kisenyi people are employed outside it and to this extent their work situation is somewhat isolated from the rest of their life. But the minority who make their living in Kisenyi are a large one. As shopkeepers, beersellers, prostitutes and concubines, petty traders and craftsmen, hawkers, hotel-keepers, headmen, or lodging-house keepers they are necessarily involved more closely and for a longer time. They give crucial continuity to what with the risk of contradiction may be called the informal structure.

Organized religion plays a rather minor part in Kisenyi. Christian observance is low, though nominal adherence is high, There are no churches in the area, but there is a small mosque. Those who profess Islam have more solidarity on the basis of religion than any other category. They are not homogeneous, but Arabs, Somalis, and all Swahili-speaking Muslims have a strong linguistic bond, while Nubian or Ganda Muslims feel ethnic unity reinforcing their religious brotherhood.[5] Other religious, ritual, and magical practices are individual and instrumental, rather than corporate or expressive. They tend to be clandestine and reflect the structure rather than contributing strongly to it.

Kinship is, of course, dissected between the traditional context of the countryside and those less certain bonds which can be picked up or developed in the town. As most of the population oscillates between these two contexts each tends to be held in abeyance while the other is manipulated. Kinship or tribal membership is still the most widely recognized bond. It is usually combined and reinforced by neighbourhood, profession, or occupation. Neighbourhood is also an adequate bond, but mere common profession or occupation without it is not. For the average low-status individual, his importance for the system

---

[5] African Muslim leadership in Uganda is split by factions, but this does not affect the warmth of informal personal relationships between Muslims.

depends on the degree, length, and type of his involvement in it. This is banal but fundamental. The segmental quality of modern life, in which a person's roles and relationships are widely dispersed in space and even in time, between numerous institutional contexts, obviously reduces his importance in any one context unless his segmental involvement is reinforced by the intrinsic significance of the role he plays. This is to some extent a vicious circle in that high-status persons are not hampered by their roles being dispersed and highly segmental. Acquaintance or relationship with other high-status persons, or possession of the objective criteria of high status, more than counterbalances the segmental dispersion of roles. But those who are restricted to minor roles have little influence if they are also segmental and dispersed. They are bound to depend on those whose social participation is more intensely local and concentrated.

The Kisenyi beersellers are a small minority in numbers but may be critically diagnostic. They are a vivid illustration of how the system works, though large numbers of other less conspicuous individuals doubtless make a similar contribution. Many of the beersellers are Ganda. This at least gives them a spatial and temporal continuity. They are longer-term residents than the average. Their occupation tends to be a key one in any community and obviously commits them at the very least to an exceedingly wide acquaintance. None the less, this could also be superficial, but the evidence suggests that this is not altogether so. These people exhibit a peculiar combination of toughness and humanity. They are hard-bitten individuals who have had to make their own way, but they are capable of real kindness and generosity in particular instances which have a strong influence on the community. Their beer bars are the prime context for the operations of prostitutes, receivers, detectives, and thieves, yet at the same time they play a part in converting the impersonal, unfriendly anonymity of town life into something warmer, more familiar and less forbidding. It is here that people meet and find fellow-tribesmen, kin, or old friends. Drunkenness and the illicit activities which beer bars do so much to facilitate constitute real social problems, though their dimensions in Kampala are probably small compared with other African towns. Possibly the widely ramifying latent functions of drinking and beer bars have something to do with the strength of their grip on the people in this sort of context.[6]

The model to which we are approximating may be outlined or caricatured as follows. Confinement to the limits of a paper must inevitably make it over-brief and crude. The overall framework has to be accepted for all practical purposes as immutable by the mass of persons within it. It consists politically of the structure of the Protectorate Government and the Buganda Kingdom, the relation between which is intricate and subject to the constant play of conflicting pressures. Economically it consists of the major employment structures of these governments, of the Kampala Municipality, of large European and Asian and smaller African business firms. Within this structure and as players of the key roles in it, Europeans, Asians, and Africans interact to an increasing degree, though still remaining rather isolated for most purposes.

Speaking more particularly of African participation in the system, the high-status categories consist of aristocratic and *nouveaux riches* Ganda, with their start on other tribes in proximity to the centre, and in wealth, education, and the power these bring. They are torn between participation in the modern secular political and economic structures and allegiance to the partially adapted traditional structure of Buganda. It is chiefly in the secular structure that they are increasingly joined by Africans of other tribes in bureaucratic, managerial, entrepreneurial, and clerical roles. Because of the distances involved, they cannot so easily attempt to fuse the secular and traditional structures as the Ganda do. They are more irrevocably committed to the secular structure and are for this reason faced with less day-to-day conflict than the Ganda in this respect, as long as they are in town.

The lower-status categories are much more diverse. Kisenyi stands for one type situation. Strategic persons with a concentrated local involvement are focal points in the field of rela-

[6] See Southall and Gutkind, 1957, pp. 57–65, 221.

tions of large numbers of others. The strategic persons must from this fact be considered to have a higher status locally. They provide links with aspects of the external structure: with the Ganda royal family and Ganda high society generally, with landowners, big chiefs, business men, and even with Asians and Europeans.

Places like Kisenyi also contribute to the social life of non-resident categories such as domestic servants and very short-term migrant workers. Short-term migrants rely more heavily on kinship and tribal links and more often try to live in local tribal clusters. They are passive pawns in the political structure and active participants in the lower reaches of the economic structure, but much of their kinship and ritual life hangs as it were suspended in their tribal homes.

REFERENCES

Leslie, J. A. K.	1957.	'Survey of Dar es Salaam'. (Unpublished MS.)
Sofer, C., and R.	1955.	*Jinja Transformed*. Kampala: East African Institute of Social Research. East African Studies, No. 4.
Southall, A. W., and Gutkind, P. C. W.	1957.	*Townsmen in the Making*. Kampala: East African Institute of Social Research. East African Studies, No. 9. (2nd impression.)

XI. LABOUR MIGRATION AS A POSITIVE FACTOR IN THE CONTINUITY OF TONGA TRIBAL SOCIETY[1]

J. VAN VELSEN

The Tonga[2] live on the western shores of the northern half of Lake Nyasa, at a distance of about 1,000 miles from the main employment centres in the Rhodesias and of about 1,500 to 2,000 miles from those in the Union of South Africa. They live in small scattered homesteads which I have called 'hamlets'. The overwhelming majority of Tonga wage-earners find work in those three countries; very few are employed in Nyasaland. Tongaland is still undeveloped and very little cash is generated locally. Compared with other tribal areas the Tonga are relatively prosperous; this prosperity is largely due to their export of labour. Their staple diet is cassava whose cultivation does not require much labour. Subsistence cultivation is almost entirely in the hands of the women and does not seem to be adversely affected by the exodus of male labour. There is no shortage of land.

Formally Tonga society is matrilineal: descent and office follow the matriline and ideally a person should reside matrilocally but wives live virilocally. In fact, however, there are many deviations from these rules and patrilateral kin play an important role in a person's life. Indeed, there are no clear foci of social and political relationships and there is ample scope for political manipulation and usurpation of offices and titles.

Absent labour migrants are an important category of Tonga; at any one time between 60 and 75% of the adult males are absent

[1] This is an abridged version of a paper presented at the International African Institute Seminar held in January 1959, at Makerere College, Uganda. I am grateful to Professor Daryll Forde, Director of the Institute, for permission to publish the full version in the *Journal of Economic Development and Cultural Change*, Chicago. I will analyse the problem of labour migration in greater detail in my forthcoming monograph *The Politics of Kinship among the Tonga*.

[2] I lived among the Tonga for thirty months from 1952 to 1955 as a Research Officer of the Rhodes-Livingstone Institute, Lusaka.

Labour Migration in Tonga Tribal Society

whilst working abroad (viz. outside Tongaland), the majority of them leaving their families behind. Indeed, even the most casual visitor to Tongaland cannot fail to notice the marked preponderance of women. In this paper I will show that these absent villagers generally maintain a stake in the social and political structure of Tongaland; that they have a vested interest in its continued functioning and try to play their social and political role despite their absence. Tonga working abroad thus belong to two contrasted and distinguishable (but not rigidly separated) economic and social environments. On the one hand there is their tribal area with the villages where they come from, where they are likely to retire and where their status is largely determined by birth. On the other hand there are the urban areas where they work (often for the best part of their adult lives) and where their status does not depend on their birth (apart from the fact that they are black).

Tonga who seek employment abroad are quite explicit about their objections to taking their families with them. These objections may refer to urban life in general (as it is experienced by Africans in Rhodesian and South African towns) or to life in particular urban areas. The reasons they give for their objections are corroborated by the literature on urban conditions for Africans. As I will describe later, it is largely for the same reasons that Tonga want to retire in the village after a lifetime in the towns. I will therefore continue to use the term 'labour migrants' because, through necessity, and hence by intention, most Tonga who go abroad retire to their villages in Tongaland. My view is that those who manage to settle in the towns permanently and have given up the intention to return to the village, are the exception rather than the rule. This view cannot easily be supported by figures from either the rural or the urban end. One would need life histories of men who have reached such a stage in their lives (or who are now dead) that one can assume that they are not likely to move from the urban to the rural area or vice versa, depending on where they are found. Considering the number of men who are away at any one time and the long average duration of a man's absence abroad, in the relatively short time that I lived with the Tonga I could not gather sufficient systematic numerical data.

The urban data in particular would be very difficult to collect because they could be reliably obtained only through the usual anthropological method of intensive study rather than through surveys which tend to lay too much emphasis on such quantitative data as the number of years spent by Africans in towns, or, alternatively, their attitudes towards urbanization. From my experience with Tonga labour migrants, it seems to me that the number of years spent in the towns by a person is not a reliable index of that person's 'urbanization'. I understand by this term a condition in which the African has given up his loyalty to his tribe and his continued dependence on the economic and social system of his tribe, and has become, as an individual and no longer through membership of his tribe, a citizen of the larger state which now contains his tribe. It is relatively unimportant whether an African has lived for one, ten, or twenty years, with or without intervals in his tribal area, in the specialized and industrialized economy of the towns if he relies for his ultimate security on his tribal society, after his limited security of urban employment has come to an end.

In the light of my Tonga evidence it might perhaps be more fruitful if in urban surveys one tried to discover a correlation between length of residence on the one hand and distance from tribal area and the nature of a man's employment (whether skilled or not or whether well paid) on the other hand. For I found a definite reluctance among the Tonga to come home frequently because their journey to their place of employment is generally long and expensive; moreover Tonga tend to have the rather better paid jobs and they are afraid that if they go on holiday too often or too long at a time they may lose their jobs.

I remarked before that the Tonga retire to the village from necessity rather than from choice. The Tonga living in the towns are all 'urbanized' in the sense that they come under the urban authorities and live in an industrial, urban, cash economy and so forth.[3] But their integration into the industrial, urban economy,

---

[3] Cf. also Gluckman, 1945.

Labour Migration in Tonga Tribal Society 233

particularly as regards social security, is only partial for reasons which are beyond their control. It seems to me that this is or should be the crucial element in any discussion of 'urbanization'. Since the majority of the Tonga working abroad maintain social and economic links with their village, they remain 'migrants' and do not become 'urbanized'. Consequently when Tonga migrants eventually retire to their village, they do not fall back upon the security of a tribal social system which *happens* to have continued during their absence; the migrants themselves, during their absence, have been contributing actively and consciously to its continuance because they know that they may have to rely on it when they are no longer usefully employed in their urban habitat. In other words, the decision of Tonga urban workers to maintain a position in their tribal society is therefore not so much a matter of choice but rather it is inherent in the social and economic system of the urban areas in which they live and work. And such variations between individual Tonga as the length of their stay abroad, the amount of money sent home, and, in general, the frequency and intensity of their contacts with the rural area,[4] are differences of degree and do not alter the fundamental fact that the majority of the Tonga working abroad look to the economic and social system of their tribal area for their ultimate security.

Tonga men who go abroad for the first time or go to a place where they have not lived before, frequently say that they do not want to take their families because the journey is difficult and they want to explore the place first. Large numbers of Tonga (perhaps half or more) go to work in South Africa where they are legally prohibited immigrants unless they sign a contract for work in the mines. But in contrast to the neighbouring Tumbuka who sign on for the mines in large numbers, Tonga never sign on as contract labourers for the mines (although many work on the mines on a monthly basis); they often enter the Union of South Africa by various illegal means. They obviously do not want to be burdened with a family; an illegal immigrant when

[4] These are the criteria which Wilson uses to distinguish between 'labour migration' and 'temporary urbanization': Wilson, 1942, p. 46.

caught may find himself working as a prisoner on a farm instead of in a relatively well-paid and certainly much preferred job in a town, as was his intention. After they have explored the new conditions, some Tonga may then fetch or write for their wives who frequently also enter the Union illegally.

Another factor which tends to discourage a Tonga from settling in the towns with his family is the fact that the minimum wage is adjusted to the requirements of quasi-bachelors without family commitments, and that in general the wages structure is based upon the assumption that families are left behind in the rural areas where they support themselves.[5] But even when wages are adequate for the maintenance of a family in the towns, the acute shortage of housing for Africans is still a deterrent to urban family life.[6]

Housing provided by employers has the great disadvantage that it offers little security—'no job, no house' is the Tonga comment on this kind of housing. Housing provided by municipalities in 'locations' or elsewhere is for various reasons also virtually 'tied housing'. In addition there is the inadequacy of social services (educational, medical, recreational, etc.) for Africans in the urban areas. Even if these services are no more inadequate than in the tribal area, the Tonga at home have at least the compensation that they live among their own kin on whose support they can rely.

RECIPROCAL SERVICES BETWEEN TOWN AND VILLAGE

The families who stay in the village have no difficulty in maintaining themselves, even if only on a subsistence level. This means that those who stay behind can feed themselves and that the money which is sent in from abroad is net income and not needed to make up for the absence of male labour (as for instance among the Bemba). This income is largely available for the purchase of goods other than the basic subsistence requirements.

[5] Bachelor-based wages are an obstacle to urban family life, particularly at the lower levels of income: cf. Thompson and Woodruff, 1954, p. 75. For African wages and family standard of living see, for instance, Dalgleish, 1948, pp. 30, 35: Hellman, 1949, p. 270: Thomson, 1954, pp. 25 *et passim*.
[6] Cf. Dalgleish, op. cit., p. 36: Hellman, op. cit., pp. 246, 268 *et passim*.

In the rising standard of living of the Tonga minimum requirements tend to include more and more manufactured goods and other items which can only be purchased with money. There are few opportunities for earning cash locally.

The Tonga who goes abroad without his family leaves them behind in the care of his own kinsmen or of his in-laws. Wherever the wife lives during her husband's absence, her relatives will see to it that she receives the treatment due to her as a wife: for instance her husband must send her money with which to buy salt, cloth, and the other necessities which a husband is expected to provide. Conversely the husband's kin take care that his marital rights are not abused.

Wives who have accompanied their husbands to the urban areas often come back to Tongaland, alone, to be confined, or to bring home their children because 'the town is a bad place for small children'. Children may also be sent home with some other returning migrant.

Money is sent from abroad for a great variety of other purposes. Relatives at home may appeal to kinsmen working abroad for clothes or for financial help (and often receive it) to pay a fine, damages, or bridewealth, to buy clothes, or to pay for the fare to go abroad. Others may help a kinsman in the country by sending him money for a gun with which he can shoot meat for his own pot and for sale to others.

The total amount of cash which is sent to the District from abroad is quite considerable and is, incidentally, larger in proportion to the population than for the other Districts of the Northern Province and perhaps of the whole of Nyasaland.[7]

Finally, labour migrants help their kinsmen at home also with other services. I mentioned already the opportunities for education which they sometimes offer. Intending labour migrants generally depend for their contacts, introduction to employment, etc., on Tonga kinsmen, and others, who are settled in the towns already. The latter will help the intending migrants with papers (genuine or forged) to facilitate their entry into the Union of South Africa.

[7] See, for instance, the *Annual Report of the Provincial Commissioners*, 1946, pp. 38, 45.

I have not tried to give an exhaustive description of the manifold reciprocal services which are expressions of the continual contact between Tongaland and the labour migrants. I merely wanted to indicate the range of these reciprocal contacts and to show that they are the result of normal kinship relationships (such as exist between persons who are still in personal touch in Tongaland), and partly the result of the special circumstance of the considerable separation, in terms of geographical distance and social and economic environment, between the two places where Tonga earn a living. Thus in spite of this separation there is still a great deal of interdependence between what one might call the rural and the urban Tonga. Rural Tonga society is geared to a permanent situation in which only a minority of its menfolk in the prime of life is available in Tongaland. The Tonga do not consider this situation as exceptional: migration to the urban centres has become part of Tonga culture. The Tonga accept it as part of life that every normal man should spend at least some years away from Tongaland. They see Tongaland as a training ground for the young and a place of retirement for the old. Young men consider their stay in the village, before they can go off to the towns, as a period of marking time.

Women on the whole do not expect to go abroad and few have ever gone. The result is that the knowledge, the experience and, one might almost say, the culture of the two sexes differ considerably. Whilst many men are literate in or can at any rate speak at least one if not several other languages (often including one or two European languages) besides Tonga, women on the whole do not have these accomplishments. Men have seen and know about the ways of Europeans and other peoples from first-hand experience, but the knowledge of the women in this respect is mostly second-hand or restricted to what they have seen in the District. On the other hand, since the women have been able to follow the developments at home during the absence of their sons, brothers, or husbands, it is the women who are more fully *au fait* in that respect. Village and town have come to represent, for the men at least, different phases of life. The same people move from one environment to another and have interests in both.

MIGRANTS' CONTINUED RELIANCE ON THE VILLAGE

I have given a short description of the links between town and village, and some of the interests they serve. We saw that the Tonga migrants leave certain interests behind which they expect their kinsmen at home to protect. It is not only a certain number of specific interests which a labour migrant expects his kinsfolk to protect, but also his total legal personality—his membership of, and his place in, Tonga society. As I mentioned before, the Tonga leave their villages for the towns with the intention of returning and they want, therefore, a niche to return to. For they know that a time comes when they will no longer be employable in the urban economy and will therefore '... relinquish their rights to be housed (in the urban areas)'.[8] Thus the same factors which make it difficult for a Tonga to take his family to the towns, also make it difficult for him to stay in the towns when he is no longer employed. Therefore, they expect their rural kinsmen to continue to consider them as members of the village and the kin-group who are only temporarily absent. And both groups of Tonga see their respective services on a reciprocal basis. The labour migrant sees his contributions of cash and goods to the rural economy as a kind of insurance premium: 'How can we expect our *abali* (kin, friends) to help us later when we are old, if we do not help them now?'

To keep the place of labour migrants means, amongst other things, that their kinsmen in the rural area must make sure that there will always be enough land for them. This is one reason why those who have, in one capacity or another, control over land, are chary of indiscriminate settlement even though there is enough land.

But a person's relationship to land, his claim for a garden, is only one aspect of his membership of Tonga society. Status in the social and political structure within the village and outside

[8] Noble, 1951, p. 128.

it is closely connected with access to land, and a person's rights to land cannot be isolated from his relationships involving other rights and obligations in the community. It is therefore his status as a Tonga in its entirety which a labour migrant wants to be preserved during his absence. Although the Tonga have been drawn into the orbit of a cash economy, those who live in Tongaland still need land as the principal source of their living. It provides them with food, fire, and building materials for their houses. As regards most basic requirements of life such as food and housing, though not clothing, the economy of Tongaland is still essentially the traditional subsistence economy. It is within this framework of basically traditional values that a Tonga occupies a position into which he is born and by virtue of which he is a member of Tonga society. And it is within this framework, too, that Tonga hold gardens, marry, have children, occupy political office, seek for protection of their rights—in brief, expect security in life. This means that a member of this society who wants to maintain his status cannot do so only in relation to one aspect of life—he is inevitably drawn into the maelstrom of the total life of the community.

MIGRANTS AND TRIBAL POLITICS

Thus Tonga, whether at home or abroad, who are interested in the preservation of rights in land, are inevitably involved in tribal politics. This explains why labour migrants continue to compete for political office at home as well as they can in spite of their absence, and notwithstanding the fact that the monetary rewards of the office, if any, are likely to be very small in comparison with their earnings abroad.

It is a common practice for labour migrants to write to the District Commissioner or the Protectorate Secretariat in Zomba asking for clarification of or protesting against political events in Tongaland.

I have seen many similar cases: sophisticated men with (as far as I could judge) quite good positions and cash incomes who come back for a few months' holiday in the village and get involved in competition for headmanships or other minor political honours or make every effort in trying to rectify what they consider is a usurpation of office.

MIGRANTS' SUPPORT OF TRADITIONAL VALUES

We have seen that the rights associated with a person's social and political status (including claims to office) require continuous vigilance against encroachment. A labour migrant expects his kinsmen at home to protect his status, though those kinsmen may be in a weak position through the very absence of male relatives. In the flexible political system of the Tonga, struggles for political power are won and lost, and titles appear and disappear. The Tonga political system shows relatively little continuity of titles of office and produces great numbers of rival claimants for political titles. And when a labour migrant's claim has gone by default (which can easily happen since many Tonga stay abroad for long periods) he loses no time to put in his claim on his return.

Whatever other effects labour migration may have upon Tongaland, it is clear that most Tonga do not cut their ties with the rural area. When they return from an urban life abroad they settle again in the pattern of Tonga life which is still dominated by traditional values. There are no obvious signs of social disorganization and the Tonga still hold together as a tribal unit, distinct from other such units surrounding them. There are indeed various factors and pressures which work towards the continuance, if not reinforcement, of tribal integration rather than towards tribal disorganization. Firstly there is the basic assumption, explicit or implicit, of the industrial economy that the average African 'is not in any real sense a wage-earner',[9] but is a labour migrant who has his tribal village to fall back upon. Secondly, the Tonga abroad have therefore a vital interest in maintaining their position in the community and the economy of Tongaland. I mentioned several factors prevailing in Tongaland which encourage the Tonga, including the migrants, to

[9] *Nyasaland*, Colonial Reports, 1954, p. 22.

conceive of their social and economic security in the rural area in terms of traditional Tonga values.

A third important factor is the Administration of the territory which is based upon 'tribal integrity'.[10] Consequently the Administration of the District makes extensive use of Tonga tribal agencies. This means in practice that some village headmen[11] receive recognition from the Administration and are appointed Administrative Headmen or Native Authorities, the latter with their own court warrants. Such Administrative appointments are on the whole made upon the assumption that the appointees hold office in the Tonga political structure. Thus Administrative recognition not only puts a premium on political leadership in the Tonga political structure, but the competition for this recognition is also largely in terms of traditional values. Consequently the tribal political structure receives powerful support from the Administration. The idea of tribal integrity is also implicit in the tax census in respect of which a Tonga who is *de facto* resident abroad, is *de jure* still a resident in his village.

I suggest that all three categories of persons—industrial employers, Administration, and the Tonga themselves—have under present conditions, an interest in maintaining the cohesion of the Tonga as a tribal community: and that there is a connexion between this interest and the fact that the social and economic systems (including the land-holding system) are still largely dominated by traditional norms.

In this paper I have tried to explain an apparent contradiction. On the one hand we have the continued predominance of traditional values; on the other hand the exodus of large numbers of men who return to the village with a great deal of sophistication and education in the ways of the Europeans, who have become in many ways a reference group for the Tonga. And I have tried to show that in general these returning labour migrants are actively stimulating the traditional values of their rural society, and the reasons why they do so.

I would like to add one 'practical' conclusion. If my analysis is

[10] Lacey, 1935, pp. 36, 40, 63.
[11] I emphasize 'some' headmen and by no means all of those who claim to have a title and to be headmen.

correct, that would mean that as long as Tonga (or for that matter, members of other tribal societies) in the urban areas are not given an opportunity to make their living entirely in the towns, in other words to urbanize themselves, so long will they have to rely on making their living partly in the rural area. And this pull of the rural area (and the economic and social system found there) will continue to exert its influence on the stabilization of the urban population, the labour turnover, the efficiency of labour, etc. The apparent failure of the majority of Africans to settle down as a fully urbanized labour force is too often ascribed to inherent personal 'failings' of the African employees; too rarely the cause is sought for in the peculiar and ambivalent lives which so many urban Africans are forced to live.

REFERENCES

Annual Report of the Provincial Commissioners, 1946. Zomba: Government Printer.

Dalgleish, A. (Chairman) 1948. *Report of the Commission Appointed to Enquire into the Advancement of Africans in Industry*. Lusaka: Government Printer.

Gluckman, M. 1945. 'Seven-Year Research Plan of the Rhodes-Livingstone Institute'. *Rhodes-Livingstone Journal*, No. 4, pp. 1-32.

Hellmann, Ellen 1949. 'Urban Areas'. *Handbook on Race Relations in South Africa*. Cape Town: Oxford University Press.

Lacey, T. (Chairman) 1935. *Report of the Commission to Enquire into Migrant Labour*. Zomba: Government Printer.

Noble, G. W. 1951. 'African Housing in the Urban Areas of Southern Rhodesia'. *Journal of African Administration*, Vol. III, No. 3.

Nyasalands 1954. *Colonial Reports*. London: H.M.S.O.

Thompson, B. P. 1954. *Two Studies in African Nutrition*. Rhodes-Livingstone Paper, No. 24.

Thompson, C. H., and Woodruff, H. W. 1954. *Economic Development in Rhodesia and Nyasaland*. London: Dennis Dobson.

Wilson, G. 1942. *An Essay on the Economics of Detribalization in Northern Rhodesia*. Rhodes-Livingstone Paper, No. 6.

XII. KAHAMA TOWNSHIP, WESTERN PROVINCE, TANGANYIKA

R. G. ABRAHAMS

Kahama is one of the smallest gazetted townships in Tanganyika and is the administrative headquarters of the most Northern of the three so-called Nyamwezi Districts. This district has itself a rather mixed population, Nyamwezi and Sukuma predominating in the east and Sumbwa mainly of Ha origin in the west. The township is not centrally set in the District, which stretches from it some 90 miles to the west but only about 30 miles east and about 18 miles to the south-east. It is thus right in the middle of the Nyamwezi part of the District and is in fact surrounded on all sides by the Nyamwezi Chiefdom of the same name. The importance of this last fact will be seen later on.

My investigations in the town have been rather brief, stretching all told over a period of about two months during which I have been engaged in other work as well. I have, however, been fairly well acquainted with the town for a little over a year. The main value of this paper will, I believe, be to present some facts about a very small town in East Africa, a subject upon which little, if anything, seems to have been written. My own main interest has been to see what such a small town surrounded on all sides by Nyamwezi Chiefdoms and villages is like.

I have said that the town is small and some population figures will help to reveal various aspects of this statement. Firstly, to compare it with other townships. Out of 33 gazetted townships in the territory, Kahama is 28th in size. The 1952 Census gave population figures as 1,497 compared with 99,140 in Dar es Salaam, the largest town, and 217 in Kilwa Masoko, the smallest. The average population of these 33 towns is 8,665 and 15 of them have a population of over 5,000, 7 of which have over 10,000. Only 3 townships have populations of under 1,000 and one of these has 990. On average roughly 0·23 of the population of

Kahama Township, Western Province, Tanganyika 243

Tanganyika townships is Non-African. In Kahama there are 310 Non-Africans out of the total population of 1,497 or roughly 0·21 of the population. These figures are all from the 1952 Census published in 1955. I have not been able to get later figures. The 1948 Census showed Kahama township with just under 1,250 African population as at 23 August 1948. This difference of 60 men, women, and children over four years would seem only to signify a fair stability of population figures though not of population over that period. It is then, I think, clear so far that Kahama is a small town among towns with a pretty average proportion of Non-African to African population for the territory.

Let us now look at the town in relation to the rest of the District of which it is the administrative centre. From the point of view of total population figures the 1948 Census will have to be used. For tax-payers more recent figures are available. In 1948 the total African population of the District was 95,813 of which 50% were Nyamwezi. In Kahama the African population was 1,250 of which 43% were Nyamwezi. These figures become more significant if one remembers the rough geographical division of the District into Sumbwa and Nyamwezi and that Kahama town lies in the Nyamwezi portion. In Kahama Chiefdom the dominant tribe was Nyamwezi who were 71% of the population. In a typical Sumbwa Chiefdom such as Mbogwe the dominant tribe, the Sumbwa, were 81% of population. In Kahama township, surrounded, as I have said, by Nyamwezi on all sides, the dominant tribe is again Nyamwezi, yet these formed only 43% of the population and the rest were apparently so mixed as not to deserve any breakdown in the census. We can see then that Kahama township in its African population structure is radically different from other self-standing units in the District, not only in relation to the small percentage of the dominant tribe but also in the fact that tribal breakdown of the remaining 57% was not made, though it presented no difficulties at all in other places. My own data support the complexity of tribal mixture as assumed above in the town.

I wish now to turn to the more recent tax-figures to discuss the Non-African population of the town and District and also the higher-income bracket African population. This last is measurable by the personal tax lists which I was allowed to examine. First then let us look at the Non-African population and, of these, first the Indians.

There are 95 Indian tax-payers registered at present in the District and of these 68 are resident in the town. The vast majority of these are engaged in business, duka (shop) owners, produce buying, and transport. The large number of owners of small dukas (or shops) in the town is surprising. One explanation is that illicit gold and diamond buying is thought to exist and at least one Indian in the town has been convicted in recent years. This trade is supported by the town's central position in relation to the Congo border, Geita Gold Mine, and Williamson's Diamond Mine at Mwadui. Until recently, there was another gold mine at Isaka some 25 miles east of the town. In this geographical position the township is unrivalled. This explanation of what would otherwise be an anomaly in a comparatively poor District economically seems to me a likely one, though more than that I cannot say. My figures here are weak. All I can add is that out of very many shops in town run by Indians only two are big enough to support general European trade.

The Arabs in the district present some rather difficult problems owing to their mobility in relation to the town. Out of 160 registered tax-payers in the district 36 are registered as resident in the town. The actual number resident in town would appear to be somewhat smaller. They are in fact to be found more stably in settlements outside the town, the larger ones being four in number. None of these, however, boast as many as 36 tax-payers though up to and slightly above 20 may be found. The reason for their settling out of town is difficult to assess. Some of the settlements ante-date the town and there is the added fact that they are reluctant to deal on credit. It is not uncommon to hear that an African prefers to buy goods at a dearer price from an Indian rather than at a cheaper price from an Arab or fellow African, and this from the mouth of an African. Availability of credit seems to be the basic reason and this may account for the reluctance of Arabs to compete in business with the Indians in town. A very small proportion of shops in town are Arab-owned in spite of their numerical preponderance in the District.

In 1948 there were some 49 Europeans in the District. These figures relate to total European population whereas the Arab and Indian figures are for tax-payers. Almost all these Europeans were and are missionaries or Government workers. Some were connected with the mine at Isaka. This figure of 49 is probably rather greater now owing to increases of Government staff in the District. All Europeans in town are Government servants.

To sum up, the largest Non-African element in the township is Indian. Second, though preponderating considerably in the District, are Arabs, and finally come the European Government workers who rarely exceed 12 men, women, and children all told.

Let us turn now to the higher-income bracket Africans in the District, that is those who pay more than the basic 12s. on the graduated personal tax scale. There are 520 such Africans in the District and of these 65 are registered as resident in town or exactly one-eight. This compared with the town's African population being roughly one seventy-fifth of total African population in the District is revealing but not surprising owing to the obvious availability of work in a township compared with the country.

The tax-registers also show one other very important fact about the town. Registered African tax-payers paying ordinary personal tax are listed in three groups:

1. Men with houses
2. Men without houses
3. Women with houses

There are 246 in group 1, 136 in group 2, and 70 in group 3. The proportion of women house-owners to men is phenomenally large when compared with figures for the country areas of the District. Thus, in the town, there are 70 such women and a total tax-paying population of 452 or just under one-sixth. In Busangi Chiefdom where I worked there were 15 out of a tax-paying population of 1,288, or roughly 1 in 85. This is, I believe, very important. More than 1 in 5 house-owners in the town are women.

The fact that some of these figures have been culled at different periods during the last ten years, to some extent weakens the analysis above. However, my general impression is that there has been a slight all-round rise in population which owing to its spread and also its slightness does little to vitiate the picture presented above.

In relation to population structure in the town I now wish to turn to some of my own data, the main source of which is a survey of some 44 houses in the township. I wish there had been more, but unfortunately, there are not. Let us, however, see what this survey reveals.

Firstly, out of 150 people interviewed 66 or 44% were Nyamwezi but many had been born as far away as Tanga and Kilwa and Kenya Colony. As well as these, there were some who called themselves Kimbu[1] and Nyanyembe[1] who might be classed as Nyamwezi. To balance these, however, are many who would normally be called Sukuma.[2] What is important is that close to 44% could be called Nyamwezi but this is not to say they are all locals by any means.

Of the remainder 21 were Sumbwa and many of these were born nearer the township than many of the Nyamwezi. The next largest group were Manyema[3] with 13. These are mostly, I believe, part of a large group of Manyema who came into the area very early in the township's history having lost their land in Tabora[4] owing to the railway. After this the numbers tail off but it is worthwhile to list them.

Nyanyembe	7	Hehe	2	Ruwa	1
Zaramu	4	Half-caste Indian	2	Bende	1
Kimbu	4	Rungu	2	Nyanja	1
Half-caste Arab	4	Ha	1	Makonde	1
Nyasa	3	Somali	1	Tusi	1
Kikuyu	2	Vinza	1	Kerewe	1
Sukuma	2	Rufiji	1	Nyiramba	1
Nyika	2	Nyaturu	1	Chagga	1
Bemba	2	Haya	1		

And all these 28 tribes were found in a sample of 150 out of

[1] Both these are ethnic groups within the Nyamwezi complex. The Nyamyembe are the people of the largest Nyamwezi Chiefdom: Unyanyembe.

[2] The Sukuma are the tribal group immediately to the north of the Nyamwezi.

[3] Manyema is a District in the Eastern Congo which was greatly influenced by Arabs and Swahilis coming up the East Coast trade route.

[4] The town which gives its name to the main Nyamwezi District.

Kahama Township, Western Province, Tanganyika

1,187 Africans. Add to this the fact that the sub-Jumbe[5] of the town is a Ganda and one begins to get a clear picture of its cosmopolitan nature. If one looks at the tribal breakdown for Kahama Chiefdom one sees the following in 1948:

> Nyamwezi 71%
> Sumbwa 12%
> Sukuma 9%
> Rest unclassified and probably mostly Tusi

Today the Sukuma have probably increased considerably. But all the three listed tribes speak interrelated languages, the difference in some cases being almost non-existent and have a body of closely related customs in most cases historically connected. The situation in town and country is clearly very different even leaving out the Non-African element. I shall try to point out in this paper some of the elements of social cohesion which exist to counter this diversity though I cannot say much owing to the short period in which my study was made.

First, however, I wish to mention a point closely connected with the figures given above, that is the large incidence of room- and in some cases house-renting to non-relatives or non-affines. Renting took place in 21 out of the 44 houses visited and 5 houses had unrelated guests, 3 of which 5 also had renting. The tribes of the householders show less variation than the total figures. 23 owners were Nyamwezi, 6 were Sumbwa, 2 Zaramo, 2 Manyema, 2 Arab Half-castes, 1 Rungu, 1 Nyasa, 1 Chagga, 1 Somali, 1 Sukuma, and 4 unknown. The possibility of the owner's tribe not being known arises out of absentee ownership. This was found in 15 out of the 44 houses, though in 6 cases there was someone, relative, wife, or in-law to look after the property. As many as 4 renters were to be found in one homestead though 1 or 2 was most common. 13 unattached women were found as either renters or guests. Of these only 4 professed to have work. The others tended to be classed as prostitutes by my assistant but some were too old for this.

The composition of homesteads varies considerably from one to another. The presence of renters, unrelated single women, and

---
[5] The assistant executive official.

also in-laws is in strong contrast to the country Nyamwezi homestead. Homesteads in town ranged from single men alone or single women and a mother or grandmother to the elementary family with odd relatives or in-laws right through to houses where only renters were found. This as I have said contrasts with the Nyamwezi homestead which, typically, can be said to be a man, his wife or wives, their children and perhaps some children of the man's sisters if they were married without bridewealth, though of course variations are found.

I did not get time to trace any picture of interrelationships within the town. However, 22 householders claimed to have relations living there. A few of the renters also had relatives. By relatives, here, I include in-laws.

Before leaving the subject of renting it is worthwhile to point out that I came across one case of a house-owner renting out his house and then renting a room for himself elsewhere. I do not know how common a practice this is, however.

So much for the population structure of the town. It only remains to say that there are clearly defined areas in which Africans, Asians, and Europeans live. Any intrusions, and these are few, take place between Asians and Africans. The European area, Uzunguni, is purely European and all Europeans live there. Arabs spread into both Asian and African areas.

I wish now to examine some of the things which appear to me to offer some social cohesion to this very heterogeneous population.

Clearly for an African population of such mixed origins, the question of language is an important one. The solution is provided by Swahili. My impression is that everyone in town can speak reasonably good Swahili and it is very common to hear it spoken there in contrast to the country areas around the town. Nyamwezi is also heard quite a lot. The importance of Swahili language seems to me self-evident here, especially when one adds that in certain cases a man may not know his own tribal language. Suffice it to say that basic communication within the town presents no problems owing to Swahili.

Whether there is a Swahili culture in the town alongside of the language is a more difficult question to answer. 'Waganga wa Kiswahili' are to be found but then so are Nyamwezi diviners. Moreover the question of defining Swahili culture is difficult for me as I have never visited the coast. Clothing which I associate with such a culture is the kanga and buibui for women and the kanzu perhaps topped by a jacket and also the white skull-cap or red fez for men. Kangas are frequently worn by women in town but then so they are in the country. The black buibui, very common in Tabora, is more rarely seen. Kanzus are worn quite frequently though to see them topped by a jacket is not so common a sight as in Tabora. The red fez is certainly more often to be seen in town than out but not so the white cap which is universal. Further, taking into account the tendency for many people, especially younger ones, to wear European-type clothes I think one can say that there is no marked Swahili culture, at least as seen in Tabora, demonstrated in the town's dress habits. More important than clothing habits, however, is the question of religion. Out of 150 people on whom material was available 116 claimed to be Muslims or roughly 71%. This large number of people sharing the same religion also seems to me to be a strong co-ordinating factor and once more in contrast to the surrounding country where if any outside religion is practised it is Christianity. One of the religious leaders of the African Muslim Community in town is a Zaramo by tribe but born in Tabora. He is, on the whole, fairly cynical about the religion of the Muslims and tells me that many drink, and pray irregularly, very few praying every day and many only on Fridays. To one less severe in judgement on such matters this seems fairly good. A man goes round the town at times of prayer to let people know, in place of a muezzin. This religious head, whom I have mentioned, has a very important role in the town courts which will be considered later.

When one comes to the question of leisure it is fair to say that the town splits up into its younger and older elements. For the older men the chief places for meeting one's companions are two, the market, which historically is the mainspring of the town, and the *pombe* (beer) club. At the market every day are large numbers of people many of whom will sit and chat for long periods. The pombe club is open during the dry season in theory four days per week, Thursday to Sunday inclusive. In practice owing to a rule allowing left-overs to be consumed, Wednesday is the only day when there is no beer to be had at that time of year. In the wet season, Saturday and Sunday are the official days but here again left-overs are consumed. Needless to say the brewers, who are women, make sure that left-overs are guaranteed. Here again a man can meet his fellows and gossip over his beer.

For the younger people politics and entertainment are inextricably interwoven. T.A.N.U. is very powerful amongst the younger elements in the town and has produced the political master-stroke of starting a youth league with community singing five nights per week, i.e. Monday to Friday. The songs sung are called 'Nyimbo za uhuru' or songs of freedom. These song meetings are very popular and as most of the songs involve getting rid of the British the singing serves a strong double function. Saturday and Sunday nights are taken up by dances at 'the welfare'. The town has two bands, neither of them good, one of them the Youth League's own band and the other called the Royal Jazz Band consisting mostly of Youth League members. Almost every sort of dancing is seen there; men and women dancing alone, or men with men and men with women, or women with women. The band makes up in energy for its lack of proficiency. Entrance is one shilling and there are always quite a few people outside, looking through the windows, unable to afford to go in.

The young women are a strong driving force in the demand for entertainment in town and recently caused the young T.A.N.U. District Chairman much worry by demanding women's football which they had seen at Tabora. He asked if songs of freedom were not sufficient and they clearly were not. Finally, they were palliated but disappointed with offers of net-ball. An interesting sidelight is thrown on this interlinking of politics and social activity and also on the position of half-castes in the town. A young half-caste girl I met had wanted to join the T.A.N.U. Youth League but had been refused owing to her not being pure African. She was not interested in T.A.N.U. politically but was clearly disappointed at being thus barred from the entertainments involved.

The picture of the town's social activities is completed by the occasional more traditional dances, the football team which plays from time to time and the Royal Bar where bottled beer is sold. This last place is frequented by both sexes and dances are sometimes held there.

I wish now to proceed to an aspect of the town which is really a qualitative one. That is that though there are so many contrasts with the country it none the less is not divorced enough to have an entirely distinct quality. One factor leading to this opinion is the lack of sophistication of the Saturday and Sunday dances compared with what one will find in Kampala or even Tabora. But there are other more concrete factors which I shall mention.

The first of these is the dependence of many of the town's inhabitants on agriculture for their living. Most of the fields are outside it and some are even in the European quarter, to the Europeans' annoyance. Here then both factually and visually is evident the persistence of the country way of life. The chief difference is the almost complete absence of stock-holders amongst those interviewed.

The second point is the conduct of the town's court, and here it may be worthwhile to give a general picture of the situation first. The town's African population is under a Jumbe, a relative of the Chief of Kahama Chiefdom. Under him is a sub-Jumbe, a Muganda. There are no subordinate headmen under these as would be found in a Chiefdom.

The position is complicated by the fact that the Jumbe is also head of a court just outside the town which covers one of the areas of Kahama Chiefdom. Moreover the same court elders are used. In theory the town court should be held in the town's baraza on Thursdays and the country court, theoretically completely separate, at the country baraza on Mondays. In fact at both courts cases are heard from within and without the town and appeals from both go to the Chief of Kahama Chiefdom who in theory has no jurisdiction over the township. This seems to me a most conclusive piece of evidence concerning the inability of the town, theoretically and legally a completely separate unit under its 'Township Authority', to divorce itself thoroughly from the surrounding countryside.

I have said that the Muslim religious leader plays a very important part in the town's court. In fact, he acts as unpaid assessor to cases involving Islamic law. Moreover, as most of these cases come to him first and if possible are settled by him out of court he plays the part very much of a headman to the Muslim community. An actual case which I witnessed will demonstrate this.

A woman, married by the man in question in the mosque, had been left by her husband when he went to work in Geita. His return home was delayed by his being jailed for raping a woman there. The woman had no respect for him on his return or for her father who wished her to carry on in the marriage. Before the court had seen the case the Muslim leader had tried to get her to go back to her husband but she was adamant in her refusal. She continued so in court and eventually a divorce was granted. Not all the bridewealth had been paid but that which had, had to be returned twofold since the woman had broken up the home forcibly and without reason. This is in accordance with Muslim law.[6] The court elders were not allowed to take any part in this case at all in which the Mwalimu was sole assessor. When the elders tried to enter the case they were silenced and told it was not their business.

The Mwalimu that day dealt with two cases and clearly does much work in this field. The fact that he is not paid for his religious work or for his work as headman and assessor does not please him. Yet he is clearly indispensable. This seems yet again an example of the town's failure to be as yet fully developed.

To sum up what I have tried to do in this paper, I have attempted to show what sort of place Kahama town is. I have shown it to be small with a very heterogeneous population many of whom are Muslims. I have tried to show some of the forces making for cohesion in the town but have pointed out that there

---

[6] I have since found out that this is not in accordance with Muslim law though the verdict was given as such.

is felt to be a lack of sufficient entertainment there and that this has been taken advantage of politically. Finally, I have tried to show that in spite of many differences the town fails to be completely divorced from its surrounding, or to be fully developed as a town.

Before I close I wish to mention two points. Firstly, it is clear that the town's population contains two main elements which can be called permanent and transitory. I have not enough evidence to speak at length on this but would suggest that roughly they coincide with house-owners and renters.

Secondly, what of the future? The town has now been surveyed and has a town plan which looks, as these things do, very good on paper. Many of the proposed improvements relate to the Indians, many of whom may be too poor to make them. This will mean a refusal to renew leases. Further improvements relate to African parts of the town. Here again some difficulty may be met since the Africans have no leases and though threats have been made in the past to evict those who do not look after their homes properly, it seems such threats do not reach fruition. Certainly the town plan brings a deal of conflict into the situation and if it is successfully carried out will work changes much more far-reaching than the widening of streets.

XIII. PARENTÉ ET AFFINITÉS ETHNIQUES DANS L'ÉCOLOGIE DU 'GRAND QUARTIER' DE NEW-BELL, DOUALA

R. GOUELLAIN

I. REMARQUES MÉTHODOLOGIQUES

Les sources d'information préexistantes à nos travaux n'étaient pas négligeables. Aux rapports administratifs, périodiques ou occasionnels, rédigés par les autorités locales ou centrales, nous avons emprunté nombre de renseignements statistiques d'ordre économique ou démographique. La quantité de ces chefferies, la diversité de leurs origines ont permis le plus souvent d'en vérifier et d'en apprécier la valeur.

Il faut cependant déplorer l'absence d'études systématiques sur ces aspects avant 1955, dans cette ville.[1] De même aucune synthèse historique n'a été tentée, nos propres essais reposent sur la consultation de multiples écrits d'intérêt limité, aussi bien occidentaux qu'autochtones. Parmi ces derniers, certains datent déjà de la fin du XIXe siècle.

Des études ethnologiques partielles existent, mais aucune à notre connaissance ne dépasse les faits culturels pour aborder les complexes et ne décrit les sociétés typiques dans leur ensemble.

De ce fait, notre travail à Douala s'est orienté d'emblée vers la morphologie (structures démographiques et socio-économiques) et vers l'écologie (implantations originales). C'est nécessairement renoncer à l'analyse en profondeur de l'objet étudié que nous eussent permis l'ethnologie et la psychologie sociale.

La méthode de base fut un sondage aréolaire au 1/10e que suivit l'étude intensive de certains quartiers. Nous avons par ailleurs effectué des enquêtes exhaustives sur le commerce de détail et l'artisanat.

En terminologie, nous avons dû recourir à des expressions susceptibles de mieux décrire les formes de concentrations

[1] See references, p. 269.

urbaines observées, les termes d' 'îlot', de 'bloc' et de 'quartier', ne répondant pas toujours à la réalité.

Nous ne pourrons nous étendre sur la notion d' 'environnement' qui, à notre avis, mérite une étude spéciale. Son aspect vécu, fort instructif, nous donnerait le processus de prise en 'possession' par les étrangers du nouveau monde qui s'offre à eux, donc le contexte dans lequel des relations nouvelles s'élaborent. L'ethnologie, la psychologie et les méthodes 'phénoménologiques' nous ouvriraient des perspectives très utiles.

Il est à noter aussi que les appartenances aux groupements résidentiels urbains n'ont pu être appréciées à leur juste valeur, tant est insuffisante notre connaissance des autres formes de groupement. Un travail sociographique scientifique sérieux devrait être entrepris par la suite. Les comparaisons entre différents groupes et appartenances seraient alors possibles.

Ainsi notre approche sociologique du milieu urbain africain, reposant sur des méthodes d'observation quantitative, exprimée par une terminologie orientée vers l'aspect extérieur mais non vécu de la réalité urbaine, nous conduit à des résultats de nature statistique et descriptive.

II. GÉNÉRALITÉS HISTORIQUES

Histoire de la ville et évolution de son administration

La concentration de population sur les bords du Wouri qui existait depuis quelques siècles n'a pas préfiguré la ville actuelle. Seule l'organisation des relations commerciales est à l'origine de Douala—organisation qui ne se fit pas dès le début des premiers contacts. Après la découverte de la côte au 15ème siècle, l'installation d'Anglais à Fernando-Po non loin de ce qui allait devenir Douala, et l'importance que prit le commerce des 'produits coloniaux' transformèrent l'estuaire du Wouri en point d'impact des relations commerciales. Mais, malgré l'existence d'une cour d'Equité, de premiers traités et l'introduction du christianisme, les firmes, jusqu'au dernier quart du 19ème siècle, ne purent s'installer à terre. La 'ville' se situait pendant cette première période dans l'estuaire, lieu des relations et origine de sa fonction.

Elle apparut vraiment quand les firmes s'installèrent à terre et que le pays passa sous protectorat, entraînant l'installation d'un Gouvernement et de ses Services. Elle prit forme quand, avec le développement économique et administratif, un plan directeur d'urbanisme fut élaboré organisant Douala et consacrant sa fonction commerciale (1906), et lorsque l'administration française réduisit 'la circonscription de Douala' qui englobait auparavant des milieux ruraux (1926). La ville se distingua des autres parties de la circonscription et eut son administration propre. A partir de cette époque, Douala se développe, se structure en zones et quartiers ayant chacun son administration avant la création récente de la Municipalité de plein exercice.

Le fait urbain implanté, la 'ville', s'est alors développée et structurée.

Développement économique

L'économie commerciale reposait au début sur l'échange indirect primitif. Quand les populations furent mieux connues, l'échange se fit sur la base du 'trust'. La Cour d'Equité règlementait les tractations. Le monopole était détenu par les autochtones qui assuraient la collecte des produits de l'intérieur. Avec l'installation des firmes à terre cet échange fut remplacé par l'échange direct, rendu possible par la pacification de l'*hinterland*.

L'économie, en général s'orienta vers la production qui s'écoulait en grande partie par Douala, dont le port assure actuellement les 95% du commerce extérieur.

Apparut aussi à Douala un autre secteur d'activité encore à ses débuts: l'industrie de transformation.

L'économie qui s'est d'abord intéressée à satisfaire les pays importateurs de produits coloniaux cherchant à faire baisser les prix de revient par l'échange direct, s'est orientée ensuite vers la production exportée dont dépend la ville de Douala.

Développement démographique

Si nous prenons la base 100 pour l'année 1924 dont le recensement parmi les plus anciens nous paraît être le meilleur, nous obtenons l'évolution démographique suivante:

Année	Ensemble ville	Etrangers
1916	66	45
1924	100 (22,772)	100 (4,396)
1932	119	201
1940	183	531
1948	298	1,047
1956	498	2,050

Evolution des structures des populations actives

Les autochtones tiraient en majorité leurs revenus hors de la ville, dans les régions où s'étendait leur influence, grâce au commerce avec les populations de l'intérieur. Après leur élimination du circuit commercial, ils reconvertirent leurs activités et beaucoup émigrèrent vers les plantations que la crise de 1928/30 les contraignit à abandonner, mais le commerce foncier, à cette époque de développement urbain, n'a cessé de s'intensifier à leur bénéfice.

Les étrangers par contre, occupèrent la plupart des postes salariés. Il en est résulté un inemploi des autochtones assez important et peut-être chez ceux-ci la volonté de le pallier par le commerce foncier des terres de réserve (extension probable de la ville) et des terrains du 'Grand Quartier' de New-Bell encore maintenant sans propriétaire en titre.

Processus écologique

La ville européenne se développant, les quartiers autochtones reculèrent tout d'abord par expropriation (1913), ensuite grâce au commerce foncier. Là où la ville s'étendait et devait s'étendre, les propriétés dites 'coutumières' étaient 'reconnues et immatriculées'. Cette transformation de la propriété modéla les quartiers autochtones qui s'urbanisèrent et se lotirent. Mais ces mesures ne furent pas appliquées en ce qui concerne les terres de réserve et le 'Grand Quartier' de New-Bell. De ce fait, celui-ci devenu le premier quartier de la ville:

— n'est pas loti;
— n'a pas de propriétaire étranger ni de propriétaire en titre autochtone;
— et se trouve donc sans statut juridique

d'où découle l'impossibilité actuelle de l'urbaniser à moins d'un règlement de la situation foncière qui suppose une politique d'ensemble.

Position du 'Grand Quartier' de New-Bell

Il est à l'Est de la ville, bloqué par les quartiers autochtones au Nord à l'Ouest et au Sud, et par les terrains classés dans le domaine privé du Territoire (piste d'aviation) à l'extrême Est.

Sa surface est d'environ 330 hectares. Il compte près des 80% des étrangers résidant en ville, soit environ 70,000. Sa voirie principale et secondaire ne représente que le 1/20ème de sa superficie. Sa densité moyenne est de l'ordre de 220 habitants a l'hectare, mais inégalement répartie selon les secteurs:

Secteur	Superficie	Densité	% population
Ouest	92 Ha.	271	39
Centre	46 ,,	217	15
Sud Est (aviation)	60 ,,	175	16
Nord Est (récent)	133 ,,	150	30

Son développement dû à l'accroissement démographique est centripète. Les équipements sont insuffisants et ne peuvent suivre son rythme d'accroissement. La voirie primaire s'élimine de plus en plus sous l'éffet de la densité.

C'est un 'Grand Quartier' assez unique du fait qu'il s'est constitué sans cadre ni aide.

III. MORPHOLOGIE

Distance

La répartition des allogènes de New-Bell suivant les régions d'origine et les distances séparant celles-ci de Douala, montre que le nombre d'immigrants en ville pour 10,000 de leur compatriotes restés dans les regions d'origine, varie en fonction de l'éloignement.

Régions distantes		de 250 Kms.	3,893
,,	,,	de 250 à 500 Kms.	1,566
,,	,,	de 500 à 750 Kms.	179
,,	,,	de 750 à 1,000 Kms.	58
,,	,,	au delà de 1,000 Kms.	15

Parenté et affinités ethniques dans l'écologie de Douala 259

Nous avons aussi remarqué que ce sont les régions ou leurs subdivisions les plus urbanisées qui libèrent, compte tenu de la distance, le plus d'émigrants. Les groupes des regions proches et déjà quelque peu urbanisées sont donc les plus mobiles.

On peut aussi constater que la structure démographique des groupes dépend aussi de la distance. Elle tend à devenir plus régulière quand les régions d'origine des émigrants sont près de la ville. En ce qui concerne les sex-ratio:

— pour les régions distantes de moins de 250 Kms.: sex-ratio: 1,044
— ,, ,, ,, ,, de 250 à 500 ,, : ,, : 883
— ,, ,, ,, ,, de 500 à 1,000 ,, : ,, : 742
— ,, ,, ,, ,, au delà de 1,000 ,, : ,, : 670

La proportion des enfants varie aussi parallèlement avec l'évolution des sex-ratio.

Autre constatation au sujet de ce facteur distance: la croyance en un retour au pays natal qui a pour corollaire la croyance que l'installation en ville n'est que provisoire, varie dans les mêmes conditions. Lors d'une opération de déguerpissement, ont accepté de se réinstaller dans un lotissement en vue de l'acquisition d'un terrain, les originaires des régions limitrophes comprises dans les zones concentriques des 250 Kms. Les autres ont préféré se replier à l'intérieur de New-Bell (la moitié se faisant héberger, l'autre achetant ou louant des cases).

Niveau de vie

Les catégories socio-économiques que nous avons retenues ont été déterminées de la manière suivante: dépouillement de tous les salaires réels distribués à Douala, par professions et ensuite par groupes de professions selon que celles-ci ne nécessitent pas de spécialisation, ou en nécessitent une obtenue avec l'expérience et le temps, ou encore réclament une scolarisation antérieure. D'où trois grandes catégories principales:

— 1 non spécialisés
— 2 spécialisés
— 3 scolarisés

auxquelles il convient d'ajouter:

— une 4ème: les isolés ou établis à leur compte
— et une 5ème: la catégorie des sans-profession que nous distinguons des vrais chômeurs

En 1956, les salaires moyens étaient les suivants (moyennes des salaires réels):

— 1ère catégorie: 5,374 Francs
— 2ème ,, : 7,855 ,,
— 3ème ,, : 9,922 ,,

Les âges moyens des travailleurs, des isolés, et des sans-profession, sont les suivants, par catégories:

— 1ère catégorie (non spécialisés): 28·3 ans
— 2ème ,, (spécialisés) : 31·5 ans
— 3ème ,, (scolarisée) : 29·4 ans

(l'expérience professionnelle, ayant été remplacée par la scolarité, explique leur âge inférieur aux précédents).

— 4ème catégorie (les isolés): 33·7 ans
— 5ème ,, (sans profession): 24·5 ans

Les situations matrimoniales et le nombre de femmes mariées pour 1,000 hommes mariés varient suivant les catégories:

Catégorie	% hommes mariés	% hommes célibataires	nombre de femmes mariées pour 1,000 hommes mariés
1ère	29	71	1,044
2ème	49	51	1,109
3ème	50	50	1,148
4ème	57	43	1,335

Chez les sans-profession nous n'avons trouvé que 13% d'hommes mariés; l'irrégularité de la progression est due à la jeunesse des employés de la 3ème catégorie par rapport à ceux de la seconde.

La répartition des enfants pour 100 femmes mariées à des hommes de catégories différentes donne:

— pour 100 femmes mariées à des hommes de la 1ère catég.: 103 enf.
— ,, ,, ,, ,, ,, ,, ,, ,, 2ème ,, : 127 ,,
— ,, ,, ,, ,, ,, ,, ,, ,, 3ème ,, : 131 ,,
— ,, ,, ,, ,, ,, ,, ,, ,, 4ème ,, : 145 ,,
— ,, ,, ,, ,, ,, ,, ,, ,, 5ème ,, : 64 ,,

(il s'agit d'enfants vivants et non de naissances).

La répartition des personnes à charge totale pour 1,000 hommes actifs des catégories 1, 2, 3 et 4, suit la même progression:

Catégorie	Femmes	Enfants	Enfants de parents résidant au village	Adultes	Total
1ère	302	310	150	88	850
2ème	550	670	248	205	1,673
3ème	580	750	410	235	1,975
4ème	760	1,140	540	185	2,625

Les pyramides d'âges tendent à devenir plus régulières au fur et à mesure que les catégories sont plus élevées. La 4ème catégorie présente une pyramide dont la base est assez importante, mais, qui accuse cependant une concavité entre les enfants et les adultes du fait que c'est la première génération d'immigrants en ville.

Propriété et occupation des logements

Une même progression peut être aussi constatée quand on répartit la population active selon ses titres d'occupation des cases à défaut du terrain:

Catégorie	Propriétaire	Hébergés[1]	Locataires	
1ère	36%	45%	19%	100%
2ème	56%	35%	9%	,,
3ème	56%	30%	14%	,,
4ème	67%	22%	11%	,,
5ème	17%	76%	7%	,,

[1] Sont logés gratuitement par le propriétaire.

Il en va de même pour les personnes à charge (femmes, enfants, enfants de parents restés au pays, adultes) selon le titre d'occupation de ceux qui les entretiennent:

Pour 1,000 propriétaires

— Femmes	743
— Enfants	1,014
— Enfants de parents restés au village	492
— Adultes	254
Total	2,503

Pour 1,000 hébergés

— Femmes	138
— Enfants	149
— Enfants de parents restés au village	40
— Adultes	56
Total	383

Pour 1,000 locataires

— Femmes	158
— Enfants	131
— Enfants de parents restés au village	5
— Adultes	7
Total	301

L'importance des propriétaires des hébergés et locataires et de leurs personnes à charge est la suivante:

		Femmes	Enfants	Enfants de parents résidant au village	Adultes
Propr.	47%	82%	86%	91%	79%
Hébergés Locataires	53%	18%	14%	9%	31%
	100%	100%	100%	100%	100%

Les pyramides d'âges établies suivant les titres d'occupation rendent assez bien compte des irrégularités de la pyramide d'ensemble; celles des hébergés et des locataires ont leur base étroite et leur forme inversée souligne l'importance des hommes.

En ce qui concerne les propriétaires dont la majorité vient des régions voisines et dont les salaires ou revenus dépassent ceux des premières catégories, les charges qu'ils assument, y compris celle de l'hébergement, sont les suivantes:

Pour 1,000 propriétaires
— 2,503 personnes à charge totale
— 1,147 personnes à charge quant à l'habitat (hébergés et leur famille)

La proximité des pays d'origine et l'élévation du niveau de vie augmentent le nombre des ménages, des femmes mariées par homme marié, des enfants par femme mariée, des enfants de parents restés au village et des adultes à charge.

Parenté et affinités ethniques dans l'écologie de Douala 263

La propriété des cases (et non du terrain) consacre la fixation en ville et favorise l'accroissement du nombre des hébergés ou des personnes co-habitantes.

Les nouvelles conditions favorables économiquement, ne diminuent ni ne relâchent si peu que ce soit les liens avec les milieux ruraux, bien au contraire; mais l'on peut constater que la grande majorité des personnes co-habitantes sont avant tout les parents les plus proches et non ceux de lignages plus étendus. L'évolution est surtout qualitative et non quantitative.

ÉCOLOGIE

Les deux aspects écologiques de New-Bell

L'écologie est surtout conditionnée au départ par la situation foncière propre à New-Bell, par les liens avec les pays d'origine que matérialise la prise en charge de parents proches et par la concentration des émigrants par affinités ethno-tribales identique chez tous les groupes ethniques. La composition de la population en actifs, parents à charge et hébergés, déterminera les habitations dans leur conception.

De même les relations par affinités ethniques qui se reflètent ou trouvent leur cadre dans différentes organisations (politico-administrative, économique et d'entraide) détermineront à leur tour, différents échelons de regroupement par ethnie, ainsi que leur implantation (îlots familiaux, aires ethno-tribales) qui auraient dû avoir pour homologues les îlots statistiques et les quartiers.

Mais ces différentes implantations à tous les échelons, qui se sont réalisées dans le contexte spécifique à la ville, ont rencontré des résistances de la part du milieu urbain, et des conditions économiques nouvelles. Ces résistances ont transformé les conceptions écologiques traditionnelles: l'habitat, habituellement multi-cases, est devenu surtout mono-case mais avec une organisation interne rappelant celle du système multi-cases; les regroupements par affinités familiales, et ethno-tribales sont devenues hétérogènes mais ont conservé le caractère d' 'îsolats' qu'ils avaient à l'origine. Quant à l'urbanisation elle s'est surtout manifestée au niveau des grandes unités.

Deux implantations spécifiques et contradictoires coexistent donc à New-Bell. Une implantation qui relève des structures traditionnelles et que l'on pourrait nommer 'ruralisme familial' et une implantation qui existe en fonction de la ville et des impératifs économiques et qui est l'aspect urbain du 'Grand Quartier'.

Disons tout de suite que c'est au niveau des petites unités que le ruralisme familial s'est le mieux réalisé, alors qu'au niveau des grandes il n'a pu s'organiser. Cette dualité se traduit en fait par l'existence de deux trames de voirie: la trame rurale qui tend à disparaître sous l'effet de la densité et la trame urbaine qui ne sert qu'à l'évacuation vers la ville sans pénétrer dans les quartiers.

Les habitations

La structure des habitations est, dans 80% des cas, en étoile c'est-à-dire que leur centre est une unité distributrice; pièce de séjour ou salon. Par l'importance de ses dimensions, elle rappellerait les cours de palabres ou de réunions familiales. Autour de cette unité se distribuent les unités personnelles lesquelles, dans le contexte d'origine, et pour beaucoup de groupes ethniques formaient des habitations séparées (système multi-cases). Cette unité distributrice est sujette à des variantes. Ses dimensions peuvent changer ainsi que sa position, souvent fonction des habitats propres aux groupes ethniques.

En ce qui concerne le groupe des Bamiléké, c'est significatif. Très fortement organisé, hiérarchisé, leur habitat traditionnel au niveau des petits lignages est centré sur la demeure du chef de famille autour de laquelle se disposent les habitations des femmes, des serviteurs, des étrangers de passage. Le *king place*, résidence du chef, en est une spectaculaire illustration. Dans leur habitat urbain mono-case, l'unité distributrice des habitations se situe au centre et ses dimensions sont assez importantes puisqu'elle occupe plus du tiers de la surface totale habitée:

Parenté et affinités ethniques dans l'écologie de Douala 265

Position de l'unité distributrice dans l'habitat urbain Bamiléké

en Coin	Latérale	Centrale	Centrale + façade
4%	8%	38%	50%

Les unités personnelles ou de repos, communiquant avec l'unité distributrice, forment avec celle-ci le 'bloc familial'. Comme toutes les unités personnelles ne communiquent pas avec le salon, il convient de distinguer ce 'bloc familial' à part. Les unités du bloc, centralisées, sont occupées par le propriétaire, sa femme ou ses femmes et leurs enfants respectifs. Il est intéressant à étudier car il dépend des relations unissant les membres de cette famille. Nous ne pouvons entrer dans le détail, mais dans plus de 50% des cas, l'époux et sa femme font chambre à part, cette dernière avec les enfants.

Ajoutons que les pièces de repos ne communiquent pas entre elles directement, mais indirectement par l'unité distributrice. Les exceptions que nous avons relevées concernent les pièces où logent l'homme et la femme, et dans certains ménages de polygames, l'homme et sa préférée. Quand les enfants sont trop nombreux et qu'ils logent dans une pièce à part, celle-ci ne communique pas directement avec la chambre de la mère.

Hors du bloc familial, mais toujours dans la même habitation nous trouvons des unités indépendantes ou satellites sans communication avec les autres pièces ni avec le salon. Elles sont occupées par des parents proches hébergés et des étrangers locataires ou non. Leur nombre est important. Dans les ménages de polygames des secondes épouses peuvent y loger.

L'organisation des habitations dépend des groupes y résidant et des relations de parenté unissant les membres de ces microgroupes. Les facilités de communication entre pièces sont fonction du degré de parenté, ainsi que du rôle familial que jouent les parents dans le contexte familial traditionnel. Un parent peut faire partie du 'bloc' ou en être exclu suivant sa position vis-à-vis de la famille restreinte, propriétaire de l'habitation.

Il faut noter une évolution dans l'habitat mono-case: l'unité distributrice a tendance à se déplacer, et à se réduire: laissant au couloir qui apparaît la fonction de distribution.

Les groupements résidentiels à base ethno-familiale

Il semble que pour l'émigrant, chaque parent proche ou éloigné résidant au pays, soit un hébergé en puissance, à charge totale ou partielle. Cette prise en charge est à l'origine des 'îlots familiaux' groupes d'habitations qui peuvent réunir entre 5 et 20 cases, et dont les propriétaires et occupants sont de même lignage d'origine plus ou moins étendue.

Ces groupes urbains ne sont pas repérables comme nos îlots statistiques, qui se délimitent par la voirie. Seule l'enquête systématique permet de les déceler. N'étant pas délimités et étant fonction du nombre d'immigrants de même lignage, leurs contours sont fluctuants. C'est pourquoi nous les nommerons '*airées familiales*' pour les distinguer des îlots aux contours nets.

L'airée familiale est le lieu où les conceptions écologiques traditionnelles transforment l'espace urbain ou 'terre étrangère' en le rendant plus familier, moins impersonnel, moins desintégrant.

C'est aussi une extension de la solidarité déjà révélée par la composition des habitations, un lieu où le nouvel arrivant de même famille peut être reçu, peut construire, et où des possibilités lui sont offertes aussitôt (entraide, adresses des employeurs . . .). C'est aussi un cadre où les comportements typiques peuvent s'inscrire, dans lequel on parle le même dialecte et où sont entretenus par tous des liens semblables avec les mêmes milieux d'origine.

Il en résulte que l'airée est un 'isolat' que les immigrants ne quittent que pour se rendre en ville, dans les différents centres d'activités. Etant des 'isolats' les airées ne communiquent pas entre elles. La voirie qui les dessert, création des immigrants, ne les relie qu'aux voies principales: les artères de la ville.

Cette voirie rudimentaire résulte de l'emplacement des nouvelles cases construites à côté de celles des parents ou leur faisant face au delà d'une cour. Ces alignements grossiers et ces cours ont formé les voies primaires constituant la trame 'rurale' de New-Bell.

La position des airées dépend aussi de leur distance par rapport à la ville et de la trame proprement urbaine. Distance et voies de

Parenté et affinités ethniques dans l'écologie de Douala 267

communication ont orienté ces 'isolats' près de la ville et le long des artères.

Il y eut une période d'étalement des airées, et des habitations à l'intèrieur de celles-ci; mais la nécessité pour les salariés immigrants d'être près de la ville, le peuplement rapide de New-Bell, et son blocage, ont favorisé le remplissage des vides qui existaient entre les voies principales par couches stratifiées suivant les arrivées et entre les airées déjà établies (très souvent aussi entre les habitations).

Les airées qui, au départ, devaient former par leur ensemble des quartiers ethno-tribaux, adjointes à des airées étrangères, se sont trouvées comprises dans des ensembles hétérogènes. Elles tendent avec le temps à perdre leur nature intrinsèque. Il n'est pas rare, au terme de ce développement, de rencontrer des blocs de quartier de plus de 20 hectares sans voirie intérieure, si ce n'est l'espace entre les cases ou ce qui reste des premières pistes.

Il n'existe aucun rapport entre l'airée et le quartier que délimitent les voies principales, entre ces deux échelons opposés, tant par leurs dimensions que par leurs caractéristiques: l'airée est familiale, vécue comme telle, mais de plus en plus impraticable, alors que le quartier est urbain et hétérogène, mais accessible. C'est ce qui fait l'ambiguité de ce quartier d'immigrants, sans voirie a l'échelon des 'isolats', sans unité à l'échelon des quartiers.

L'urbanisation rencontre de sérieuses difficultés car elle signifie dans beaucoup de cas, l'éclatement des 'isolats'. Mêmes difficultés quant à la formation des quartiers soit ethno-tribaux, soit simplement urbains, grâce aux équipements de voirie, commerciaux scolaires, sanitaires et sociaux... Il existe bien des 'aires d'implantation ethnique', mais leur unité tient surtout à la majorité de leurs ressortissants par rapport aux autres immigrants; elles sont sans relation, ou presque avec les ensembles urbains à équiper.

Il existe aussi un équipement commercial assez important, mais sa structure est encore schématique: les produits bruts de consommation quotidienne, sont vendus a l'échelon du 'Grand Quartier'. A l'échelon des quartiers, le long des voies, sont vendus les produits importés qui peuvent s'acheter hebdomadairement. A l'échelon des 'ilots' ne sont vendus que les produits prêts à être consommés mais qui ne constituent pas l'alimentation de base quotidienne.

CONCLUSION

Nous sommes partis d'une situation d'ensemble qui nous a permis de définir la position du 'Grand Quartier' de New-Bell (géographique, démographique, domaniale). Nos recherches sur la population allogène nous ont révélé des structures sous-jacentes allant s'améliorant au fur et à mesure que l'étranger croit davantage en son installation définitive en ville, que son niveau de vie s'élève et qu'il devient propriétaire d'une habitation à défaut du terrain.

Mais les liens avec les pays d'origine, s'ils se ramènent aux liens les plus proches, n'en entraînent pas moins des devoirs devant lesquels les étrangers sont tous égaux, quels que soient leur appartenance ethnique, leur niveau économique et l'indépendance de leur habitat en ville.

Les implantations originales reflètant cette dépendance à l'égard du milieu d'origine est compréhensible, la déstructuration ne pouvant être totale.

Si les changements structuraux et culturels sont peu visibles dans les micro-groupes familiaux qui composent les habitations, ils deviennent réels, dans les groupements résidentiels plus étendus, où 'l'isolat' s'avère de moins en moins conforme aux nouvelles personnalités. L'éclatement écologique des 'isolats' et leur éclatement sociologique semblent dûs aux nouvelles formes de regroupements des individus qu'une sociographie exhaustive pourrait décrire et évaluer. Les groupements de voisinage interraciaux, les groupement de camarades, d'individus de même profession ou de même niveau culturel incitent les immigrants à sortir de leur isolement familial ou tribal et à prendre possession de la ville. D'ailleurs c'est dans la mesure où ces nouvelles formes de vie sociale apparaissent que la prise de conscience de la contradiction écologique de New-Bell se rèvèle.

Le retour aux anciennes structures et la 'destructuration' qui s'est faite normalement dans le nouvel environnement sont à l'origine des deux aspects urbain et rural, de New-Bell, qu'une

Parenté et affinités ethniques dans l'écologie de Douala

're-structuration' essaie de dépasser. Mais de ce retour aux anciennes formes il restera quelque chose: dessin des nouvelles unités de voisinage, par exemple, qui sera comme une variante apportée au phénomène urbain en général.

REFERENCES

Cameroun: Service de la Statistique Générale	1955-6.	*Recensement de la Ville de Douala.*
Diziain, R., and Cambon, A.	1955-6.	*Etude sur la Population du Quartier New-Bell à Douala.* Yaoundé: I.R.CAM.
Gouellain, R.	1956.	*New-Bell, Douala: Etude Sociologique.* 1ère pàrtie. Yaoundé: I.R.CAM.

SUMMARY

Kinship and Ethnic Affiliations in the Ecological Context of New-Bell, Duala

The present study does not claim to have explored with any thoroughness the influences of 'environment', nor to have analysed in depth the psychological and sociological aspects of the existing situation in New Bell, where a traditional rural conception of living persists in an increasingly urban environment. This paper presents and analyses descriptive and statistical material derived from a scrutiny of official documents and a sample survey of one-tenth of the population by areas, supplemented by a more detailed study of retail trading.

The peculiar constitution and characteristics of the 'Greater Sector' of New-Bell, the chief area of African, particularly immigrant, habitation in Duala, derive from the historical conditions which brought it into being, and the haphazard manner of its development.

Although for some centuries there had been settlements on the banks of the Wouri River, the present city of Duala owes its existence entirely to the fact that the estuary of the river became the centre of a considerable trade in colonial products, carried on initially by the 'trust' system, whereby African traders were responsible for the supply of produce from the hinterland. It was not till the end of the nineteenth century that trading firms were able to operate on shore. The establishment of a Protectorate and of government services was followed by economic and administrative development and the initiation of a planned urban economy culminating in the recent attainment of full municipal status. The former 'trust' system was replaced by direct exchange between European traders and African producers. With the expansion of commercial activity the population of the city, and especially the immigrant labour force, increased very rapidly. Many of the indigenous African inhabitants, who no longer acted as middlemen in the European trading system, turned to trading in land in the reserves and on the outskirts of the city. On sites where the city was extending or likely to extend, so-called 'customary' titles to land were recognized and registered. This procedure, which shaped the lay-out of the urbanized African quarters, was not applied to New-Bell, the chief area of immigrant habitation. Here there are no legal titles to land, no delimitation of the land into plots, and the district has no administrative status. Planned urbanization cannot be carried out until the land question has been regularized.

The superficial area of New-Bell is about 330 hectares (750 acres); the road system covers no more than one-twentieth of the area; 80% (70,000) of the inhabitants are immigrant wage-earners, the population density is 220 persons per hectare, but unequally distributed. The sample survey showed that the distance from the city of the places of origin of the immigrant workers bears a direct relation to the proportion of migrants to persons remaining in the country, the social composition of migrant groups, and the permanence of their residence in the city. Those who come from a distance of about 250 kms. or less, are as a rule more numerous in proportion to the persons who remain in the country, bring with them more women and children, and are more disposed to take up permanent residence in the city. All these figures decrease *pari passu* with the increase of distance.

A classification of immigrant workers according to educational and professional qualifications, and average earnings, showed a similar progression. The categories of better qualified and higher paid workers included a higher proportion of married men, a larger number of children in proportion to married women, a larger number of dependent relatives, and a higher proportion of owners of houses as opposed to lodgers or tenants.

The ethnic affiliations of immigrant workers have affected in various ways their life in the city and their reactions to the urban environment. The strength and persistence of the ties linking them with their home country are shown by the numbers of dependants, both adults and children, residing with their relatives in the city. Traditional ways of life have also influenced the type and internal arrangement of houses—many of which reproduce the pattern of the traditional homestead accommodating members of a lineage or extended family. In New-Bell this has resulted in the establishment of 'family tenements' which form self-contained units, in which traditional relationships, behaviour, and language persist. Originally these family tenements, grouped together, according to ethnic affiliations, formed tribal areas. But with the continuing influx of population, vacant sites between earlier habitations and between the main roads are being filled up, so that areas of tribal settlement are becoming heterogeneous. Thus there exists a contradiction in the material and sociological situation of New-Bell. On the one hand, the persistence of traditional modes of life expressed in self-contained kinship units, having little or no communication with each other; on the other hand, the pressure of the urban environment, new economic conditions, new forms of association. On the mercantile level, the same division appears: the raw materials of everyday consumption are sold in the 'greater sector'; imported and processed goods are marketed in the urbanized blocks. The planned urban development of the area faces considerable difficulties, involving as it does the breaking down of these self-contained units, the reconstruction of roadways—some of which have been obliterated by the density of population and the reorganization of areas of tribal settlement which at present bear no relation to urban aggregates. At the same time, though structural and cultural change may not be readily detected in the smaller family units, in the larger residential groupings the self-contained kinship unit is seen to conform less and less to the existing personal situation. Already new forms of association based on neighbourhood or common employment or the practice of the same trade are inclining the immigrants to emerge from their family or tribal isolation and become part of the city. As new forms of social life appear the physical contradictions of New-Bell become manifest. The harking back to the social structure of the past, and the breaking down of that structure by the pressure of a new environment are at the root of the two aspects—rural and urban—of New-Bell. What is required is the building of a new structure to which the traditional way of life can still make a contribution—for example, the conception of a unity based on neighbourhood.

XIV. CHANGES IN THE COMPOSITION AND STATUS OF KIN GROUPS IN NYASALAND AND NORTHERN RHODESIA

D. G. BETTISON[1]

Two studies undertaken by the Rhodes-Livingstone Institute during 1957 and 1958 offer an opportunity for comparative study. Blantyre-Limbe, Nyasaland, is a commercial area growing in the midst of land held under individual and also communal African title. Lusaka, Northern Rhodesia, is a commercial and administrative town growing in the midst of Non-African controlled, individually titled, smallholdings and farms. The present study discusses the effects on traditional villages around Blantyre-Limbe of the presence and growth of the urban area and compares the importance of kinship groups in the respective urban centres.

As these studies were commissioned by Governments or statutory bodies, and were made with the knowledge that results had to be available by specified times, full use was made of survey techniques and mechanical sorting. To some extent they lack the detail that other, but less speedy, techniques would provide. In Blantyre-Limbe, in particular, surveys have been supplemented by more personal and intimate methods.

The areas studied: The 1956 Census revealed there to be in Blantyre-Limbe Municipal area 23,590 males and 790 female Africans in employment. Possibly a third of male African workers reside outside the municipal area in the peri-urban villages and commute to work daily. Similarly, the same census revealed there to be 21,800 male and 300 female Africans in employment in the municipal and suburban areas of Lusaka. There are perhaps 70,000 Africans resident in Lusaka. It will be observed that the size of the two towns is approximately equal in terms of Africans in employment.

---

[1] I would like to acknowledge the help given me by Dr. Raymond Apthorpe, Research Secretary of the R.L.I., in the preparation of this paper.

Both towns have experienced very rapid growth since 1937, but especially since 1950. In Lusaka, for example, the municipal valuation in 1937 was a mere quarter of a million pounds. In 1957 it was over £21 million. In both areas, though to a somewhat different extent, the most pronounced features are the development of the economic resources of the area, the growth of the town backed by a wage economy, the presence of extensive civil engineering enterprises, increasing land values, and the prominence of industrial and commercial interests in local government. Growth is largely the result of non-African initiative.

The indigenous Africans in both areas are organized on a matrilineal, uxorilocal basis (the Yao and Nyanja in Blantyre and the Lenje, Soli, etc., in Lusaka). Both have received as immigrants, during somewhat different times, a considerable number of originally patrilineal and virilocal Ngoni. These have moved from the Central Province of Nyasaland southwards to Blantyre and from the Eastern Province of Northern Rhodesia westwards to Lusaka. Blantyre is somewhat more homogeneous than Lusaka in its tribal composition. The Yao and Ngoni together comprise some 60% of people in Blantyre-Limbe, whereas in Lusaka the Nsenga, Ngoni, and Chewa together comprise only an approximate 42% of the total. Over 60 different tribes were recorded in a 10% random survey of Lusaka.

In Lusaka all significant ethnic and tribal groups must be considered immigrant, with the possible exception of Europeans who have held authority over the land in and adjacent to the town since the time its development became significant. In Blantyre-Limbe this is not so markedly the case. The Nyanja and Yao in particular, but also the Ngoni since the turn of the century, are traditional land-holders over a considerable proportion of the peri-urban area. Even where land around the townships was granted to non-African interests for plantation purposes, only a very small proportion of these estates were developed. It was in the interests of estate owners, who required seasonal labour, to leave relatively unmolested the indigenous inhabitants, or tenants, on their estates. Thus, despite some variety in tenure over the land, the peri-urban area of Blantyre-Limbe was until recently, and in some areas still is, under the occupation of Africans attempting to live in a traditional manner.

This is in marked contrast to the peri-urban area of Lusaka. With the exception of the Lenje reserve, some eight miles from the town, and a selected area of poor quality farming land under individual title, where the owners have but little interest in it, the entire peri-urban area is under intensive smallholding, farming, or industrial propositions. An African resident in this area is a wage-earning farm hand. The settlement of a larger social group than a worker and his family is difficult as it tends to conflict with the interests of non-African developers in the same area. In Blantyre-Limbe the presence of land under traditional African settlement adjacent to the built-up area has enabled social structures of considerable size to remain intact in a village or series of villages in close juxtaposition to the town.

These arrangements affect also the distribution of the immigrant population attracted to the town. In Lusaka these immigrants have to leap-frog over the non-African controlled peri-urban area and seek accommodation within the built-up area of the town. In Blantyre-Limbe they may take up residence in the peri-urban area in addition to the town itself. To some extent this is responsible for the presence in Lusaka of high-density, low-standard, slum or near slum housing estates on land under non-African control and known as 'Unauthorized Compounds'. These compounds house possibly 30,000 to 40,000 persons, or over a third of Lusaka's African population. This phenomenon makes only a limited appearance in Blantyre-Limbe, and takes the form of what might be described as squatter camps on Crown Land. These are much more easily cleared up by the authorities than are the Unauthorized Compounds of Lusaka.[2]

THE PERI-URBAN VILLAGES OF BLANTYRE-LIMBE

The town's labour force is made up of a mixture of local and immigrant males. An approximate third of this force commutes

---

[2] Mr. H. A. Fosbrooke has pointed out to me that Unauthorized Compounds are rare in East African towns generally. On the other hand, they appear to have been, and in some instances still are, a commonplace in many towns and cities to the south of Lusaka.

daily from village to town. Ecologically it tends to be concentrated residentially within easy walking distance—62% reside within four miles of the built-up area. Within this high-density, peripheral zone, villages tend to be large and many of their households are heavily dependent on a wage to supplement village horticulture.

Mitchell's[3] description of the political organization of traditional villages serves as a background against which our findings may be compared. He writes:

> These village settlements are inhabited by groups of kinsmen. In general there is a matrilineal core of kinsmen of whom the village headman, who has the same name as the village, is one. In some more complex villages there are subsidiary matrilineages related to the matrilineal core agnatically through one of other incumbent of the position of village headman. Succession to posts of authority, including that of the chief, is matrilineal. Ideally the succession should pass to the first born son of a man's eldest sister, but this is not always followed, for the personal qualities of the successor are most important.

Our study revealed the presence of four types of village composition:

Type 1: Those conforming to Mitchell's description. In these the founding matrilineage comprised more than 80% of the village population. Villages of this type were found both adjacent to the built-up area and far removed from it. Thus it appears that ecological factors alone cannot account for the changes from traditional structures that the following types comprise.

Type 2: Where members of the founding matrilineage comprise about half of the village population. The remainder consist of unrelated accretion groups varying markedly in size and composition from fairly large-scale matrilineages to a number of primary families. To some extent these variations are accounted for by the length of time an accretion group has been resident in the village. The authority of the headman is acknowledged by his own kin and by the accretion groups, yet accretion groups possess a considerable degree of social and economic autonomy. This type of village is found almost exclusively within a radius of

[3] Mitchell, 1949, p. 141.

eight miles from the town, and should be thought of as an adjustment to the pressures introduced by the urban area.

Type 3 have much in common with Type 2, save that they contain varying proportions of persons paying a monthly rental to some villager or other in return for the right to reside in a hut in that village. Thus a village of Type 3 possesses:

(*a*) a founding matrilineage,
(*b*) groups of varying composition, having taken up residence with the founding matrilineage as accretion villagers,
(*c*) groups, usually primary families, resident in a village as rent-paying tenants.

There is a right, acknowledged by the headman, for a villager to let his house at terms to be decided by the villager. It is the operation of this right which facilitates the entry of rent-paying tenants. The right is applicable to members of the founding matrilineage and accretion groups as individuals. All headmen are emphatic that it is the duty of a villager intending to let his house to introduce the tenant to the headman. Yet, in practice, we found cases where the headman was ignorant of the actual occupants though he knew the person who 'should' be occupying it.

Type 4 villages are still under investigation. In the one village completed to date, accretion groups of varying composition, but mainly primary families, have moved into the land formally under the control of the founding lineage, and have established themselves without the apparent permission of the headman. They are resident on village land by tacit permission. Some such groups now let accommodation to others or 'sell' a vacant hut to any applicant. Many are making money from lodgers, i.e. groups hiring a room as distinct from tenants who hire a house. The phenomenon of tenancy is present in addition to the lack of permission to reside from the headman. It is as if residents by tacit permission assume the right to let houses or even portions of garden land, without regarding the headman as in any way involved. In this type the authority of the headman over portions of his original domain is virtually nil, though he retains authority over his lineage and any accretion groups recognizing his authority. It appears that this type of village is found only in selected areas and generally closely adjacent to the built-up area of the town.

Thus in all types of village the founding matrilineage remains present. In fact, the only circumstances which appear to remove it are the expansion of the town and voluntary removal by government for re-settlement purposes. However, although present, the lineage's functions and those of the headman are attenuated in all save Type 1 villages. Unrelated accretion groups with the status of villagers are viewed by their members and members of the founding lineage as socially distinct. Their allegiance is to themselves in the first instance and then to the village headman. They are also marked off socially from groups resident as tenants in the village or present by tacit permission.

A difference exists between residents with the status of villagers and those who are mere tenants or present by tacit permission. A villager has rights to land and cannot be removed merely at the termination of a lease. He has consolidated his position by winning the acceptance of the headman and his sisters and sisters' sons. A village can remain intact so long as the headman's authority is acknowledged by members of his matrilineage and by the accretion groups. When a villager wishes to let his house he is under an obligation to introduce the prospective tenant to the headman. In turn the headman introduces his sisters and sisters' sons 'so that they may know them and not cause trouble with them'. Tenants rarely give the headman beer and tend to view the contract with their landlord as of adequate substance to ensure their presence in the village.

A tenant anxious to take up permanent residence in the village will attempt to procure his status as a villager through gifts to the headman, by being exemplary in behaviour, and by supporting the headman or matrilineage in his or its disputes. The status of villager is achieved when he is shown land by the headman on which he may build a house free of any obligation to pay a monthly rental or when he purchases the house he is renting and the rights to any gardens that may be agreed to with the landlord.

Such a purchase requires the landlord to decide on the relationship he intends retaining with the headman. On the other hand, a house would not be purchased by the tenant unless he were sure of being accepted as a villager by the headman and his lineage.

At least two administrative provisions support the authority of the headman. The Town and Country Planning Committee has control by licence, within the area of its jurisdiction, over the construction of houses. Thus the uncontrolled building of tenant accommodation is theoretically impossible. Further, an application to reside as a villager must be acceptable not only to the village headman but to the superior Native Authority also. Permission to leave the Native Authority from which he came is required in addition to permission to reside in the new one. Any dispute beyond the competence of the headman to settle is referred to the Native Authority Court with the headman present at the case, or at least his awareness of the trouble indicated by a letter or substitute in person. A headman acknowledges some obligation to a tenant as he is resident within his domain, but his attention to his case and his attitude generally would be casual, and official rather than intimate and sincere. On the other hand, persons resident on village land by tacit permission are ignored entirely by the headman.

The existence of a right to let accommodation provides a means whereby residence in one's village can be avoided for a considerable time without losing rights within it. Formerly, unresolved conflict necessitated fission of the lineage and the exit of one or other group with consequent removal of privileges. Tenancy permits the exit of primary families, who may in fact gain from the rentals paid for their vacated accommodation, and the retention of village rights if not formally abrogated.

In the process of change the features of the traditional system retained most noticeably are the sibling group with the headmanship given to an acceptable male member; uxorilocality of marriage for members of the founding matrilineage and others with the status of villagers; and the wish to build up a large village composed of the founding lineage as a first choice and of acceptable unrelated accretion groups as a second. Tenants and persons resident by tacit permission appear at least to the headman as adjuncts and are viewed with varying degrees of favour or disfavour. The features of the traditional system which appear to be changing are the status of the headman in so far as the village domain is concerned, and the right to reside thereon; the willingness of village segments to break from the lineage has decreased due partly to the possibility offered primary families to let accommodation and move out temporarily; the use of village gardens as an essential attribute of village life as income from wages commonly supplements and occasionally replaces sustenance from village horticulture.

THE URBAN DWELLERS OF BLANTYRE-LIMBE AND LUSAKA

Nowhere in the urban areas of Blantyre-Limbe and Lusaka did we discover groups organized in such a way as to suggest the existence of anything more than a slightly extended primary family occupying premises together or in adjacent premises. Where additions are present they tend to be related to the husband almost twice as frequently as to the wife. In Lusaka, at least, more than 70% of additional persons have been resident for less than six months. We obtained some evidence to suggest that primary families deliberately seek accommodation in those suburbs, particularly the unauthorized compounds, where they may more readily associate with kin. But only to a limited extent have urban families a choice as to where they will reside. The type of job procured by the husband and the availability of accommodation at any given time are largely responsible for the place of residence.

Nonetheless, social relationships can persist without regard to spatial propinquity. Urban kin relationships have inevitably to seek non-spatial methods of expression. These can connect kin resident in the urban area, or connect persons in the town with their kin in the rural or peri-urban areas.

Within the urban context it appears that kin assemble socially to celebrate vital events. Kin give gifts at such events, but so also do friends and neighbours who are not kinsmen. A tendency exists for leisure hours to be spent with kin or tribally common companions, especially with work-mates. There appear to be few permanent economic relationships between kinsmen in urban areas, though temporary borrowings and the formation of associations for the rotational distribution of pay are common. A kinsman already well established in the urban area will assist another to settle in.

In times of domestic tension or economic misfortune, kin are the source of comfort and relief. In Blantyre it was noticeable that a woman during domestic disputes frequently sought the aid of her brother if he resided in or near town; though the wish to return to the village where the security of mothers and sisters could be felt immediately—as distinct from the more protective and conciliatory role of the brother—caused ambivalent feelings.

Differences between Blantyre and Lusaka are most marked in the relationships between persons in town and their kin in the country. This is brought about largely by the relative closeness of kin in Blantyre. In Lusaka, labour is drawn from remote areas. In Blantyre women particularly move to and fro, from village to town, for social and economic purposes. This contact is much less in Lusaka and often takes the form of an annual visit. Women in particular are cut off from kin as visits involve transport costs and women have not taken to or cannot afford bicycles. Kinship ties are most frequently expressed in terms of gifts sent to the country from the town. In Lusaka very little is sent from village to town, but a considerable movement occurs in Blantyre. However, it is thought to be somewhat less than the value of goods sent from town to country.

Under conditions characteristic of Lusaka, women become increasingly dependent on their husband's wage. Sources of income are particularly restricted in municipally controlled suburbs, where a tighter administration makes beer-brewing, etc., difficult. Women in unauthorized compounds often have garden allotments outside them, and have greater freedom to earn from morally doubtful sources. A small amount of trading is undertaken by them. In Blantyre many urban women retain rights to peri-urban village gardens, and make elaborate arrangements for their cultivation if unable to do so personally. Their traditional role of cultivator and supplier of household food is not entirely thwarted, and some manage to earn a cash income from the sale of produce.

Thus African urban residents maintain relationships with kinsmen, but they do not assume, as a general feature, a co-residential pattern. The exchange of gifts and services within the urban context and between town and country is common. To some extent this method of expression is a response to the lack of complete adjustment to urban conditions. Some important phenomena inhibiting this adjustment are, briefly:

(1) wage rates at levels which support a single man but not a two-child primary family at minimum levels of subsistence. Living thus remains largely a struggle for subsistence.
(2) the lack of permanent and negotiable rights to property in many centres. Africans, unlike other races and local governments, are largely denied opportunities to benefit from speculation and increases in land values. The accumulation of capital is made difficult.
(3) the absence of adequate social welfare services which are an inevitable outcome of a total dependence on a wage. Thus an attachment to the land must be retained despite its inefficient character.

The facilities offered an urban resident themselves influence the process of urban adjustment. They are, therefore, an essential to the study of urbanization.

THE DETERMINANTS OF FUTURE TRENDS

We have observed that the presence of growing commercial and industrial centres has affected the composition of many peri-urban villages; that kin relationships of some kind persist in the urban complex but they are increasingly attenuated the further removed the urban dweller becomes from the village in which he was formerly resident. It is now necessary to consider one or two urban phenomena, principally of an economic character, influential in determining the degree to which kin relationships can persist or change.

The continuous growth of an industrial town leads sooner or later to an authority assuming responsibility for town planning, and also for the provision of financial services for the housing of the lower income groups. Non-African influences attempt to conserve land values by a judicious placing of African suburbs.[4] Financial security necessitates the construction of dwellings capable of standing for at least the length of the loan raised to build them. Planning at the rate of six or eight dwelling units per acre with adequate open spaces speedily leads to a considerable enlargement of the built-up area. It also leads to rising standards in the urban home. Thus the distance between urban worker and the peri-urban village increases—in the case of Blantyre-Limbe—thereby straining the retention of face-to-face relationships between kinsmen. The increased cost of rental, the journey to work and the rising standards within the home reduce the available resources for expenditure on absent kin. Thus not only are the facilities offered by a spatial propinquity of kin largely denied, but the expression of relatedness through gift exchange is likely to suffer also. This process is already well advanced in Lusaka where the geographical separation of urban dwellers from rural kin was achieved from the start.

The utilization of savings for productive ends is somewhat more difficult in the Blantyre situation than that of Lusaka—though Blantyre offers a wider range of opportunity for investment through the provision of freehold land and other immovable assets found less frequently in Lusaka. An economic investment in a peri-urban village in Blantyre is hindered by the uxorilocal character of marriage. A son will not invest in his own village if he has to marry out of it. Similarly, an investment in his wife's village suffers from the insecurity of his position in that village. Yet it would be unwise to consider the urban dweller of Lusaka to be in a much more advantageous position. In his case the range of activities tends to be prescribed by administrative regulations, town plans, and subtle means of control. In Blantyre hindrances appear to emanate from kinship ties and marital rules; in Lusaka they tend to be prescribed by Non-African agencies.

[4] See Irving, 1958.

The man anxious to make use of the profitable aspects of modern economic conditions in the Blantyre situation seeks residence in that environment where the disintegration of village organization has proceeded furthest. (The European and Asian environment, while best suited, remains too remote to him.) This is where Type 4 villages occur most frequently, i.e. in the Ndirande area. In this area the independent primary family can claim to itself the right of independent economic action in admitting lodgers and tenants, in starting businesses, and in the economic utilization of its assets. Yet resident also are traditional matrilineages. The area contains two social systems and two sets of values juxtaposed physically and interacting to some degree. In the Lusaka situation such a man is not seriously affected by traditional village organization or even by kin. His problem is essentially to operate successfully within the unfamiliar nexus of non-African devised administrative provisions. He tends to reside in a variety of suburbs throughout the urban area. He is found in unauthorized compounds and in municipal suburbs. In both situations the preconditions he requires are relative freedom of action, whether from kin or legal enactments, and the utilization of a social system providing him with security for his assets and with avenues of productive activity.

To conclude, the circumstances within which African settlement occurs in Lusaka demand that change is abrupt and relatively complete. The intensity of change is great, but the steps through which it is achieved are few. In Blantyre the old methods of kin and village organization persist despite changes occurring within and around them. Change under these circumstances involves many steps to reach a given end, but is persistently required. The differences between Blantyre-Limbe and Lusaka in this connexion do not lie in the traditional African structures undergoing the change, but in the differing circumstances under which it is occurring. These circumstances have been, and still are, determined largely by decisions made in terms of non-African methods of organization, values, and needs. This is an essential for the development of a modern industrial and commercial town.

REFERENCES

Irving, J. 1958. 'Ecology of City Growth in the African Context', in *Proceedings of the 11th Rhodes-Livingstone Conference, January 1958.*

Mitchell, J. C. 1949. 'The Political Organisation of the Yao of Southern Nyasaland', *African Studies*, Vol. VIII, No. 3.

XV. TRADE AND THE ROLE OF WIFE IN A MODERN WEST AFRICAN TOWN

D. McCALL

The division of labour between the sexes in Akan society allotted most of the work on the farm to the woman. A man helped clear the forest with fire and machete but the woman did the planting, weeding, harvesting, and transporting the produce from the fields. The woman also kept the household area clean, did the cooking, and cared for the children. Sometimes she also made pottery or other handicrafts, but farming was her main occupation.

A wife was allocated land from her husband's lineage on which she was required to raise food for the support of the family. She could if she wished farm some land of her own lineage and whatever she raised here she could sell in the market and the profits would be her own and not her husband's. However, the duties on her husband's farm would not leave her very much time for this supplementary work and she would have to get her brother to clear the land for her unless she could hire someone or make use of a slave.

The husband controlled the dispensing of food from the supplies his wife or wives had harvested and stored. It was he who decided what would be used to feed the family and what would be used to entertain friends which was a necessary expense for a politically ambitious man. Thus, at this period a husband controlled the product of a wife's labour.

Markets were held every fourth day and on market day a woman could leave her farm work and sell whatever foodstuffs she had as a surplus. If it came from her husband's land, the income should be spent to procure some item in short supply for the family larder, and this amounted to little more than an exchange of one agricultural product for another. If it had been raised on her own land, however, it was pure profit and she had to account to no one for it. Clay pots she had made or chickens which she had fattened on termites that she had collected could also increase her personal saving. Strings of cowrie shells and weighted amounts of gold dust used as media of exchange made possible the accumulation of savings; or she could buy cloth or trinkets or use it as she pleased.

Women's trading in the market was restricted to foodstuffs and a few handicraft products. The more valuable commodities were handled by men. Gold, slaves, kola nuts, monkey fur, ivory, and cloth were the prerogative of the men traders. Thus the profits which men made through trade normally exceeded those made by women traders.

Both husband and wife contributed money or services or goods for the support of the family, but in addition each kept a private account and income was not put into a family pool. The maintenance of separate accounts by husband and wife reflected the tenuousness of the marriage tie in Akan society. The elementary family was split by the cleavage of lineage. The wife and children were of one lineage, this being a matrilineal society, and the husband of another. The lineage tie was stronger than the marriage tie. A man expected to confide in his sister or his mother rather than his wife, who was an outsider, and might eventually leave him. A wife likewise expected to confide in her brother rather than her husband. In the event of a divorce, a wife had to return to her husband all gifts which he may have given her during the marriage. Wives sometimes for this reason refused to accept gifts from their husbands.

As long as the marriage continued, however, the husband–wife relationship was one of superordination–subordination. The husband was dominant and not only controlled the product of his wife's labour as noted above but expected to have maintained a supervision of his wife's behaviour. That is, if he had paid all three parts of the brideprice, the women of the bride's lineage, particularly her mother, should see that she was not unfaithful, and if necessary the men of her lineage, particularly her brothers, should exhort her to mend her ways. Fidelity, however, was not incumbent upon the husband.

Thus in the period of the Ashanti Kingdom, a woman was

primarily a farmer but had some experience in trading and was accustomed to the idea of taking charge of her own property; and she was under the dominance of her husband economically and sexually, her lineage being prepared to support the husband's rights.

At the present time, although rural women are still farmers, the women in the towns of Ghana are essentially traders and make only a token effort to fulfil their traditional duty of working on their husband's farms. Trade has become a predominantly feminine calling and women handle not only foodstuffs and handicrafts but also the expensive items of trade which are now usually imported goods.

This change is only one of many changes that have occurred in the society and it is of course related to many of these other changes. The growth of towns is of pre-eminent importance. One quickly perceives here that the size of the market and the number of women traders is a function of the size of the town. In the town are 'stranger' women who have no access to local land; the town may be so large that it has grown out over the land of some of the lineages, or it may be too far to walk from some parts of the town to the farms. The town at the same time has a need for a system of distribution of goods which the women can operate.

In the towns, a new kind of economy exists today. This is the exchange economy which has intruded into this area and linked it with a network of world trade. In the countryside, a subsistence economy persists. Food-farming is little affected but trade has been revolutionized. The trade that existed in the days of the Ashanti Kingdom is what Polanyi[1] calls 'administered trade'. This was a trade largely of luxury goods which was regulated by the political authority. Men had to have permission of the Asantehene or of one of his authorized representatives before he could engage in trade. He had to trade with the Asantehene whose goldweights were considerably heavier than those used by commoners and so no trader could ever become richer than the king. At the present time there is no need to obtain permission to trade and of course the chiefs cannot impose their unequal system of trading any more.

[1] *Trade and Markets in the Early Empires.*

In the description of markets in the accounts of early visitors to the area there is scarcely a mention of the presence of women: now women traders are ubiquitous and could not be missed. Of course, the earlier visitors did not interest themselves in the food market and foods for family consumption which the women sold at that time. Now that the women sell all types of goods, the change is a remarkable one.

Several factors contributed to the decline of masculine participation in trade. Some of the commodities formerly handled by men are no longer available. Gold is now mined by European companies which control the movements of this commodity. Slavery has been abolished and so this commodity no longer exists. The type of monkeys whose fur was exported in such quantities at the end of the nineteenth century is now virtually extinct and so are the elephants that furnished the ivory. And the social conditions of trade are different. The Asantehene and his entourage were exiled and for nearly a generation his position in the society was vacant. And the authority of the remaining chiefs was less extensive than it had been. The system in which the Asantehene or a lesser chief distributed, at the time of the *Adae* ceremony, quantities of gold dust to subordinates to be used in trade and later accounted for to the lender, now fell into disuse. The use of slaves as porters to carry back into the interior the European goods obtained in exchange was now forbidden, and the men could not afford to pay free porters if they were to make a profit.[2]

There seems actually to have been a decline in trade in the inland area for a while. Gradually this revived as the railway and then motor highways penetrated the interior and brought in the goods formerly head-loaded in by slaves. Meanwhile the attention of men was diverted to other occupational opportunities presented by the presence of the Europeans. Men have been able to avail themselves of these new jobs to a far larger extent than women because boys earlier got a start in education, and schooling is indispensable for a clerk, storekeeper in a European firm, or for a lawyer or medical doctor. These positions had begun to acquire

[2] Cf. Caseley Hayford, 1903, p. 97.

the prestige that formerly went to military and commercial success. Some men continued to trade but they were no longer as significant as they had been and as the mechanized transportation system was extended men who remained in trade were inadequate to the need for the distribution of goods. Women traders, who had continued to trade in their traditional type of goods, added new items to their inventory and expanded their trade to fill the vacuum left by the neglect of trade by men. As far back as the turn of the century, some women were receiving credit from European firms for items like tobacco, canned fish and cloth, and many other women were trading in imported goods but the credit was held by their husbands.[3]

The women no doubt benefited from their experience in trade on a smaller scale; they knew the process of exchange, and were familiar with a medium of exchange. Some of the coins in use are now called by terms which formerly referred to units of exchange in the Akan system, e.g. *taku* for sixpence. But the women from the coast also moved inland with the opportunities for trade and the Ashanti women were initiated into the peculiarities of this kind of trade by the Ga and Fanti women who had come in contact with it earlier on the surf ports along the coast.

Peter Bauer has written[4] that the present system of distribution is efficient. Perhaps this is true in the economist's sense even if it is socially wasteful of energy and labour-time. But, however one views it, the fact is that the majority of women in the towns engage in trade and for the most part do so as a full-time occupation—to the exclusion of farming.

The scale on which a woman trades varies greatly and depends upon the amount of money or credit that she has available, for this determines the kind and amount of goods she can stock. Credit can be obtained from overseas firms if a woman is known to be a good trader. She is given a passbook which states the amount of her credit. Some women have credit of thousands of pounds sterling. These bigger traders are middlemen, or middlewomen if you prefer, who sell to smaller traders. Mothers give their

---

[3] Personal communication from Ione Crabtree Acquah, 1954
[4] *West African Trade.*

daughters money to get started in trading. A husband may give his wife a small weekly stipend which she uses to trade and thus to support herself, or he may give her a sum of £50 to £100 at the time of their marriage and she is expected to support herself from that through trading for the rest of her life. Some of these women who have small amounts handle the inexpensive food products traditionally sold by women; those who can, buy and sell imported goods where the profit is greater.

Whatever the scale of their trading, whether the profits be enormous or trifling, town women are under a compulsion to trade. There is an expectation that women will support themselves even after marriage and that they will contribute to the support of the children. In the old days and even today in the rural areas, a woman can do this by farming. In the towns, farming is not always possible for a woman who may be a 'stranger' and therefore not entitled to local land, or if she is a member of a local lineage or married into one, the town may have expanded until buildings have been erected on the fields formerly used for farming, or the distance from the urban dwelling to available farmland may be too great to make regular trips feasible. Furthermore, it is quite apparent that women if they have a choice between farming and trading will choose the latter.

Trading is relatively pleasant in comparison with farming. Although market women work hard, there is also a social atmosphere to the market. It is their club as well as their place of business. Women plait each other's hair while waiting for customers to buy their goods; they gossip or nurse their small children or otherwise occupy themselves. The market has become virtually a woman's world. The few men who are still in trade tend to have stores which on a smaller scale are like European stores. However, some men sell in the market; and hardware, meat, and imported drugs are usually handled by men. Some women also have stores and there is a certain prestige attached to such elegance. Many women rent stalls in the market by the month, paying two shillings to the N.A., and others pay a smaller fee for the day and take their places in the lanes between the lines of stalls. Women also install themselves at a crossroads or along the side of a busy street. They may set up a little table to display their goods, or perhaps build a small fire on a sheet of metal and fry plantains to sell to passers-by. Other women walk along the byways with head-trays carrying lotions, perfumes, head-ties, and such things.

Educated women sometimes have an opportunity for other types of employment, as teachers or telephone operators, and a small number of women are completely supported by their husbands who prefer that they do not trade, but the greatest number of women are engaged in trade.

In Koforidua in 1952, I counted in the market nearly 3,000 sellers on a market day. This did not include the numbers of women selling at the various crossroads and in the streets. Since the population of the town is somewhere between 25,000 to 30,000 that means that about 10% of the total population or perhaps 40% of the adult female population was engaged in selling in the market and an additional undetermined percentage engaged in selling outside the market at a given time. One could estimate from this that not less than 70% of the adult female population was engaged in selling.

In the following tables is presented some information obtained from interviewing a sample of 78 women in this market.

Of the 78 women, slightly more than half were local women:

    41 local women
    35 strangers
    2 no information on origin

Of the stranger women, at least 6 ethnic categories were present:

    8 Akan women from other Oman
    11 Ga-Adangme women
    8 Ewe women
    3 Yoruba women
    1 Hausa woman
    1 woman from the Northern Territories
    3 of doubtful identification

Of the 78 women, 68 had been married:

    59 were currently married
    7 were widows
    2 were deserted
    10 were unmarried

so that 19 were currently without husbands, and several more had husbands who lived in other towns so that an even larger number were living as 'single' women.

Of the 41 local women,

> 29 were married
> 3 were widows
> 1 was deserted
> 8 were unmarried

Of the 35 stranger women,

> 28 were married
> 4 were widows
> 1 was deserted
> 2 were unmarried

And of the 2 women for whom we have no information as to origin, both were married.

Of 68 women who are or have been married,

> 28 had monogamous husbands
> 40 had polygamous husbands

Of the 29 local women, currently married,

> 16 had monogamous husbands
> 13 had polygamous husbands

Of the 28 stranger women, currently married,

> 9 had monogamous husbands
> 19 had polygamous husbands

Of the 7 widows,

> 2 had had monogamous husbands
> 5 had had polygamous husbands

Of the 2 women with no information on origin,

> 1 had a monogamous husband
> 1 had a polygamous husband

And both of the deserted women had polygamous husbands.

There is a somewhat higher proportion of polygamy in the stranger group than in the local group, which may indicate that it is easier for a woman to go away to trade if she leaves co-wives at home to care for the husband.

The occupations of the husbands of the 68 women who are or had been married run almost the entire gamut of vocations in the society, only the professional men being conspicuously absent.

> 18 worked for the Government
> 11 were artisans
> 15 were in commercial or clerical positions
> 16 were farmers
> 4 were Native Authority
> 4 were drivers

The 78 women were supporting or helping to support 224 *dependent* children:

> 29 married local women had 111 dependent children
> 28 married stranger women had 80 dependent children
> 7 widows had 7 dependent children
> 2 deserted women had 11 dependent children
> 10 unmarried women had 12 dependent children
> 2 no information women had 3 dependent children

The local married women had considerably more dependent children than the stranger married women; this may be because more of them were living with their husbands. The 7 widows were supporting an average of 1 child each, but 3 had no dependent children and 4 had the total number for this category. The deserted women have a high proportion of dependent children, but whether or not this is a factor in their desertion I do not know. Of the 10 unmarried girls, half had children, 2 had 1 and 2 had 2 each; in both of the latter cases the 2 children were by different fathers; one had 6 (3 each by 2 different fathers); none of the unmarried mothers received any support for the infants from the fathers of their children.

Four husbands (2 of local women and 2 of stranger women) gave nothing to the support of their children by the women in this sample; one had 5 children; one, 4; one, 3; one, 1. Six women wouldn't say how much their husbands gave them.

None of the unmarried mothers got any money from the fathers of their children, but one got 1s. each from both her mother and father; one of the widows received something regularly from a son, and another widow received something occasionally from her children. Neither of the deserted women received anything from anyone.

> 25 women received less than 2s. per day
> 26 women received from 2s. to 4s. per day
> 13 women received 5s. or more per day
> 1 woman received 2s. per month
> 6 women wouldn't say how much they received, if anything

But some received certain sums daily, one received it weekly, and 8 received them monthly:

0	1	2	3	4	5	6	7	8	shillings per day
16	3	8	9	9	3	8	0	1	no. of women

1 woman received 10s. weekly; and of the women who received money monthly:

> 5 received £1 per month
> 1 received £2 to £3 per month
> 1 received £5 per month
> 1 received £4 10s. per month
> 1 received 2s. per month

The woman receiving 8s. per day is the wife of a chief and receives that only when cooking for him; other days she receives 6s. to cook for the children. Responses indicate that the husbands are not consistently reliable; several women added the word 'sometimes' after giving their reply. In polygamous marriages, this may be related to the days on which they cook for the husband (as in the case of the chief above), but in any case allowance must be made for what is spent on the husband's meal from these amounts. There seems to be no correlation between the amount and the number of children or between polygynous or monogamous marriage.

One woman would not say how many hours daily she spent in the market; of the 77 others the responses ranged from 6 to 11 hours daily.

6	6½	7	7½	8	8½	9	9½	10	10½	11	12	hrs. per day
3	3	16	7	11	8	10	3	5	2	7	2	no. of women

52 out of the 77 spent from 7 to 9 hours; only 6 spent less than this and none less than 6 hours; 19 spent more than 9 hours, but none more than 12 (one woman who spent 11 hours weekdays

stayed for 12 hours on Sundays). Two of those who spent only 6 hours sold food ready to eat and spent time at home preparing it.

Of the 78 women, 70 spent 5 or more days a week in the market:

>9 women spent 7 days a week in the market
>56 women spent 6 days a week in the market (Mon. through Fri.)
>5 women spent 5 days a week in the market
>3 women spent 4 days a week in the market
>1 woman spent 2 to 4 days a week in the market
>1 woman spent 3 (Tues., Thurs., and Sat.)
>1 woman spent 2 (Mon. and Thurs.)
>1 woman in this market for the first time (stranger)

Thus it can be seen that trading is a full-time occupation for these women and that there is little time for farming, yet of the 41 local women 37 maintain some kind of a connexion with a farm: 26 of the 29 married local women, all but 1 of the 8 unmarried local women, and all 3 of the local widows and the 1 deserted local woman claim to have a farm. But of the 32 strangers, only 3 have a farm; one is a widow who lives in Accra where she has her farm and comes for the day with a load of fish; two others were married women who go to their farms in Kwahu about once a month. The farm work is just a token; of the 26 married local women who farmed nearly all were vague as to how often they visited their fields:

>6 were so irregular they couldn't say how often
>5 went once a month (on Saturdays)
>5 went some Saturdays
>2 went most Saturdays
>1 went every few weeks
>1 went every 2–3 weeks
>4 went every Saturday
>1 went Wednesdays and Saturdays
>1 went Tues., Wed., Fri., and Sat.

The last woman is more of a farmer than a trader since she spends only two days in the market, Mondays and Thursdays.

Though many of the women make trips to buy things to sell in this market, only a few of them go to other markets to sell.

Of 29 married local women,

>25 don't sell in any other market
>4 sometimes go to sell elsewhere

Of 28 married stranger women,

> 25 don't sell in any other market
> 3 sometimes sell elsewhere

Of the 4 stranger widows,

> 3 don't sell in any other market
> 1 lives in the other town, came here for first time

Of the 3 local widows none sells elsewhere and none of the unmarried or deserted women go elsewhere to sell. The local women who sell elsewhere seem to have a different pattern from the stranger women; the local women go to the smaller surrounding towns on market days; the stranger women all go to the big food market where many of the others go to buy to bring back and sell in the town. Items taken for sale elsewhere are usually light in weight except for fish. Some go elsewhere 'in the cocoa season,' once a month, when they 'feel like it', sometimes, and two go every Friday.

These responses show that for this sample of women there has been a practically complete change in the means of obtaining a livelihood; they are essentially full-time traders. Farming, when done at all, is only a token to traditional expectations and even this affects only the local women.

The information shows furthermore that the women support themselves, that they sometimes entirely support their children and always are contributors to that support, that they receive relatively little from their husbands and that what they do receive is partly for the husband's meals and the remainder for the children's, and that typically they do not give any money to their husbands.

Trading has been substituted for farming and inasmuch as the women continue to support themselves the difference in the means by which they accomplish this may not be important, but whereas while they were farmers their husbands controlled the product of their labour, now that they are traders he does not do so.

Men typically do not know the conditions of the market, the seasonal fluctuation of goods and prices and could not tamper with the woman's profits without endangering her future capacity to trade advantageously. It is the type of economic activity rather than the value of the product which has enabled the women to escape the supervision of husbands in this respect.

The economic independence and particularly trading have often been seen as related to a sexual independence on the part of the women-traders.[5] The farm activities of the women were done in the old days in company with other women to each of whom the wife had a definite relationship either through her own lineage or through her husband's. All of these to a greater or lesser extent would protect the interests of the husband which had been paid for in the brideprice. In the small markets of that time, she would find the same women there to watch her.

The scale of the markets and the towns that they serve have so expanded that the trader is often a stranger to her neighbour who has no interest in her husband's welfare. The trader can pick her friends in the market by personal preference and is not restricted to relatives and affines. Those women who carry their goods through the streets to sell can be least supervised.

The lineage is now less effective in guaranteeing the interests of the husband to the extent expected before 1900. The members of the lineage are more scattered and less able to assert their controlling influence. In any event, the woman is inclined to be less ready to accept such direction from her lineage. She will not want to alienate her kinsmen but she is in a better position to temporize and procrastinate until the husband is tired of pressing the matter on the lineage head.

This freedom is one of the contributing factors to the prominence of a form of extra-marital affair known locally as 'jollying'.

The rise of towns, and the role which women play in the trade of these towns, has modified the role of the wife in that it has diminished the dominance of the husband both in regard to his ability to control his wife economically and sexually.

[5] Cf. Nadel, 1942, pp. 168, 334; and Little, 1948.

REFERENCES

Bauer, Peter	1954.	*West African Trade*. Cambridge: University Press.
Hayford, Caseley	1903.	*Gold Coast Native Institutions*. London: Sweet & Maxwell.
Little, K. L.	1948.	'The Changing Position of Women in the Sierra Leone Protectorate'. *Africa*, Vol. XVIII, No. 1.
Nadel, S. F.	1942.	*A Black Byzantium*. London: Oxford University Press for International African Institute.
Polanyi, M.	1957.	*Trade and Markets in the Early Empires*. Glencoe (Ill.): Free Press.

XVI. SECOND GENERATION MIGRANTS IN GHANA AND THE IVORY COAST[1]

JEAN ROUCH

Migrants come from West African savannah territories: Upper Volta, Sudan, Niger, northern Ivory Coast, Ghana, Togo, Dahomey, and Nigeria. They leave their homelands to go to the coastal area of the Gulf of Guinea, mainly the forest zone of the Ivory Coast and Ghana. Most are young men temporarily engaged in various occupations and trying to return to their own territories every year. The movement is encouraged by the fact that the season for the cocoa crop corresponds to the dry season in the northern territories. The young men are therefore able to go south between October and March to work on the cocoa farms when they would otherwise be unoccupied at home, and in the cocoa off-season they can return north for the rains when farm work is heaviest. A certain number of wealthy migrants settle temporarily in the south, but even after years without going back they preserve very close links with their original group. On a rough estimation there are from 2,000 to 3,000 migrants in Ghana and 150,000 to 300,000 in Ivory Coast during the season.

From the historical point of view these movements to the coast are the answer to a very old wish of the Sudanese empires to reach the sea. The landing of Europeans about the sixteenth century on the West African coast reversed the direction of the great trade routes. Empires, which until then had their main commercial links with Europe and the Near East across the Sahara, started trading with the south. Important exchange markets developed on the edge of the forest at Kong, Bondouke, Kintampa, Salaza, Zugu, and later Kumasi. Cattle and slaves were exchanged for clothes and European goods. The famous nineteenth-century raiders, the Sudanese Samori and the Nigerian

[1] Part of the general survey of migrations being conducted as a joint C.C.T.A./C.S.A. project in Ghana and Ivory Coast with financial support from the governments of Ghana, Ivory Coast, Togo, Dahomey, Upper Volta, Niger, and France.

Second Generation Migrants in Ghana and the Ivory Coast 301

Babaku, trying to extend their influence further southward, attracted a lot of young and determined men to the middle part of the Ghana and Ivory Coasts. After the establishment of European settlements the military movement changed into migration in search of a job and the adventures of the long journey to the south became substitutes for the old military saga. From the middle of last century it has become accepted in the savannah that to be a real man you have to have been to the Coast at least once.

From the ethnic point of view the migrations involve mainly Upper Volta tribes. In rural parts of Ghana and Ivory Coast the Moshi are the most important group. They are mainly employed in manual work and play an important part in local farming. The Sudanese in the Ivory Coast started as labourers on European plantations, buying their own land after about five years. They are now traders and farmers, whereas the Nigerian migrants are exclusively traders, mainly dealing in cloth both in urban and rural areas.

These migrations have a considerable influence on the economy of both countries of origin and destination. In Ghana it seems that 60% of the labourers are from the northern territories of Ghana and Upper Volta. In the Ivory Coast 90% of plantation labourers are from Upper Volta. The territories of origin receive a very important contribution to their revenue. In the western districts of the Niger territories 80% of income tax is paid out of money sent back from Ghana and Ivory Coast by the migrants. Obviously there are also political implications.

The majority of migrants are single, either in the sense of being unmarried or of having left their wives and children in rural areas. Very few women migrate from the north, although by contrast coastal migrations appear to attract more women than men, as in the case of Yoruba and Calabar. The result is that many relationships spring up between northern men and coastal women. The unskilled and the poor most frequently cohabit with professional prostitutes whose fees are low and uniform. Amongst returning migrants and those with more stable incomes longer-term relationships are established with indigenous women. A young Gao man employed by an Ashanti mammy may become her boy friend after a time. Or a young Divule from Treichville may ask a Baoule mammy to lend him her daughter during his stay.

Finally, amongst the more settled migrants, marriages with women found in the city are relatively frequent. There are many cases of migrants with wives and children in both northern and coastal areas. In fact, the migrant does not try to marry a woman of his own or a neighbouring group. Northern migrants seem to favour certain indigenous groups of women. That is why in the whole Ivory Coast Baoule women enjoy a particularly high reputation and become the preferred wives of migrants. Children born from such unions find themselves divided between the two kin groups.

If the woman comes from a matrilineal and the man from a patrilineal society their child belongs by custom to both groups. The conflict emerges at marriage according to the customs then followed. Young migrants tend to adopt the customs of the coast, because they are more flexible than those of the north. Verbal agreement followed by the making of a small gift is sufficient to give a union legal sanction, but it is regarded as a state of concubinage or temporary cohabitation rather than marriage, and is damaging to the prestige of the older migrants with more secure incomes. They therefore attempt to marry women according to their own Islamic customs, which include dowry payment and expensive ceremonies. Acceptance of Islam by the wife is also necessary. However, women know that acceptance of Islamic marriage involves the loss of all claim to the children by them in case of separation, so they frequently hesitate to marry or insist on very high dowries.

Even among settled migrants such inter-tribal marriages do not usually last long. The more frequent causes of separation are the husband's return to his country, or the constant interference of the wife's family in domestic affairs. Whatever the system of marriage followed, both parents attempt from the start to take the children. In the case of most migrants interviewed in Ghana and the Ivory Coast, it was apparent that they wished to send their children to their own villages as soon as they were weaned, on the pretext that coastal conditions are not good for children. This is a precaution by the father, more or less frustrated, to prevent his wife from taking their children. In the father's village the child will be brought up as a member of the patrilineage. He will be initiated and eventually receive the tribal markings. Should he return to the coast he will always be a member of his patrilineage.

With the slightest excuse, such as illness, mothers try to send their children to their own family. When migration first started, husbands allowed themselves to be caught out in this way and there were many complaints from them about lost children. The most striking example of this kind is to be found among the Kotokoli women of Middle Togoland, who come to South Ghana for the express purpose of prostitution in order to have children and, of course, the money. Most of them are married women, but nevertheless many marry young northern migrants, who are considered to be the most handsome men. As soon as the children are of an age at which they may travel, they run away with them. If the father pursues them he often arrives only to find his children with Kotokoli tribal markings, belonging to the family of their Kotokoli mother.

Most frequently the children who are torn between their parents in this way settle on the coast, casually brought up by the mother and educated by the father at minimum expense. They are called *dankasa* meaning 'born in foreign lands'. In both Ghana and the Ivory Coast they form a distinct mixed group held apart by both the indigenous coastal people and the migrants. Belonging to neither the maternal nor the paternal group they have no tradition and attempt to create customs of their own. This marginal category is considered by all informants to be unintelligent, unambitious, and lazy. Migrants attempt to eliminate them and coast people discourage their scholarly pursuits.

Those who have reached adulthood form a sort of intermediary class concerning itself with petty trading and semi-skilled occupations, bad taxi-drivers, non-specialized fitters, semi-literate clerks, and shop assistants.

Rejected by all, they have formed themselves into separate groups, finding compensation in creating voluntary societies where loneliness, despair, and dreams are shared. This has led to the creation of *goumbe* societies in the Ivory Coast. Initially similar to the many mutual societies found on the coast, the *goumbes* rapidly become young people's dance societies. There are membership fees and general meetings which elect numerous office-bearers; they meet every Sunday to dance and to elect the best couple. But the *goumbes* go even further; more recently they have replaced the maternal and paternal kin groups. Young *goumbe* boys and girls intermarry by preference and the marriage ritual has little similarity with the parents' customs. For example, one frequently finds free unions preceding marriage; and the traditional dowry has been replaced by a 'domestic grant' ('subvention du ménage') given by the *goumbe* to enable the couple to buy necessities such as furniture, kitchen equipment, etc. This suggests the development of a new type of community; a community of the rejected, but of people who have withstood contempt and are creating a new way of life.

XVII. FAMILY LIFE AMONG THE YORUBA, IN LAGOS, NIGERIA

ALISON IZZETT

Lagos is the political and commercial capital of the Federation of Nigeria and according to the last census in 1952, had a population of 267,407 (143,280 males and 124,127 females), of which the Yoruba numbered 195,974 and the Ibo 31,887.

Among the Yoruba in Lagos, there is a great variety of family pattern as can be seen in considering the composition of different households. The traditional Yoruba household contains a large patrilineal and patrilocal extended family. The head of the family is usually the most senior male member, but in families where particular emphasis is laid upon the position of the first-born, the head of the family may be a first-born woman. The men are normally polygamous, each wife having a separate room. The husband provides capital with which the wives trade, and with the profits, they feed themselves and their children, and take it in turn to feed the husband. The wives have a share of the farm products for food and the husband may trap and hunt and thus provide meat. The affairs of the household are run by the family meeting, usually held monthly, of which usually only men of the most senior generation of the lineage are members.

Family households adhering closely to these traditional ways still exist in Lagos. In some cases, a lineage or segment of one still has a common residence, and individual members strongly assert their rights to accommodation, rights which under crowded urban conditions with consequent high rents entail considerable financial advantages. In most cases, however, the members of the extended family cannot all be accommodated in the family house, or may prefer to live separately, but may continue to acknowledge the authority of the head of the lineage and accept the traditional duties of membership.[1]

[1] See Schwab, 1955, pp. 353 ff. for rights and duties of membership.

Nowadays young couples tend to live away from their families, both the husband and wife finding the authority exercised by the senior members as irksome, and regarding the interest shown in all the intimate details of their married life as interference. Young wives are no longer willing to take so subservient a part in the family life as custom allots to them and resent having to shop for the older women, fetch water, carry out the more tedious culinary work, such as grinding pepper, and be at their beck and call to run errands at any time.

Thus the younger married couples form a separate, usually monogamous, household, together with their children, and in most cases, including one or more dependent siblings or young relatives of either the husband or wife. Such junior relatives often act as house-servants, although the majority will be sent to school or to literacy classes.

Married couples in such households are, however, members of their own 'family meetings' and if senior enough must attend regularly. Among families consisting of many educated people, living in separate houses, the tendency is to lower the age limit, and to allow all male adults to attend. On the other hand, where the component elementary families have become more individualized, the wider family meetings does not regularly concern itself with the affairs of individuals but is largely a social gathering, where the members of all the generations can get to know each other better.

Yoruba women are very keen traders, and many are well-to-do. Such women may be heads of their own households, their husbands often living with them in an inferior position. Such a home may be shared with other female relatives, and the wealthy woman may have been sent the children of her less well-to-do relatives to bring up, while her own children may be in the homes of better educated relatives.

Prosperous women may live with male relatives in patrilineal households, but nevertheless obtain a very powerful position. In such homes, the daughters may marry or have sexual relationships with men for whom they bear children, but they do not leave their mothers' homes and remain very much under their control.

Such mothers may make and break the daughters' marriages to suit their own wishes. They often prefer their daughters to have temporary liaisons with well-to-do men, rather than marry men of lower social status. They wish to be able to boast that they are connected with such and such wealthy or socially respected families, who will be represented at their family functions and ceremonies.

Other households centre around women, whose 'husbands' may be married under the Marriage Ordinance, which implies monogamy, to other women. These are known as 'outside wives' and have a definite status as such, but the dignity of the legal wife is maintained in that she does not admit them to her home. Other women have fleeting unions with men whose homes they never enter. The men visit them in their rooms and pay their rents. But the recognized wives of polygamous unions may also live separately, if the home of the husband is too small to contain all the wives together. Wives of some men may also be left, in Lagos, to fend for themselves and their children, when their husbands are sent on transfer to other parts of Nigeria. This may also occur when a man who is older than his wife retires and returns to a rural area.

Some households consist of men without wives, but with their own children, some of whom may be married. Such men may have no wives, this usually being an indication of poverty, or their wives may be in their parental homes, during the one- or two-year period of breast-feeding a child. During his wife's absence, such a man frequently has a temporary liaison with a woman, but she continues to reside in her home. In such unions, difficulties arise in that the man sees the union as primarily for the purpose of sexual relationship, and definitely not for procreation, while the women regard the men as husbands and primarily desire to become pregnant. So when children are born, the men attempt to evade paternal responsibility, while the women do not understand their motives, and bring the children to the notice of the men's relatives, seeking assistance and acceptance.

It is rare for a single woman to live on her own, for she would then lay herself open to charges of being a loose woman who will not submit to any control. There are, however, many young men living alone or sharing with other single men, each of whom usually has a young brother, sister, niece, or nephew living with him, who is sent to school, and in return does the cooking and housework. The emphasis that Yoruba culture lays upon seniority gives these young men the right to demand implicit obedience and to exercise full parental control.

The variety of households found in Lagos thus expresses the variety of unions which characterize urban life. Couples may be married under the Marriage Ordinance in a Registry Office. Such a marriage, as in English law, entails monogamy. It carries with it some social prestige and for women a certain security, in that it is felt that wives so married cannot be quite so summarily or easily dismissed as can wives married under native law. With men, and with their parents, marriage under the Ordinance is less popular. They complain that women so married are insubordinate and headstrong, and parents dislike the rights of inheritance that it gives to the wife and which deprive the family of rights they have under native law.

Marriage by native Yoruba custom is still deemed important by first generation residents of Lagos, as well as those who have come as adults to work in the city. The latter normally return to their native towns for the necessary ceremonies. The essential aspect of marriage by customary law is that it unites two families and gifts are given to cement the new union. The amount of money paid at marriage varies with the different localities; Egba pay £5, Ijebu pay £12 10s., and Awori people pay £10. But the actual money is not the main part of the marriage gifts. In some families, and especially in chiefs' households, no money may be paid, and there is a growing tendency among educated parents either to refuse all money payments, saying their daughter is not for sale, or to give the money to the bride for her own personal use.

The gifts sent with the money are regarded as more important than the money. These vary from family to family but include 40 bitter cola and 40 cola nuts, 10 guinea-pepper, 1 bottle of gin, 1 bottle of each type of mineral water (this replaces home-made wines), or various wines. Christians also include a Bible, an engagement ring and a purse, containing two guineas, which goes to the bride. The bridegroom is also expected to give the bride a gift of £10 to £30, according to his financial position. At the wedding, the groom is expected to give 10s. 6d. to be divided between the children of the house, and approximately one guinea for the women married to men of the family.

The actual bridewealth is normally divided into two, half going to the bride's mother's family, and half going to the bride's father's family. The distribution is not fixed, but it is customary for parents and all half or full siblings of the bride's parents to accept some of the money. Other close elderly relatives may also accept a portion, but it is not usual for any relative of the bride's generation to receive anything. It is equally important—if not more so—that these relatives should share in the cola or pepper and the drinks, and these may be kept for two or three years in the bride's parental home, if elderly relatives are away and prevented from taking their share earlier. If an individual is not in agreement with the marriage, he refuses to accept his share. Acceptance indicates approval of the marriage and a willingness to render assistance if the bride's husband dies or turns out to be unreliable, the assistance being given to the bride and her children. Nowadays, relatives are less willing to fulfil these obligations.

Whether or not bridewealth is paid or the ceremonial gifts provided, the man who marries or cohabits with a woman has full custodial rights over their children, even when another man has paid bridewealth which has not been refunded. Marriage entitles the husband to exclusive sexual rights over the wife, while still alive, but if he does not exercise these rights, the wife's cohabitation with another man for the purpose of child-bearing would be largely condoned. Custom decrees that a husband should not cohabit with his wife for the two years or more that she is breast-feeding a child. Husbands do however give consent for their wives to take up paid employment in a different town from wherein they reside, and the couple will then each have a young relative or ward to carry out the domestic duties, the children of the couple being placed with relatives or in boarding schools. The Yoruba lay emphasis on marriage being first and foremost for procreation, and as long as children are born regularly, many couples appear content to reside apart.

A wedding ceremony in a Christian Mission church carries the condition of marriage under the Marriage Ordinance. Couples who do not desire this, or do not qualify, can however come to the church for a blessing. Church weddings are notoriously lavish and both families incur a heavy expenditure. These weddings are not popular with young, ambitious people, who desire to use their money for a more lasting purpose. Church marriage does, however, afford considerable social prestige, which one or other of the families concerned may greatly value. Muslims may marry by Muslim rites and certificates are provided. The ceremony often takes place in the home, but where a display is desired, a hall is hired for the purpose. As with marriages under the Ordinance, traditional Yoruba ceremonies are also observed.

Among some Yoruba in Lagos, the ceremonies and expenditure attendant on traditional marriages are no longer being observed, but the formal expression of family consent is usually retained. The heads of both families or the parents of both spouses consent to the proposed union and give the couple the blessing of their families. The first signifies the couple's right to call upon the family when in matrimonial or personal trouble, while the blessing is thought to ensure the well-being of the couple.

Other more casual and temporary marriages are described as being by mutual consent. This means that the couple have decided to live together as man and wife, but that although they may be introduced to each other's families, there is no formal acceptance by the latter. Such unions are frequently not the first marriage of either party, and indicate that the parties have become divorced to some extent from their family responsibilities and liabilities and are being left to fend for themselves. In such unions, both the man and woman will regard themselves as husband and wife, using the same Yoruba words as are used for those entering into more permanent relationships, and the woman is expected to remain faithful to the husband of the moment.

The Yoruba stress on marriage being primarily for the procreation of children means that a girl becomes a wife in order to

Family Life among the Yoruba, in Lagos, Nigeria

become a mother, and she sees herself essentially as a future mother. The preliminary step of first becoming a wife is now tending to be transposed, and the illiterate girl aims first at becoming pregnant, and then considers how to make the man marry and maintain her. Young men equally wish to make sure that girls are capable of bearing children before they marry them. This tends to depreciate the role of a wife, and the modern girl pays little attention to fitting herself to become a good one. When the child has arrived, she tends to judge her husband according to his ability to provide for her and her child, and continues a demanding relationship, which provides little emotional satisfaction for the husband, who may then go in search of other women. The wife accepts her husband's infidelity and sees it as the price she has to pay for ceasing sexual relationships with him while breast-feeding her child. She is mainly concerned with how to ensure that the new woman does not get too much of her husband's money.

When husband and wife are living together on their own, the wife does not have the status and companionship among other wives that is to be found in an extended family. Her domestic relationships are less satisfactory, and she looks outside the family for amusement and prestige. The husband may find himself thrust into the unfamiliar position of bread-winner, and not much more, and is likely to resent her constant demands, and his need to feel superior may make him go out to court another woman, since nowadays it is in courtship, rather than in marriage, that he can play a dominant role.

In the traditional household, income is derived from farms or property held in common by the extended family, and the wives and children help either with the farming or in the trading of the product as participants in a co-operative effort. But the urban father today has to face a new pattern. He is being forced into the unfamiliar role of bread-winner for his wife and children, and is alone held responsible for their financial support. This he frequently finds difficult to accept, and he does not regard his wife and children as having first claim on his wage or salary. He often feels that his mother, his siblings or his cousins have prior claims.

He expects his wife, as under rural conditions, to contribute substantially to the family income, but the urban wife may have no qualification to obtain paid employment, and has insufficient capital to trade profitably.

The wife equally desires to be economically independent of her husband, and is frustrated and unhappy when she cannot achieve this. In the smaller households, she has to accept personal responsibility for the physical care of the children, there being no one with whom she can share this task, and her own economic activities are thereby limited.

Traditionally, as has been said, marriages are between two families and they were frequently arranged by the elders. Today young people are more and more claiming the right to choose their own spouses, but still lay great stress upon the choice being approved by the families. When a young man has chosen a girl, he writes to her family head for permission to marry her. His letter has to be endorsed by his family elders. The girl's family will then make inquiries regarding the character and position of the young man, and that of his family: insanity, criminality, and physical defects are all taken into consideration. If the inquiries are satisfactory, the young man's family is informed that the proposal is acceptable and the two families meet for the 'Thank-you' ceremony. The risk involved in making prolonged inquiries lies in the fact that unless the young man signifies his intentions very early in the friendship, he may be debarred from seeing the girl.

Young people from unreliable and unstable homes do not seek the family consent, and the young man then asks the girl direct. But if she consents, there is a preliminary period before she joins the young man in his house. It is at this time, both with the family approved marriages and the individual unions that the girl tries to get what she can from the man. She may ask for a monthly maintenance allowance of £1 upwards, and for special gifts such as cloths, sewing machines, household articles, and money. During this period the girl frequently becomes pregnant and she may not join the man in his house until after the child is weaned.

Because of the insecurity of marriage today, the more sensible girl from a stable family tends to rely on parental judgements, knowing that if she marries without her family's consent, she will not be able to fall back upon it if the marriage fails.

Once a young man has written to the girl's parents, he is regarded as the father of any children she may have. Virginity at marriage is becoming rarer, but this is largely because marriage is only the final stage in a relationship which is regarded as established at an earlier stage. Ability to bear children must be proved, and it is no longer as important for an unmarried pregnant girl to get married as for the paternity of her child to be acknowledged. Immoral girls, in the local phrase, 'hawk around their pregnancies', trying first to get the most esteemed of their lovers to accept paternity, and if he refuses, continuing their efforts until one man accepts. Equally, if a girl quarrels with her boy friend, or her husband, she may try to punish him by refusing to allow him to claim paternity, and may offer this to another man with whom she agrees to have sexual relations in the future.

Nowadays, Yoruba society is very mobile, and both men and women are concerned with improving their status. Women seek to do so partly through marriage. They wish primarily to improve their standard of living, and this means marrying men with money. Formerly educated girls hoped to marry men in the senior service of the Government, but experience has shown them that such men have many financial commitments. They now aim at marrying rich business men or professional men with plenty of ready money. Previously, the older educated families formed a type of élite. Chiefs attempted to marry their children into other chiefs' households, but nowadays such distinctions are fading away, and whoever has money which he is willing to spend lavishly on entertaining will be accepted in any society.

Illiterate girls look for men who are better educated than they are and who hold permanent rather than casual jobs. The semi-literate girls, brought up in a family home of one room, look for educated men able to give them 'a room and a parlour', i.e. a separate bedroom and living-room.

A plurality of wives no longer enhances the status of men, and men who formerly spent money on bridewealth now spend it on building houses, first one in the town of their origin, and then secondly, in the town of their residence. A double-storey house carries more prestige than a single one, and in the Juvenile Court, many fathers who are shown to have failed to maintain their children financially will state in justification that they cannot do so, as all their money is being spent on building a house.

The following are the main factors responsible for the breakdown of marriages:

With the emphasis on childbearing in Yoruba marriage, a husband who found his wife was barren would look for another. Formerly, the first wife had a say in the choice. Nowadays economic factors make it difficult and unrewarding to maintain several wives, and the dissatisfied husband tends to turn away the first one, when the second bears a child. The first wife is also economically more free and may feel that she will have better luck with another man and so leave.

Another factor is the man's desire for a change. Men married under native law not infrequently report that they are tired of their wives and wish to get rid of them, adding that no one can make them keep a woman they no longer want. Such an attitude is often associated with falling in love with another girl, when the man then picks a quarrel with his wife until she leaves in desperation. A man may also bring a new wife into the home without the warning which custom requires, favour her and neglect the former one.

The most common reason give by women for leaving their husbands is failure of the latter to support them. In such cases, a woman would normally find a new 'husband' before leaving the old one. If a husband loses his means of livelihood, the wife feels justified in leaving him, since he is not fulfilling his prime duty of maintaining her. Women will similarly give as their reason for marrying that they must have someone to pay the rent. Other marriages also break up because, having previously suffered neglect, the wife is afraid to accompany her husband when he is transferred elsewhere to work. The husband then usually takes another wife, and neglects the first one—and her children—more and more.

Married women often complain of physical cruelty—usually of frequent beatings without any justification. On the other hand, men complain that their wives bully and nag them, or that they are disobedient, going out without permission and not preparing meals as told.

Parental interference is also a common cause of marital failure. The couple may have married without the consent of their respective families and the parents of one or the other try to break up the marriage and make their child marry according to their choice. Other parents use their daughters for bargaining, handing them over to any man who gives or promises financial help, and taking them away from those whose help proves meagre.

The women are often credulous and great believers in luck. They often marry without thought, only to find that their husbands have given them false accounts of their financial position. Such women often leave to try their luck elsewhere.

At the same time, the idea of reconciliation, in human relationships is deeply ingrained in the Yoruba. Wherever there is disharmony or disagreement, there will be persons coming forward to re-establish good relations. For relationships within the extended family, it is the duty of the male or female head, or any elderly person who is asked, to effect reconciliation. Theoretically anyone who has accepted a part of the bridewealth may be called upon. With families more widely dispersed, the individual who feels wronged will go to elderly people on both sides and relate the circumstances. Such relatives will send for the accused person and attempt reconciliation. In settlement, the aggrieved party is asked to accept money as compensation for the alleged harm but in all cases, the dignity of the man will be upheld, and he will only be blamed in secret.

REFERENCE

Schwab, William B. 1955. 'Kinship and Lineage among the Yoruba'. *Africa*, Vol. XXV, No. 4.

XVIII. SOCIAL CHANGE AND THE STABILITY OF AFRICAN MARRIAGE IN NORTHERN RHODESIA

J. C. MITCHELL

MEASURES OF MARRIAGE STABILITY

It is possible using appropriate statistical devices, to predict how long a given marriage will last. These statistical devices are analogous to those used in the life table and with suitable material a marriage duration table can be prepared (Barnes, 1949). In these tables divorce is analogous to death and the tables are constructed from an analysis of the periods marriages have survived before being dissolved by divorce or death, in the same way that life tables are constructed from the analysis of the ages at which people die. In this paper I am not concerned with the termination of marriage by the death of one of the spouses, so that when I discuss the duration of marriage I mean the duration of marriage before it is ended by divorce or legal separation.

Failing measures of this sort, which are the only true comparative statistics we can work with, we must use the divorce ratios of the sort we have suggested elsewhere (Mitchell and Barnes, 1950), but we must appreciate that these measures may be seriously disturbed by differences in the average age of first marriage or in the age distribution of the population.

Eventually when the standard of collecting divorce statistics has advanced sufficiently we will be able to compare the stability of marriage from one society to another, as Barnesh as started to do. He has been able to say, on the basis of his analysis, that the average Ngoni marriage will last for 15·5 years while among the Americans it will last 20·4 years.

This figure, like the life expectancy, is a general average arrived at purely empirically. It is obvious that the causes of death are numerous but the overall operation of these causes results in an expectancy of life which does not vary much from one year to another in the same community. The life expectancy, however, differs widely from one society to another. Demographers look beyond the life curve itself and are able to isolate from the myriad causes of death several significant factors and use these to explain the differences between societies. The high infantile mortality rate, for example, in non-literate societies, is instrumental in reducing the general life expectancy.

We may approach the analysis of the stability of marriage in the same way. There is no doubt that whether the marriage breaks up or not depends on a variety of factors, economic, social, and personal, and that these factors operating simultaneously give rise to an overall divorce rate which does not differ much within the same society from one year to the next. The multiplicity of factors, therefore, operate adventitiously and not systematically, in the same way that random factors affect the trajectory of a missile to give rise to a cone of fire and not to a constant error. But from one society to another certain major determinants of the divorce rate can be isolated. In other words we may adopt the same type of reasoning as used by Durkheim in his analysis of suicide. A variety of factors he argues affects the *incidence* of suicide but the *rate* is determined in different countries, and at different times in the same country, by a few major sociological variables.

KINSHIP AS THE MAJOR DETERMINANT OF MARRIAGE STABILITY

Therefore, in trying to assess the probability of divorce in any particular marriage we should take into account a wide range of relevant factors but if we are interested in trying to understand, say, the trend in divorce rates in general, then we need to be able to assess the influence of the major determinants and knowing these trends so deduce the trend in the divorce rate.

There have been many attempts to do this for Western European society but these studies are not directly relevant to the situation in Africa. Here we need to take account of the fact that tribal societies are organized on a different basis, and indeed we should make this the starting-point of our analysis.

Marriage is essentially a relationship between two persons which fits into a larger pattern of social relationships. Marriage, therefore, operates within a social system and being itself part of it we should expect that the social system would determine its nature. In tribal societies in Africa, as in other parts of the world, the kinship system is a dominant feature of the social structure so that it is reasonable to suppose, as Gluckman (1951) has done, that the major determinants of marriage stability in tribal societies lie in the kinship system.

Basically Gluckman's argument is that in societies which are organized on the basis of corporate patrilineages marriage becomes the institutionalized means whereby new members are recruited to the patrilineages. Given rules of incest and exogamy, the patrilineal groups can survive only by securing rights over the reproductive powers of women from other groups. This they do by marriage, involving as it does the payment of bridewealth and the performance of appropriate ceremonies. These rights over the reproductive powers of the women are transferred permanently to the husband's group so that the marriage cannot easily be dissolved. On the specific reason why the rights should be transferred permanently Gluckman is not clear, but I would suggest that it is related to the prolonged infancy of the human child and the fact that in general the child needs its mother for several years before it can safely be separated from her. Before this stage is reached the woman is usually pregnant again and therefore will not easily be released by her husband's group.

In societies in which there are corporate matrilineages the woman produces children for her own descent group. Her reproductive powers are therefore not transferred and the duration of the marriage does not affect the welfare of the child nor the rights of its matrilineal kinsmen over it. The duration of marriage here is therefore determined mainly by the personalities of the spouses and divorces usually are relatively frequent.

In bilateral societies kinship alone cannot be the basis of corporate kin groups and therefore the possession of rights over a woman's reproductive powers is not a live issue. Marriage therefore, as in matrilineal societies, is brittle and of short duration.

In general these hypotheses have been upheld and we are able to use them in interpreting the trends in societies where the kinship systems are changing. In order to do this we need to emphasize some general features of kinship systems.

Marriage, we have argued, will assume different forms within different kinship systems. We may approach the analysis of the rôle marriage plays in different kinship systems by considering the sorts of rights and obligations which the formal act of marriage confers upon the contracting parties. Bohannan (1949) on the basis of her analysis of Dahomean marriage has suggested that we can approach the problem from the point of view of the rights a man or his kinsmen acquire over a woman through marriage. One set of rights are those held in her as a *wife*. These are the rights to her services both domestic and sexual and they may be termed *uxorial* rights. The other set of rights are the rights in the woman as a *mother* and refer particularly to the ownership of the child. These are the *genetricial* rights.

Now it follows that where there are corporate agnatic descent groups the patrilineage as a whole acquires the genetricial rights in the woman while the uxorial rights are usually held by one of their number. In this situation, as Gluckman has argued, divorce is rare and difficult. In matrilineal societies the uxorial rights are acquired by a man who is not a member of the matrilineal descent group while the genetricial rights in the woman are permanently held by the woman's mother's brother, or her own brothers. As Gluckman points out the uxorial rights may easily be transferred from husband to husband without affecting the genetricial rights in her so that divorce here is easy and frequent.

In bilateral societies recruitment to corporate groups is not by kinship alone, so that the genetricial rights in women are not relevant. Here uxorial rights as in matrilineal societies are easily transferred from husband to husband and divorce is consequently easy and frequent.

In order to appreciate fully the significance of genetricial rights as rights over the reproductive powers of the woman, we should consider the rights and obligations which the possession of these rights confers over the children born to the woman. In a society where corporate groups exist the possession of genetricial rights over a woman implies that her children will belong to the group which possesses these rights. The children, therefore, may expect the succour and protection from the other members of the group and they in turn must be loyal to their fellows. As Bohannan points out, the acquisition of genetricial rights confers jural authority over the child. The word 'jural' here presumably means that the sanctions behind the implementation of the obligations of the child to its group lie in force either through the mechanism of the courts or through the feud. In other words genetricial rights, being linked particularly to corporate relationships, operate in a political field.

Where corporate groups exist, the genetricial rights are held, as I have pointed out, by the group as a whole. But some genetricial rights may also be held by an individual as, for example, among the Bemba of Northern Rhodesia. The Bemba are a people amongst whom succession to office and membership of the non-corporate association of clanship is determined by matrilineal descent. The most important political unit is the village. Villages are built up on the basis of matrilocal extended families (Richards, 1950 : 227), i.e. they are made up of the village headman and his married daughters. There may also be several of the headman's sisters and their daughters in the village. The Bemba practise shifting cultivation of a slash-and-burn type in rather poor soils and the size to which each village may grow is limited by this ecological factor. As the trees become exhausted in its vicinity each village must shift its locale approximately once in every five years and this is the time, as Richards points out, at which villages are particularly liable to fragment. The economy of villages is based upon the cultivation of eleusine in ash patches prepared from the burning of branches lopped from the trees by the young men of the village. The labour of the young men is crucial in the ecological balance between the Bemba and their somewhat inhospitable agricultural environment because pollarding the trees as against cutting them down completely allows a much more rapid regeneration of the trees and thus ultimately a higher carrying capacity of the land. The prosperity of a Bemba man, therefore, in a land where the margin between subsistence and starvation is narrow, is counted in food, and the labour of young men is essential to the production of food. This labour is provided by the husbands of the man's daughters. A man, therefore, is heavily dependent on his daughter's husbands for economic security, or as Richards (1956 : 46) graphically puts it: 'Wealth consists of the power to command service.'

A Bemba man's dependence on his daughters' husbands is limited not to economic relationships only: it extends also into the social and political field. Within the social field, prestige in Bemba society is associated with the economic independence of the man. As Richards points out (1956 : 42) a man can eventually acquire status and prestige as head of his own extended family with sons-in-laws working for him whether he moves to one of his own relatives or stays where he is. But if he wishes to increase his renown he must try to become a village headman. Among the Bemba as amongst other Central Bantu, the ambition of every man is to become a village headman. In order to do this he must have the right to remove his wife and her children from her village. With his daughters' husbands then, provided that he has the permission of the chief, he will be able to set up his own village.

Genetricial rights amongst the Bemba therefore centre on a man's jural authority over his daughters and their husbands.

In Bemba marriage three payments are made (Richards, 1940). The first, a trifling amount of say 2s. 6d., called *nsalamu*, confers uxorial rights upon the man. The second payment, called *chisungu*, is made during the girls' initiation and is made once only in respect of each girl. We can look upon it as a ritual payment which releases the mystical sexual powers of the girl. The third payment, *mpango*, formerly made up of barkcloth, hoes, or arrows, conferred genetricial rights upon the husband. It was through this payment that the man established his rights to remove his daughter from his wife's village and thereby established his rights to the services of his sons-in-law. As Richards (1956:44) puts it: 'The *mpango* gave the father those limited rights he secured over his children although it did not, in this matrilineal society, give him complete control over his wife's reproductive power as does the cattle *lobola* among the Southern Bantu.'

But these rights the Bemba man held personally: his brothers, for example, could not enforce them on his behalf, and from this point of view they differ from the genetricial rights acquired by a man in a patrilineal society with corporate kin groups. Divorce was easy and apparently frequent among the Bemba during the early years of marriage (Richards, 1940 : 101) but less frequent and more difficult after children had been born (Wilson, 1941 : 42). It was when the children were born that the man's ambitions became capable of being realized and it was to his advantage therefore not to seek a divorce at this stage: he could only build a village with the assistance of his daughters' husbands. The genetricial rights a Bemba man acquired over his wife, therefore, only became effective when his daughters were old enough to form the nucleus of a village and the divorce apparently became more difficult and less frequent as this stage was reached.

This argument links the stability of marriage with a man's realization of the genetricial rights he acquires in his wife whether this is in a society organized in corporate patrilineages or in a matrilineal society in which a man may personally acquire genetricial rights over his wife. In societies organized in corporate matrilineages such as among the Yao and Chewa a husband never acquires genetricial rights over his wife and therefore marriage is never stabilized by this factor. In bilateral societies also, as amongst the Lozi, genetricial rights are not involved so that we would expect the divorce rate to be higher than say amongst the Bemba. The rights which are disputed amongst the Yao and the Lozi are uxorial rights—particularly adultery—and not the rights over children. Among the Bemba, while adultery cases clearly figure prominently, the rights of a man to the portion of the marriage payment made for his daughter and the rights to the children are also involved. Note for example Richard's record (1940 : 57) of the case where a woman screamed: 'We shall take the baby . . . . That is no father that! He paid us no *mpango*.'

Amongst bilateral peoples, in fact, the kinship system may operate to increase the instability of marriage. Gluckman (1950 :

201) in fact describes how the Lozi system encourages the wide ramification of cognatic and affinal ties and how a person uses these ties to exploit the resources at its command. He writes:

> Because their productive activities are varied and many fall in distant places in the same month, they require co-operation and help from many people. Kinship provides the framework for getting this help, but since neighbours in the various parts where they have economic resources are linked to them by patrilineal, matrilineal and mixed ties, they emphasize his links with many lines: therefore marriage does not tie a woman's procreative power to one line. She produces for many lines.

It follows from this that from the point of view of any one individual the less his kinship links coincide with another's the better his chances of operating these links to his personal advantage.

In other words in bilateral systems the emphasis is on filiation while in matrilineal or patrilineal societies the emphasis is more likely to be on corporate relations. Where the emphasis is on filiation we expect to find high divorce rates.

To summarize we should expect:

In patrilineal societies with corporate groups, i.e. genetricial rights acquired by *groups*	marriage duration *long*
In patrilineal or matrilineal societies where genetricial rights are acquired by *individuals*	marriage duration *medium*
In matrilineal societies with corporate groups, i.e. where genetricial rights are never transferred or bilateral societies where genetricial rights are not relevant	marriage duration *short*

In order to test this hypothesis we need detailed information on the duration of marriage such as to enable us to compute expectancies of marriage duration and this we cannot yet do.

MARRIAGE STABILITY AND MODERN CONDITIONS

In broad terms we have tried to relate marriage stability in tribal areas to social structure: in particular, following Gluckman's lead, we have tried to relate it to the kinship system and the rights which marriage confers within these kinship systems. Therefore when we turn to modern conditions we must try to relate changes in marriage stability to changes in the kinship system whether through time (historically) or from place to place (situationally). Richards' (1940) study of Bemba marriage and Barnes' (1951) study of Ngoni marriage are studies of the historical sort. I intend, however, to try to consider marriage stability not in historical but in situational change, i.e. to look at marriage stability where the kinship system is altered fundamentally by the social situation in which it is set. The most striking examples we have are in the newly created industrial towns.

In these towns we may isolate two main types of related variables, i.e. the demographic and the sociological. Demographic factors influencing marriage would be such factors as the disproportion of sexes which Wilson (1941) emphasized so much. Another is the tribal heterogeneity of the towns and a third is the relatively high mobility of the town dwellers. All of these demographic characteristics have their influence on marriage stability as such, but the social structure, itself influenced by demographic variables, also affects marriage stability. Fortes (1953 : 24) has pointed out that there is evidence that 'unilineal descent groups break down when a modern economic framework with occupational differentiation linked to a wide range of specialized skills, to productive capital and to monetary media of exchange, is introduced'. The unilineal descent groups under these conditions tend to become reorganized in nuclear families and the descent tends to be reckoned bilaterally (Gough, 1950 : 85). This is particularly true in the industrial towns where the demographic and social conditions militate strongly against unilineal corporate group activity. As Fortes (1953 : 36) remarks: 'A lineage cannot easily act as a corporate group if its members can never get together for the conduct of their affairs.' In these towns where the emphasis is on heterogeneity and on mobility the conditions prevent the daily participation of unilineal kinsmen in joint activities. There are no cattle, there is no land to focus the activities of say a patrilineage, and the working hours and conditions preclude their participating in joint ritual and ceremonies for protracted periods. The emphasis in town is on individual success in a competitive environment and this emphasis cuts across the ideology of corporate descent groups.

Kinship instead remains important in the form of filiation—as an ever-ramifying network of personal relationship which links any given person to others in haphazard fashion across the township. Kinsmen, who in tribal conditions played an unimportant part in the life of a person, assume a new importance in town where the overwhelming majority of contacts are with strangers. A person may call on distant kinsmen for help in town whom he would not consider approaching in his tribal home (Wilson, 1941 : 53; Epstein, 1953 : 11; Mitchell, 1957 : 27). Though kinship is still important in the new industrial towns it possesses qualities different from kinship in tribal areas. Wilson (1941 : 51) has drawn attention to an example of the way in which the relationships between kinsmen must inevitably alter in the urban situation. He points out that in the tribal areas the economic bond between Bemba men and their daughter's husband was particularly important. We have seen that the Bemba men acquire rights to the services of their daughters' husbands through the *mpango* payments. He writes:

the wife's parents were the skilled foremen, the young couple were the relatively skilled labourers of those times, and both couples alike benefited from their co-operation. . . . The domestic group formed by the old couple and a number of daughters and sons-in-law was the main factory of Bemba wealth and their living depended upon it.

But in towns, of course, this essential link between a man and his daughters' husbands cannot exist because: 'the main productive relationship in which the urban Bemba are involved is that between European capital and skill on the one hand, and African unskilled labour on the other; it is on getting a job, not on getting married that a young man's living now depends.' We must therefore look at marriage and marriage stability in the matrix of urban social relationships of which it is a part.

In this situation genetricial rights in a woman fade in favour of uxorial rights. The rights by means of which kin groups are able to recruit new members are not significant where these groups cannot exist nor are the rights viable where the essential economic and political bond between a Bemba man and his daughters' husbands cannot exist. Instead where men are involved in wage-earning all day and individual households, as against joint households of the tribal type, are the pattern, the personal domestic services of the women achieve new importance. The emphasis on the personal services of the women is increased by what Wilson calls 'disequilibrium' or 'disproportion' (1941 : 40), i.e. an unbalanced sex ratio. The adult sex ratio in the towns of Northern Rhodesia does not depart from equality as much as it does say in Southern Rhodesia or South Africa. On the Copperbelt, for example, there are 142 adult men per 100 adult women. Yet this is enough to give rise to a certain amount of competition among the men for the sexual and domestic services of the women.

It is not surprising, therefore, that the question of the custody of children or of a man's rights in them are seldom raised in court. Instead the emphasis is rather on adultery or from the woman's point of view, on her husband's neglect of her. The uxorial rights appear to be most significant in urban areas, and this accords with the different forms that kinship in towns has taken there.

As we may expect in towns the significance of the marriage payment differs from that in tribal areas. The initiating gift (*nsalamu*) and the 'virginity' (*chisungu*) payments are substantially the same but the *mpango* payment understandably appears to have lost its tribal function of fixing a man's right to the services of his daughters' husbands. Instead the *mpango* payment has become, as I have expressed it before as 'a sort of insurance policy against the possible dissolution of marriage' (Mitchell, 1957 : 25). An aggrieved husband is able to sue for the return of his *mpango* payment if his uxorial rights have been transgressed. Those kinsmen who accept a marriage payment on the Copperbelt therefore, do so in the full knowledge that they may be called upon to refund the amount if a divorce takes place. They will therefore become guardians of the husband's uxorial rights and will bring pressure to bear upon their kinswoman, the wife, if she deviates from the norms of accepted behaviour. This is the point made by a Lala man, quoted in an earlier paper (Mitchell, 1957 : 25) who paid six times as much in marriage payment as he would have done in his rural home. He said his wife would not be as 'proud and cheeky' as she would have been had he only paid the usual amount. It is significant that three of four kinsmen who accepted the marriage payments were in fact living on the Copperbelt. They were themselves part of the social system in which the norms operated and were able to take a personal interest in the marriage.

We are, also, thus able to interpret the fact that even tribes which traditionally make no marriage payments, such as the Bisa and the Yao, fall into line on the Copperbelt and make substantial *mpango* payments. In the urban situation uxorial rights are as significant to them as other tribes and they endeavour to protect these rights both with their wives' kinsmen and in the courts by making the formal payments (Mitchell, 1957 : 27).

MARRIAGE STABILITY IN TOWNS

We are now able to turn to the question of marriage stability in towns. Wilson was convinced that: 'the instability of marriage is greater in town than in the country' (Wilson, 1941 : 41). This he relates to the lack of traditional restraints, in town, the idleness of the women making them 'all the more ready for sexual adventures', the disproportion of men and women and to the number of inter-tribal marriages.

When Wilson wrote it was not generally realized that marriage was unstable among the matrilineal and bilateral peoples of Northern Rhodesia even in the rural areas. It seems likely that this had been so even before the advent of the Europeans. Richards had just published her figures (1940 : 120) on Bemba divorce in the rural areas but Wilson was not able to collect comparable figures in Broken Hill. Since 1946 we have been able to make considerable advances in collecting the quantitative material on marriage stability and we have been able to clarify the methods of using this data to best advantage (Barnes, 1949; Mitchell and Barnes, 1950). The collection of data still lags a long way behind the sophistication of analysis Barnes has proposed but we are still in a better position to get at least a first estimate of the relative frequency of divorce in tribal and in urban areas.

I have published some information (1957 : 10) which suggests that urban marriages may be more stable than tribal in Northern Rhodesia. The figures, however, are not strictly comparable because of the possible effects of differing age structures in the samples. More refined work is necessary.

Nevertheless on the basis of our general analysis we might well have predicted this. Our argument, following Gluckman, has been that the main stabilizing influence in marriage is the legal transfer of genetricial rights to the husband. We would expect, therefore, that in the towns where corporate groups cannot operate as they do in tribal areas marriage duration will be shorter and the divorce rate will be higher. On the same reasoning since the legal transfer of rights over the services of the daughters' husbands is not significant in town we would expect the probability of divorce among urban Bemba couples to increase in the later years of marriage as against tribal couples. The overall duration of marriage may possibly be slightly shorter and the overall divorce rate will then be larger.

We would expect the duration of marriage in town to be longer, however, than among the strongly matrilineal people and the bilateral. Here the very assaults on the stability of marriage which Wilson emphasized have generated their own stabilizing reaction in the form of substantial marriage payments which protect the uxorial rights of the men. The result will be increasing reluctance to face divorce and a consequent lowering of the divorce rates.

These predictions are derivations from the hypothesis we have built up on the basis of viewing marriage as an element in a total social system in which certain clear-cut rights and obligations are involved. The next step is to proceed to test these by the use of refined quantitative techniques. I am able to do this for the urban side on the basis of social survey material from the Copperbelt but, except for material on the Ngoni, we are not yet in a position to compare this with measures in the rural areas.

REFERENCES

Barnes, J. A.	1949.	'Measures of Divorce Frequency in Simple Societies'. *Journal of the Royal Anthropological Institute*, Vol. LXXIX, pp. 37-62.
	1951.	*Marriage in a Changing Society*. Rhodes-Livingstone Paper, No. 20.
Bohannan, L.	1949.	'Dahomean Marriage: A Revaluation'. *Africa*, Vol. XIX, pp. 273-87.
Epstein, A.L.	1953.	'The Role of African Courts in the Urban Communities of the Northern Rhodesian Copperbelt', *Rhodes-Livingstone Journal*, No. 13, 1-17.
Fortes, M.	1953.	'The Structure of Unilineal Descent Groups' *American Anthropologist*, Vol. LV, pp. 17-41.
Gluckman, M.	1950.	'Kinship and Marriage among the Lozi of Northern Rhodesia and the Zulu of Natal', in Radcliffe-Brown, A. R., and Forde, D. (eds.), *African Systems of Kinship and Marriage*. London: Oxford University Press for the International African Institute.
Gough, E. K.	1950.	'Changing Kinship Usage in the Setting of Political and Economic Change among the Nayars of Malabar'. *Journal of the Royal Anthropological Institute*, Vol. LXXXII, pp. 71-87.
Mitchell, J. C.	1957.	'Aspects of African Marriage on the Copperbelt of Northern Rhodesia'. *Rhodes-Livingstone Journal*, No. 22, pp. 1-30.
Mitchell, J. C., and Barnes, J. A.	1950.	*The Lamba Village: A Report of a Social Survey*. Communications from the School of African Studies, University of Cape Town, New Series, No. 24.
Richards, A. I.	1940.	*Bemba Marriage and Present Economic Conditions*. Rhodes-Livingstone Paper, No. 4.
	1950.	'Some Types of Family Structure amongst the Central Bantu', in Radcliffe-Brown, A. R., and Forde, D. (eds.), *African Systems of Kinship and Marriage*. London: Oxford University Press for International African Institute.
	1956.	*Chisungu: A Girls' Initiation Ceremony among the Bemba of Northern Rhodesia*. London: Faber.
Wilson, G.	1941.	*An Essay on the Economics of Detribalization in Northern Rhodesia*. Rhodes-Livingstone Paper, No. 6.

INDEX

Abidjan, 11
Absenteeism, 43
Accra, 23, 41, 47, 296
Acholi, 40, 222
Administration, 101, 225–6, 240, 251–2
Adultery, 65, 94, 326
Aga Khan, H.H., 101
Aged, and migration, 42
Agriculture, 2, 4, 6, 7, 128, 230, 275, 280, 286, 288, 290, 291, 296, 297, 298, 300, 320–1
Akan, 41, 286–7, 290, 292
Arabs, 226; in Kahama, 244, 246, 247; in Mombasa, 99–102 *passim*, 110
Asantehene, 288, 289
Ashanti, 2, 56, 287, 288, 290, 301
Asians, in Mombasa, 99–101
Associations, 36, 37, 68, 78, 111, 116–20; appointment of officers in, 119–20; behaviour in, 119–20; credit (*ikelemba*), 168–9; in Gwelo, 136; in Kahama, 251; Luo Welfare, 111; migrant in Ghana and Ivory Coast, 303–4; Ratepayers, 40; tribal, 38–9; *see also* Clubs, social; Unions
Authority: of elders, 71, 72, 73; of family, 41, 42, 43, 45; of headmen, 276, 280; Native, 240, 279

Babuku, 301
Bakweri, 52, 64–5, 84–96
Balandier, G., 153
Balong, 92
Baltzell, —, 155
Baluyia, 102
Bamileke, 34, 264
Banana production, 85
Baoule, 49, 302
Barnes, John, 317, 326
Barotse, *see* Lozi
Bassa, 118
Bauer, Peter, 290
Beer: bars, 28, 136, 140, 227–8, 249–50; brewing by women, 59, 56, 57, 281; sale and sellers of, 213, 218, 222, 227
Bemba, 39, 74, 234, 246, 320–2, 324, 325

Bende, 246
Benin, 56
Bicycles, 194–5, 281
Bisa, 39, 327
Blantyre, 33
Blantyre-Limbe, 43, 273–84
Bohannan, Laura, 318, 320
Bondouke, 300
Brazzaville, 33, 46, 153, 182–204
Bread, as status symbol, 188–9
Brideprice, bridewealth, 4, 62, 65–6, 287, 328; Bakweri, 93–4; Bemba, 321–2, 326–7; Luo, 65–6; repayment by women, 51–2; Yoruba, 308–9
Broken Hill, 327
Bua, 49
Budgets, household, 163–6, 170, 176, 177
Buganda, 20, 145, 217, 228; social class in, 149, 150, 151; 1949 riots in, 156
Building, *see* Housing
Bulawayo, 10
Burial, 111
Busia, K., 147, 152

Calabar, 301
Cameroons Development Corporation, 85, 87, 89
Camps, in plantations, 90
Cassava, 230
Cattle, 300, 324
Chagga, 246, 247
Chastity, premarital, 52–3, 65
Chewa, 39, 274, 322
Chiefs, 78, 79, 154; Bakweri, 84; in Blantyre-Limbe, 276; Ganda, 151; in Kahama, 251; in Kisenyi, 221, 222, 225; in Mombasa, 112; *see also* Headmen
Children, 5, 37, 42–3, 44, 47–8, 77, 88, 106, 118, 162, 235, 259, 260, 261, 262, 291, 294, 307, 309, 310, 311, 312, 313, 314; rights to, 47, 56, 62, 63, 65, 302–3, 309, 319–20, 322
Christianity, Christians, 22, 39, 52–3, 88, 109, 110, 111, 150, 152, 216, 308–9, 310; *see also* Missions

'Chronicles of Kilwa', 99
Class system, 111, 121; African, defined, 148-55
Cloth, 287, 290, 301
Clothes, clothing: as status symbol, 22-3, 75, 109, 121, 140, 157; expenditure on, 175-6, 177, 178; Muslim, 118; Poto-Poto, 195-7; Swahili, 249
Clubs, social, 28-9, 210-16, 249; *see also* Associations
Cocoa, 84, 300
Cola, kola, 287, 308, 309
Colour bar, 127, 133
Compounds, 'unauthorized', 10, 11, 275, 280, 284
Concubinage, concubines, 94, 111, 213, 226, 302; *see also* Liaisons, extramarital; Prostitutes, prostitution
Congo, 10, 11, 12, 33, 43, 46, 49
Conquest States, 3
Consumption patterns, among Congolese *évolués*, 160-80
Contraceptives, 24
Copperbelt, 7, 10, 33, 37, 43, 46, 48, 70-6, 117, 326, 327, 328
Courts, 92, 251, 252, 279
Credit, 244-5, 290; — system (*ikelemba*), 168-9
Creole, 118, 119
Crops, 7, 84-5
Currency, 287, 290

Da Gama, Vasco, 99
Dancing, 74-5, 118, 214-15, 250, 251, 304
Dar-es-Salaam, 12, 33, 37, 38, 39, 40, 43, 46, 48, 224
Debts, 164, 165
Descent, double, among Bakweri, 92-3
'Detribalization', 69, 89
Diamond buying, mining, 7, 244
Diet, *see* Food
Digo, 102
Diviners, 249
Divorce, 60-1, 65, 93, 94, 252, 287, 316, 317, 318, 322, 323, 327, 328; *see also* Marriage, stability of
Djerma, 39
Douala, 33, 254-72
Dowries, 302
Dress, *see* Clothes, clothing
Drugs, imported, 291

Drunkenness, E., 227
Durkheim, 317

Ecology, Douala, 263-4
Economy: Brazzaville, 184-202; Cameroons plantations, 84-5; Congolese, 159-60; Douala, 256; Ghana, 288; influence of migrants on, 301; Lusaka, 274
Edo, 56
Education, 22, 108, 110, 123, 134, 138, 139, 145-57; *see also* Schools
Elders: Bakweri, 92; Kahama, 251, 252; Luanshya, 71, 72, 73; Yoruba, 312
Elisabethville, 46
Élite: definition of, 146-55; Ghana, 147; Nigerian, 151, 152; Temne, 117-18; Yoruba, 313
Eleusine, 320
Embu, 103
English language, use of, 140, 150, 151
Enugu, 12
Epstein, A. L., 70-4, 80, 216
Ethnic groupings: in Gwelo, 126; in Mombasa, 103; in Lusaka, 274
Europeans: 'black', 149; in Cameroons, 91; in Gwelo, 129-30, 142; in Kahama, 245, 251; in Lusaka, 274; as 'models' for Africans, 115, 118, 156-7, 179, 180; and prestige, 121, 122, 123, 136, 139, 140, 141, 152; in West Africa, 289
Évolués, Congolese, 159-80
Ewe, 292
Exports, from Cameroons, 85

Face-to-face relationships, 25, 29-30, 40, 283
Facing Mount Kenya, 156
Factories, 15-16
Fallers, L. A., 149-50, 151
Family, 109, 165, 166, 170, 233-4, 276-7, 280, 284, 287; authority of, 41, 42, 43, 44, 45; as unit of social class, 149-151; Yoruba, 305-15; *see also* Kinship
Fanti, 290
Farmers, 85, 128, 184
Farming, *see* Agriculture
Fertility: in Cameroons, 87; Yoruba, 314; *see also* Children, Marriage

Fish, 296, 297; canned, 290; consumption of, 174
Fishermen, 184
Food, 187, 191, 286, 287, 290, 295-6, 297; consumption of among *évolués*, 170-5; as status symbol, 21, 109, 157, 188-9; traditional, 161, 230
Football, 250, 251
Fortes, Meyer, 324
Freetown, 37, 46, 117, 120
French language, use of, 24, 209
Friendship, as indication of social status in Gwelo, 137-9; in Kisenyi, 217-29
Fulani, 2, 3
Furniture, 191-3; expenditure on, 175-6, 177, 178

Ga, 290
Ga-Adangme, 292
Games, 250, 251
Ganda, 2, 24, 38, 39, 43, 48, 60, 64, 150, 151, 217-29 *passim*, 247, 251
Gao, 301
Gauri, 60
Germans, in Cameroons, 83-4
Ghana, 36, 51, 147, 152, 286-98 *passim*, 300-4
Giriama, 102
Gluckman, Max, 318, 319, 323, 328
Gold, 7, 287, 289; — weights, 288
Gough, E. K., 324
Gussmann, B. W., 10
Gwelo, 19; social stratification in, 126-43

Ha, 242, 246
Half-caste, 246, 247, 250
Hardware, 291
Hausa, 2, 292
Haya, 40, 49, 218, 219, 222, 223, 246
Head ties, 292
Headmen: authority of in Blantyre-Limbe and Lusaka, 276-80; Bemba, 320, 321; in Cameroons, 92; in Kahama, 251; in Kisenyi, 222; in Sierra Leone, 118, 119; Tonga, 240; *see also* Chiefs
Hehe, 246
Hellman, Ellen, 67
Hindu, 101

History: African, general, 2-3; of Douala, 255-6; of Mombasa, 88-100; of Southern Cameroons, 83-5
Homesteads, *see* Households
Hospitality, among Congolese *évolués*, 165-6
Households: of Congolese *évolués*, 162-80 *passim*; in Kahama, 247-8; in Stanleyville, 207-8; Yoruba, 305-8, 311
Houses, housing, 8-13, 33-4, 40-1; Blantyre-Limbe and Lusaka, 275; Cameroons, 92; Douala, 264-7, 271; Mombasa, 106, 107, 110, 111; Stanleyville, 206; Tonga, 234; ownership of, 221, 223, 246, 247; renting of, 247, 248, 277, 278, 279
Hunting, 305

Ibadan, 11
Ibo, 23, 38, 56, 90, 305
Ila, 39
Illiteracy, of women, 162
Immigrants, *see* Migrants
Income, African, 160 n., 162, 163, 184-7, 202-3; 245; *see also* Wages
Indians, 61, 244, 246
Inheritance, 93, 308
Investments, 178, 180, 283
Islam, 2-3, 52, 53, 117, 118, 153, 302
Ismaili, 100
Ivory, trade in, 99, 287, 289
Ivory Coast, 6, 36, 37, 300-4

Jazz Band, 250
Jinja, 48, 223-4
Joking relationships, 38-9

Kabaka, 221
Kachin, 60
Kahama, 48, 51; — township, 242-53
Kalela Dance, The, 70, 74-6, 117, 216
Kamba, 102
Kampala, 28, 33, 38, 40, 43, 44, 46, 48, 51, 61, 64, 217-29
Katanga, 7, 33
Katikiro, 221
Kenya, 6, 7, 9, 10, 11, 12, 156
Kenyatta, Jomo, 156
Kerewe, 246
Kikuyu, 102, 103, 153, 246
Kimbu, 246
King's African Rifles, 221

Index

Kingwana language, 209
Kinship, 31–45, 59–60, 64, 317–27 passim; Akan, 287; Bakweri, 92–3; Blantyre-Limbe and Lusaka, 273–84; Douala, 254–72; among évolués, 165, 169–70; Gwelo, 130–1; Kahama, 248; Kisenyi, 217–29; Mombasa, 106–7, 108, 109; Tonga, 230, 235, 237; Yoruba, 305–28 passim: — terminology, 35–6: see also Marriage
Kintampa, 300
Kisenyi, suburb of Kampala, kinship, friendship and relations in, 217–29
Koforidua, 41, 51, 59, 286–98
Kong, 300
Kongo, 24
Kotokoli, 303
Krapf, L., 3
Kru, 118
Kumasi, 37, 56, 300
Kunda, 39
Kwahu, 296

Labour, 4, 102, 103–4, 230–41 passim, 275–6, 281, 301; division of, 286–8; see also Migration, Occupations
Lagos, 33, 38, 41, 59, 64; family life among the Yoruba in, 305–15
Lakher, 60
Lala, 326
Land, use of, 8, 36, 237, 275; — rights to, 78, 79, 93, 238, 257–8, 270, 281, 283, 286, 301
Land Husbandry Act, 19–20
Landowners, 221
Lango, 222
Languages, literacy in, 236
Law, Islamic, 251-2
Lay-preachers, African, 110
Leith-Ross, Sylvia, 151, 153
Lenje, 274
Leopoldville, 11, 33, 36, 51; expenditure study of Congolese évolués in, 159–80
Leya, 48
Liaisons, extramarital, 50–1, 58, 65, 93, 109, 223, 289, 301–2, 304, 307, 310, 311; see also Concubinage; Prostitution
Limba, 119
Lineages, 31–2, 54–5, 60, 61, 65, 92–3, 120, 276–9, 286, 287, 298, 303, 319, 322, 324; see also Kinship; Marriage

Linguae Francae, 36, 89, 248
Liquors, alcoholic, 118; see also Beer
Little, Kenneth, 152
Livingstone, 48
Loans, 164, 165
Lozi, 39, 74, 322, 323
Luanshya, 70–4
Luganda, 150
Lukiko, 221
Lunda, 2, 39
Lungu, 39
Luo, 24, 38, 39, 40, 65–6, 102, 111, 218, 219, 222
Lusaka, 10, 11, 273–5, 280–4

Madagascar, social class in, 152, 153
Makerere College, 147, 154
Makonde, 246
Mambwe, 77
Manyema, 246, 247
Marketers, women, 50, 286–98
Markets, 300
Marriage, 33, 75, 109, 155, 213, 224, 279, 283; Akan, 287, 293; Bemba, 320–2; exchange, 61; migrants, 302, 303, 304; Northern Rhodesia, 316–28; Southern Cameroons, 88–9; stability of, 46–66, 314–15, 316–28; Yoruba, 305–15; see also Kinship; Monogamy; Polygyny
McCulloch, Merran, 132
Meat, consumption of, 174–5, 291
Mende, 152
Merton and Kitt, 156
Meru, 103
Methodology, 68–70, 80–1, 113, 162, 182–3, 254–5, 273
Migration, migrants, 5, 6, 7, 19, 28, 36–7, 49, 126, 127, 160; Southern Cameroons, 85, 89, 90; children of, 37, 41, 77, 235, 259, 260, 261, 301, 302, 303; Douala, 257–72 passim; Ghana and Ivory Coast, 300–4; Gwelo, 128; Kisenyi, 229; Tonga, 230–41
Military service, 219
Milk, free, 106
Mines, mining, 7, 13, 70–4, 77, 233, 244, 289
Missions, 2–3, 8, 9, 102, 110, 111, 152; teaching of, 52, 53, 110
Mitchell, Clyde, 70, 74, 75, 121, 131, 157, 276, 326, 327

Mombasa, 33, 40, 46, 98–112
Monkey fur, 287, 289
Monogamy, 306, 308
Moshi, Mossi, 39, 301
Mothers, unmarried, 294–5
Muslims, 22, 39, 61, 100, 117, 118, 226, 249, 251, 310

Nadel, S. F., 146, 147
Nairobi, 33, 46
Nandi, 49
Ndebele, 39, 126
Neighbourhoods, in Stanleyville, 206
Neighbours, 208–9, 218, 219
Netball, 250
New Bell, quarter of Douala, 33–4, 254–72
Ngoni, 2, 39, 274, 324, 328
Norms, of conduct, 14–24, 113, 115–16
Nsenga, 39, 274
Nubi, Nubian, 218, 219, 221, 226
Nyambo, 40
Nyamwezi, 48, 242, 243, 246, 247, 248, 249
Nyanja, 246, 274
Nyanyembe, 246
Nyasa, 39, 246, 247
Nyasaland, 6, 23, 67; changes in kin groups in, 273–84
Nyaturu, 246
Nyika, 102, 246
Nyiramba, 246

Obrebski, J., 155
Occupations: in Brazzaville, 184, 185, 186; in Cameroons, 90, 91; European in Mombasa, 101; in Gwelo, 130; in Ghana, 289, 294; Indian in Kahama, 244; of migrants, 303; rank order in Gwelo, 135–6; in Stanleyville, 208; in towns, 7–8
Onitsha, 56
Oshogbo, 11, 23, 41

Pagans, 102, 109, 111
Perfumes, 292
Periplus of the Erythraen Sea, The, 99
Phonographs, 193–4
Pidgin English, 89–90
Plantains, 292
Plantations, 12, 27, 34, 46, 83–96, 257, 301
Polanyi, M., 288

Police, 221
Politics, African, 143; tribal, 238, 239, 240
Politics in an Urban African Community, 70–4, 216
Polygamy, Polygyny, 52, 153, 293, 295, 305; *see also* Marriage
Popularity, in Kisenyi, 222
Population: age structure of, 5; Blantyre-Limbe and Lusaka, 273; Brazzaville, 184; Cameroons, 85, 86, 87; censuses of, 5; Douala, 257, 258; ethnic variation, 49; Gwelo, 126; Kahama, etc., 242–3; Kisenyi, 217; Lagos, 305; Leopoldville, 160; Mombasa, 103; plantations, 87–8, 91; Stanleyville, 206; *see also* Sex ratio
Portuguese, 3, 5
Poto-Poto, 182, 204
Pottery, 286
Pregnancy, pre- and extramarital, 47, 55–6, 294–5, 311, 313
Property, rights to, 60, 61, 311; *see also* Land
Prostitutes, prostitution, 47, 49, 51, 94, 109, 110, 111, 223, 226, 247, 301, 303; *see also* Concubines

Quislings, 156

Racial discrimination, 155; tensions in Mombasa, 111; *see also* Colour bar
Radios, 193–4
Razafy-Andriamihaingo, Pierre, 152, 153
Reference Group theory, 155–7
Relationships: social, restructuring of, 113–25; in Stanleyville, 205–16; *see also* Face-to-Face relationships; joking relationships
Reserve, Lenje, 275
Rhodesia, Northern, 6, 7, 10, 39, 67, 77; changes in kin groups in, 273–84; marriage in, 12–13, 63–4, 316–28; — Southern, 6, 7, 10, 126, 142; villages in, 127–8
Rhodes-Livingstone Institute, work of, 67–81, 273–84 *passim*
Richards, Audrey, 320–3, 327
Ruanda, Rwanda, 38, 40, 218, 220, 222
Ruanda-Urundi, 24, 36
Rubber plantations, 84
Rufiji, 246

Rungu, 246, 247
Ruwa, 246

Sahara, 300
Salaza, 300
Salisbury, 8, 33, 46
Samori, 300
Savings Banks, 163, 164, 180
Schapera, I., 67
Schools, 150, 152, 153, 154; — nursery, 106
Seck, Assane, 153
Seniority, Yoruba, 308
Separatist Churches, 22
Servants, employed by Africans, 24
Sex ratio, 5, 46, 47, 48, 86-7, 89, 109, 259, 273, 324, 326; see also Population
Shona, 126
Shops, 244-5
Sierra Leone, 37, 118
Sikh, 101
Singing, 250
Slaves, 102, 287, 289
Slave trade, 99
Sociology of Rising Nations, The, 155
Soga, 48, 60, 218, 223
Soli, 274
Somali, 226, 246, 247
Songhai, 39
Stanleyville, 12, 20, 28, 46, 51; social relations in, 205-16
Status, 20-4 *passim*; Cameroons, 91; Gwelo, 133, 134-9; Kisenyi, 227; Tonga migrants, 231, 237-8, 239; Yoruba, 313-14: — symbols, 20-4, 120-4, 157; Brazzaville, 187-201 *passim*; Buganda, 150, 153; Congolese *évolués*, 161, 180; Gwelo, 139-41; Mombasa, 109, 111, 112: of women, 21-2, 26-66 *passim*, 93-4
Stratification, social, 114, 115; in Gwelo, 126-43
Strikes: on Copperbelt, 71-4; in Mombasa, 104
'Sub-systems', in society, 159-60
Suburbs, 280, 283, 284; Kisenyi suburb of Kampala, 217-29
Sudan, 3
Sudanese, 301
Suicide, 317
Sukuma, 242, 243, 246, 247
Sumbwa, 242, 243, 246, 247
'Supertribalism', 39

Swahili, 43, 110, 223, 226, 246 *n.*; culture and language, 248-9

Tabwa, 39
Tanga, 20
Tanganyika, 6, 7, 9, 38-9, 154, 242, 243
Taxes, 221, 301
Tea, 85
Teita, 102
Temne, 38, 117-18, 119
Tenants, see Houses, renting of
Teso, 222, 223
Timber, 85
Titles, 118, 207, 208, 239
Tobacco, 118, 290
Togo, 300, 303
Toka, 48
Tonga, 23, 39, 48; labour migrants, 230-41
Toro, 38, 40, 44, 218, 219, 223
Towns: attraction of, 224; growth of, 1-13 *passim*; kinship in, 32-45; stability of marriage in, 46-66 *passim*, 323-8; see also Urbanization
Town and Country Planning Committee, 279
Trade, 215, 256, 269, 270, 301; 'trust' system, 256, 269, 270
Traders, women, 49, 51, 57-8, 163, 167, 213-14, 286-98, 305, 306
Treichville, 302
Tribalism, 1-4, 31-45 *passim*, 67-8, 75-7, 79, 131, 139, 271
Tribal markings, 303
Tswana, 31
Tumbuka, 233
Tusi, 246, 247
Tutsi, 23, 24

Uganda, 3, 6, 7, 10, 13, 15, 38, 44, 46, 49, 53, 146
Unemployment, 184, 257
Unions, 40, 72-4, 65, 66, 85; see also Associations
Upper Volta, 300, 301
Urbanization, 31-45 *passim*, 67-81, 95-6, 160, 232-3, 241, 267, 271, 281-4
Usumbura, 11, 24

Value system: in Gwelo, 132; traditional, 161, 238, 240

Vernacular, use of, 24
Villages, 92, 273, 276-80, 320
Vinza, 246

Wages, 105, 108, 129, 136, 185, 186, 234, 260; *see also* Income
Watson, W., 77
West African Institute of Social and Economic Research, 85
White-collar workers, 104, 152
Widows, 292, 293, 294, 296, 297
Wilson, Godfrey, 121, 324, 325, 327, 328
Witch doctor, 129
Women: education of, 111, 123, 124, 150, 155, 162; fertility of, 42-3, 47, 87, 314; in Kahama, 250-1; in Kisenyi, 221, 223-4; migrants, 49-50, 236, 301-2; property of, 60-1, 93, 245, 247; status of, 21-2, 26-66 *passim*, 93-4; work of, 43, 50-1, 57-8, 163, 167, 230, 281-2, 286-98; Yoruba, 54-6, 305-15; *see also* Concubines, Marriage, Prostitutes
Working pattern, in Mombasa, 105

Yao, 39, 43, 274, 322, 327
Yoruba, 23, 31, 35, 38, 41, 64, 292, 301; — women, 54-6, 305-15

Zanzibar, 99-112 *passim*
Zaramo, Zaramu, 38, 43, 48, 246, 247, 249
Zugu, 300
Zulu, 62